O9-AID-544

TRUE BLUE

POLICE STORIES BY THOSE
WHO HAVE LIVED THEM

Sgt. Randy Sutton

Edited by Cassie Wells

St. Martin's Paperbacks

NOTE: If you purchased this book without a cover you should be aware that this book is stolen property. It was reported as "unsold and destroyed" to the publisher, and neither the author nor the publisher has received any payment for this "stripped book."

TRUE BLUE

Copyright © 2004 by Randy Sutton.
Excerpt from *A Cop's Life* © 2005 by Randy Sutton.

Cover photo © Brand-X Images.

All rights reserved. No part of this book may be used or reproduced in any manner whatsoever without written permission except in the case of brief quotations embodied in critical articles or reviews. For information address St. Martin's Press, 175 Fifth Avenue, New York, NY 10010.

Library of Congress Catalog Card Number: 2003058650

ISBN: 0-312-99537-7
EAN: 80312-99537-7

Printed in the United States of America

St. Martin's Press hardcover edition / February 2004
St. Martin's Paperbacks edition / March 2005

St. Martin's Paperbacks are published by St. Martin's Press, 175 Fifth Avenue, New York, NY 10010.

10 9 8 7 6 5 4 3 2 1

PRAISE FOR RANDY SUTTON'S
TRUE BLUE

"A simply great new book . . . Funny, sad, and, at times, haunting, the essays capture mundane events, as well as tragic ones. Some of these 55 stories are lyrical, some are gritty, some so heart-breaking they make you cough up a tear, and others laugh-out-loud funny, and some more thrilling than top suspense fiction. But they all come right from the heart that beats beneath the badge."

—*New York Daily News*

"If you want to enter the hearts and minds of the men and women sworn to protect us, read *True Blue*. These intimate episodes, written by the law officers who lived them, are funny, sad, moving, and powerful . . . Everybody should own this memorable book."

—Joseph Wambaugh, author of
The Onion and *Fire Lover*

"If you want an adrenaline rush, forget about intricate mysteries and so-called thrillers. These pages bring to vivid reality the real stories of cops whose guts and glory are seldom seen and rarely heard."

—John Langley, creator of *COPS*

MORE . . .

"Wanna know what cops really think when they're under stress, and what makes them act and react? These stories will tell you. Most telling their stories in these pages are first-time authors; some are polished, some are gritty, but all have a story worth reading."

—Dan Mahoney, author of
Justice: A Novel of the NYPD

"I've been a Las Vegas cop for twenty-five years and I got a rush reading *True Blue*. This book achieves what all the police shows strive for, hard-hitting action combines with genuine emotion. These stories are real, the cops are heroes."

—Sheriff Bill Young, Las Vegas
Metropolitan Police Department

"Heartrending . . . Some are hilarious . . . All [the stories] demonstrate that cops, who have reason to reflect on their experiences, are wonderful philosophers and storytellers."

—*Booklist*

"An effective overview of police work. Recommended for specialized collections in criminology."

—*Library Journal*

"Candid true-life tales of officers from places as diverse as downtown Los Angeles to small-town America . . . illustrate 'the heart behind the badge' and bridge the gap of misunderstanding and distrust that often tarnishes the public perception of the police."

—Michael Ratcliff, *The Times* (Trenton, NJ)

DEDICATION

True Blue began as a dream, but became a reality through the positive energy of all of those who contributed their time, their work, and their heart. When this project began, I had no idea of the incredible scope of knowledge and skill it would take to complete. It was a humbling experience to realize how much I did not know and how much I needed to learn. But perhaps because of the mission of this book, I found nothing but support from my fellow authors and police officers, from police organizations and from those publications that got the word out. Without their support, this book would have been impossible to create. In the months that were spent in promoting the project and doing the many things necessary to obtain such quality stories, I worked closely with one person who was led to me by providence. Without her, *True Blue* would not exist, and without her guidance, support, skill, and friendship I would not have been able to see my dream become a tangible reality. Cassie Wells, who began as my editor and became my writing mentor, has given me the support and encouragement that only a person of her qualities could accomplish. I am proud to have her as my friend. I further believe that the memory of my father, Arthur, and the love and support of my mother, Lillian, provided the inspiration I needed to complete this important project. I know *True Blue* will come to mean as much to those who read it as it has to those who wrote these stories and lived their tales.

ACKNOWLEDGMENTS

There are a number of people who gave of themselves in the creation of this book. I gratefully acknowledge their support: Lt. Candy Byrd, Diane Ferriolo, Gerrie Daly, Kathleen Zaccara, Mike Blasko, Tom Keller and Patrick Taylor of the Las Vegas Metropolitan Police Department, Karen Parker of Skaggs Police Equipment, Cynthia Brown of *American Police Beat,* and Joanie Smith of S&W Literary Editors, Inc. Special thanks to Antoinette Kurtiz of the La Jolla Writers Conference for her support and great connections.

I also wish to acknowledge some of the writers/contributors who helped to make *True Blue* a reality:

Jeremy M. Williams	John Morehead
John E. Kolberg	David Pomeroy
Keith J. Bettinger	John Carpino
Cheryl Schulte	Gary Replogle
Craig Fisher	David Kahler
Robert "Robin" Vercher	Brent Larson
Jeremy Rosenthal	John Schembra

and all the rest of those who submitted so many wonderful, engaging, and powerful stories.

CONTENTS

PREFACE xiii
INTRODUCTION xvii

Little Boy, G.I. Joe by Scott Harmon 1
Her Name Was Jackie by Randy Lee Sutton 5
Blue & White Graveyard by Charles R. Martel 9
A Little Less Than Smart by Al Gibson 11
Your Husband—My Partner (A Letter to Lesa)
   by Ron Corbin 13
Staging Point for the Alien Invasion
   by Robert Banks 19
Bert & Ernie by David A. Rogers 22
The Show-up by Gavin Keenan 28
The Emotional Switch by Rocky Warren 35
The McBungler by Melinda Walker 41
Death on the Border by John Malone 45
Lieutenant Dad by O'Neil De Noux 52
The Grocery Scam by Joseph Kaiser, Jr. 56
The Potential by Mark Falcione 66
The Christmas Gift by William Seyfried 71
Jimmy by Ponzio Oliverio 74

Standoff by Gina Gallo   76

Danny by Shauna Bragg   81

My Reminder by Chris Bolton   86

The Lonely Years by Don Cossean   92

Land of Oz by Dennis N. Griffin   94

Not in My House . . . an Officer's Lament
  by Dennis McGowan   97

Shots Fired by Jack Comeaux   102

Eugene by Tim Gardner   105

Retrospect by Scott Partridge   114

Kung Fu Curt by Andrew Borrello   118

Of Life by David Pomeroy   120

Season's Greetings by Charles R. Martel   122

Yes, It Is Part of the Job! by Michael Summers   124

Directing Traffic by Stan Damas   127

Sweet Sixteen by John Schembra   129

Fear in Children by Dave Cropp   135

The Morning After by Phil Dunnigan   149

Hearts in Barbed Wire by Ricky D. Cooper   152

Twenty-seven Times by Justin Paquette   167

The "Routine Stop" That Changed My Life
  by Richard Augusta   171

A Pair of Jeans by Brian Parr   174

August in December by George Booth   176

Another Day, Another Quarter by David L. Wood   186

The Cycle of Violence by Phil Bulone   191

The Boot by Jack Sommers   196

My Survival by Tom Schulte   198

Heads & Tails by Chuck Springer   204

What Seeds We Plant by Ray Majeski   207

WTC Rescue 1982 by Robert Gates   213

Insomnia Revisit by Harry Fagel   217

Heroes by Paul Rubino   219

I'm Walking and Talking, I'm Not Bitching
  About Anything by Patrick Zwiebel   223

Contents

Firefighter, Cop, Marine, Friend, Hero
  by Lou Savelli   232
Loss of a Child by James Scariot   238
Untitled by Peter DeMonte   243
Untitled by Robert Brager   247
Untitled by James Bogliole   255
Soul Food by Bob Dvorak   260
There's So Much Hope by Joe McAdams   268

EPILOGUE   279
IN MEMORIAM   281

PREFACE

It seems a lifetime ago when I first put on the badge of a police officer. I solemnly swore to uphold the laws of our country, to defend our citizens, and to protect the rights of all. It was the proudest moment of my life and, unexpectedly, it was the beginning of a journey of self-discovery that continues to this day. I soon learned that there is no more challenging a profession than law enforcement. I also came to believe there is a huge chasm between those who enforce the laws and the people that they serve, a chasm of misunderstanding, distrust, and prejudice. I now believe that it is part of my job to bridge that dangerous gap one person at a time. My efforts have been worthwhile, for I never stopped believing that the success of a civilization can be measured by the strength of its laws and by the unity of those who uphold the laws with those who live by their grace.

For me, the years have passed swiftly. The collage of my long life as a police officer unfolds before me. I see mental snapshots of those I arrested, of their victims, of the bystanders standing curiously in the streets just beyond the police barricade. I catch myself smiling at memories of moments of laughter shared with long-ago partners whose names I've forgotten but whose faces, whose presence, I never will. In my mind's eye, the crack of twenty-one rifle shots, the snap of white-gloved hands in salute, and the mournful tone of taps being played as another murdered cop is being laid to rest, is replayed again and again, filling me with sadness, yet also with pride.

All of us, citizens as well as my brothers and sisters in law enforcement, have our own reservoir of private memories and private burdens that we must bear alone, but the events of September 11, 2001, we must bear together. When our nation came under attack and the World Trade Center was consumed in a fiery hell, when the unthinkable occurred and our world altered, the changed reality became ours to share. The chasm existing between law enforcement and those they serve was spanned instantly through tragedy that day: more police officers lost their lives on September 11 serving their community, their country, than on any other day in history, and everyone has felt that loss along with their own.

So in the aftermath of that unforgettable day, I suddenly found the answer to the question that has been eluding me for more than a quarter of a century: How can we show who we really are to those we are sworn to protect, and perhaps to one another? It came to me that the way to shore up this bridge across the divide, the way to offer solace in this terrible time, is with words. Not to argue, or preach, or pontificate, or rail, but to tell our stories. The book that you are holding in your hands was born from this idea. Within its pages are true stories written by law enforcement officers from all over the United States. Those in big cities, those in small towns. Suburban, rural, and the heart of the biggest metropolis—they are all represented here. Men and women of law enforcement share with you profound, startling, or amusing moments of their lives on the job. In many cases, moved to do so by the events of September 11, they are offering you something they've never revealed even to their fellow officers, much less to the public at large: a glimpse into their hearts. No one who wears a badge can be unaffected by what he or she has seen or experienced, though often it is a matter of survival to appear unfazed and dispassionate. The abject cruelty and inhumanity to which police officers are exposed cause them to build a fortress around their emotions so that they might still function effectively and objectively. But now we've all been exposed to cruelty and inhumanity and destruction on a massive scale. This experience, shared by all Americans, has prompted all these current or former members of law enforcement, these men and women with stories to tell, to step forward and build this monument for the fallen with just their words.

Many of the contributors to this book had never before written anything other than a police report, and they struggled courageously to put their stories down on paper. Some of these contributors are professional writers who have a great ease with words and, in fact, make a living writing, yet they also donated their stories for the same good cause. All proceeds from the sale of this book will go to the families of the law enforcement officers killed in the line of duty during the attacks of 9/11. I only hope you see what I have seen within these extraordinary pages: the heart behind the badge—strong, resolute, and over-flowing with a compassion that the uniform, by necessity, must often hide.

True Blue: Police Stories by Those Who Have Lived Them is dedicated to my brothers and sisters in law enforcement who gave their lives on that terrible day. Lest we forget.

SGT. RANDY SUTTON

INTRODUCTION

The stories fall loosely into five categories and are identified as:

THE BEAT

Some walk a foot beat in the inner city, others patrol rural highways or the small towns that fill the map from coast to coast. Some wear blue uniforms, others wear khaki. Their patches are as different as their badges, but their hearts all beat to the rhythm of law enforcement. What they have in common is that every time one of them puts on his uniform, straps on his gun, and pins on his badge, he knows that he will be facing the unknown. The hours of his shift may crawl along with nothing more than checking out a broken burglar alarm to break the monotony. Or time may sail by with lights and sirens from one emergency to the next. You just never know, and that's why it takes a certain kind of person to do the job. There are some certainties: heartache, cruelty, and death are constant companions in the career of every law enforcement officer. So are humor, irony, and courage. At the end of the day there are stories to tell. Some are amusing, some are touching, some are gripping tales of heartache and loss, and some are hysterically funny. But they are all a part of life on the beat.

WAR STORIES

Every cop has them. You will hear them in the locker rooms of police stations in the largest cities, in station parking lots in the smallest towns. You will hear them in neighborhood bars and hangouts where off-duty cops let off steam after the end of their watch. They're called "war stories," and from the first day a rookie pins on his shiny new badge until long after the day he hangs up his cracked and worn leather gun belt for the last time, these are the tales that will work their way into his private conversations with other cops, and with those lucky enough to be taken into his confidence. Some are poignant, some revel in absurdity, others might offend delicate sensibilities. Some will make you laugh out loud, some will make you shake your head in amazement, others will make you wonder about the mysteries of life and the inexplicable actions of human beings. These stories are a cop's way of sharing the moment, a snapshot from his album of memorable moments of a long and riotously varied career.

OFFICER DOWN

"Officer down!" These words chill the blood of even the hardest and most cynical of cops. Sometimes these dreaded two words are heard cracking over a police radio from the disembodied but bursting-with-tension voice of a dispatcher. Or perhaps they come from another cop, a partner even, who has rolled up on the scene and through the tinted windows of his patrol car seen the sight that will haunt him forever . . . his brother or sister officer lying on the dirty sidewalk or sprawled in the street, their blood seeping into the dirt. Sometimes cops casually pick up a newspaper or turn on the television and to their horror find that a fellow officer, maybe their own partner, was killed the night before. And sometimes the words are the last sounds uttered by an officer himself into his radio after he has felt his body penetrated by a bullet, ripped by a blade, or bludgeoned by a bat or tire iron. No matter how or when they come, they herald the worst thing a cop can experience in his tenure on the streets. These stories are from those who know what it means to hear, "Officer down!"

LINE OF DUTY

Much of a police officer's work is routine; it is simply interacting with people who have problems, or issues, or even illnesses. The truth is, the majority of the calls for service that an officer attends to won't even be remembered at the end of the week. But there is always that one call, the one that changes your life. The call itself may be dramatic or traumatic; it may be violent or bloody. But it also may seem routine and the revelation experienced by the cop may come from inside, when suddenly he "sees" something in someone or in himself that he never saw before. These stories are epiphanies—they are the stories from a cop's life that will never be forgotten by those who have lived them. Some cops are haunted by what they've experienced, others are liberated. What these stories have in common is that they define the "line of duty": the line that separates cop from civilian, the line that no cop can retreat from, where every cop makes his stand no matter what it costs him.

GROUND ZERO

Never before in our nation's history has a single event touched the lives of so many. The terrorist attack on the World Trade Center literally changed the world. The lives of thousands of men, women, and children were lost and among them were more than seventy law enforcement officers, making it the deadliest day in law enforcement history. The horror of 9/11 will be forever felt by those who witnessed the tragedy, by the survivors, and by the rescuers. These riveting and unforgettable stories attest to the toll extracted from those on duty that terrible day.

LITTLE BOY, G.I. JOE

by Scott Harmon

*Police Officer, Galena PD and Kankakee PD,
Illinois, twelve years.*

It was an early afternoon and I was pulling a double shift because I was ordered over. It was a beautiful July day, not too hot, about seventy-five degrees with a perfect breeze. I remember thinking how nice it would be to take the bike out for a cruise, but I was stuck working.

Then my reverie was over and I found myself thinking about an incident that happened the night before, where a guy had gotten shot in the chest when he was holding a gun by the barrel while approaching me. I was contemplating how I could have made the situation better, while at the same time thinking about how I got called into the office for a "beef" I had received from a citizen. It just seemed like this was not my month. The week prior, a guy had jumped off a train bridge into a shallow river embedded with rocks. His family was blaming the police department and my name was at the top of the list.

I was thinking all this as I was patrolling up Evergreen Street and saw a little boy sitting on the curb and crying. He had blond hair and was wearing a white-and-blue-striped shirt and blue jeans. Normally, since the kid was obviously not in any danger, I would have just driven away without asking what the problem was, but for some reason I was curious as to why this little boy was sitting all alone and sobbing his heart out on such a beautiful summer's day.

"Hey, kid, what's the matter?" I asked before I had considered that this might be opening a can of worms.

The boy pointed to the sewer drain at the corner and said, "My G.I. Joe fell in the drain!"

I could see the tears streaming like tiny rivers on his cheeks as he relived this horrible occurrence. "Oh, that's not good," I said.

Hey, what can you say in response to something so trivial? Don't get me wrong, I'm not heartless, I was just in one of those moods. But I radioed dispatch, "City K-13."

"K-13?" dispatch replied.

"I'll be out at Evergreen and Oak with a juvenile," I said and exited my squad.

I walked with the boy over to the drain and looked down. "Don't worry, kid, we'll get him out."

He sniffled and wiped his eyes and then looked up at me with absolute confidence. "Okay, you're a policeman, you'll be able to help him!"

Hey, no pressure, kid, I was thinking. Then I wondered how the hell I was gonna get down there. You know how your mind starts racing with different thoughts? I was thinking, I really don't wanna get dirty and "un-tucked." Stupid, huh? Yeah, I know. But I looked again at the boy's trusting face and something happened—it was as if something cracked open inside me and I too felt the urgency and gravity of the G.I. Joe-in-the-drain situation. Suddenly all the things I'd been thinking about earlier seemed trivial. I knelt down and first put my hand, then my whole arm, all the way into the drain. I had maneuvered myself so that I was just barely able to touch G.I. Joe's crewcut head when my sergeant drove up. He rolled down the window in his squad, looked at the two of us for a moment, and said, "Hey! What the hell are you doing?"

The boy and I, excitement evident in our voices, responded in unison, "Getting G.I. Joe out!"

I could hear Sergeant McCabe mumbling as he exited his squad, "You gotta be shittin' me."

But I said, "Hey, Sarge, your arm's longer than mine, give it a try!"

McCabe just stood there for a second staring at me, unamused. I could see the wheels turning in his head as he considered various stinging retorts, but then he looked in the drain and at the boy who was now standing next to me. "Oh, man!" McCabe said as he knelt down on the pavement.

We discovered that McCabe's arm was longer than mine, but apparently not quite long enough. As McCabe tried to reach our American Hero in the drain, my sister beat car pulled up. Officer Brian Coash is not only my partner but also my best friend, and when he saw the three of us alongside the drain he just started to laugh. But he got out of his squad and assessed the situation, laughing the whole time, and then said, "Let's just pull the drain grate out!"

Why didn't I think of that, I was muttering in my head.

"There's no way we can pull that thing out, we'd need a crowbar," McCabe said, appraising the grate.

Without hesitation I reached for my radio's lapel mike. "City, K-13!"

"K-13?" dispatch replied.

"City, will you contact the city crew and have them twenty-five my location with a crowbar."

"Nice!" McCabe said, smiling.

Then another squad pulled up and then another just to find out what we had going on. Moments later the city crew arrived. I grabbed the crowbar from them and went over to the drain and started prying. But it was a lot harder than I thought.

"Get on this!" I said to no one in particular. Brian leapt forward, grabbed the end and started prying.

"It's moving!" the boy cried.

"Yeah! Keep it up!" McCabe was as excited as the little boy.

Finally the grate slowly lifted up and gave a low suction noise. As I knelt down to reach into the drain, I bumped heads with Brian and Sergeant McCabe.

"I got it, I got it, spread out!" I cried, realizing that we were experiencing a Three Stooges moment. I felt the soft cotton fabric of G.I. Joe's uniform and grabbed him in a tight fist.

"I got him!" I shouted with joyous triumph. And at that moment I saw myself as someone I hope I'll always be. I looked over at the boy and his face was almost angelic and his smile simply brightened my existence and warmed my heart. I stood up, dusted myself off, walked over to the boy and presented him with G.I. Joe, no worse for his experience in the drain.

"Here you go, sir," I said.

"Thank you so very much!" the boy said with utter joy and gratitude. I realized at that moment what this job is all about. It's not about the contract negotiations, or how much comp-time you have accrued, or how you get called into the office for pointing your finger into some guy's chest. It's not about the fact that your favorite food hangout rang up full price and now you gotta bum five bucks from your partner, or that your uniform got a little ragged from a long tour of duty.

I realized right then and there, you do it for the little ones.

HER NAME WAS JACKIE

BY RANDY LEE SUTTON

Sergeant, Las Vegas Metropolitan PD, Nevada, seventeen years; Princeton Borough PD, ten years.

The four-year-old compact car was stopped at the traffic light. The neon lights from the casinos flashed their staccato rhythm and reflected on the faces of the family in the cool Las Vegas night. Times were getting better for the young couple. Steady work, a small home, and the addition of the little one-month-old baby girl now happily burbling in the infant seat gave the young family hope that the American Dream might just become a reality. They were on their way to the store to pick up some formula and diapers and the new father glanced over to watch as his young wife turned around in her seat to stroke the baby's face with the back of her hand. He smiled as he returned his concentration to driving and was just about to ease down on the accelerator in anticipation of the light turning green. He had no reason to pay any attention to the lowered primer-gray Buick idling next to them.

The shaved heads of the two men inside the Buick glistened with sweat even though the brisk winter nights in Las Vegas had people donning their coats. The cocaine surging through their systems had raised their body temperatures and reduced their ability to think or feel. There was no reason to do what they did next. They shared the same ethnic heritage of the young couple in the car beside them, but certainly not their values, not their hopes. And maybe that void was why they chose that moment to raise their 9mm semiautomatics and empty them into the car beside them. The bullets tore into the glass and metal, devastating everything in their path.

In the four-year-old compact, the baby, who moments before had been innocently waving her little arms in the air, enveloped in the warmth and love of her parents, now lay motionless. She was still strapped into her car seat, but now blood was pouring from the horrible gash where the bullet had ripped into her face. The mother screamed as shards of glass imploded into the car, while the father punched the gas pedal in a frantic attempt to escape the fusillade. Without a backward glance, the two gang punks sped off, laughing, proud of the "courage" it took to indiscriminately open fire on the innocent, not giving a damn.

My patrol car glided through the night on a collision course with this family's destiny. I had more than twenty years of experience behind the badge, but this night I would always remember. I was first alerted that something was wrong when I approached the intersection and saw the compact car parked at a weird angle. I noticed the panicked, jerky movements of the people surrounding it before I heard a woman screaming. As I climbed out of my unit, I heard someone yell, "My God, my God, the baby's been shot!" It was then that I saw the infant car seat on the sidewalk next to the car. My flashlight illuminated the tiny face awash with blood and my heart fell as I saw the little body jerking spasmodically.

I was alone on this call. I needed three heads and ten hands. Who shot her? Were they still nearby? I needed to get medical attention for the baby. Procedure is clear:

summon the paramedics and begin the investigation. But people were shouting, crying, and all I could think of was that I must help the baby. I radioed for assistance but as I kneeled beside her, I found she wasn't breathing. Then, as if in answer to a prayer, another patrol car pulled up. It was all instinct after that—I didn't give another thought to procedure—I just snatched up the limp and bloody bundle, jumped into the front seat, and shouted to the young cop to get to the hospital. As I cradled the infant in my arms I saw that the bullet had inflicted so much damage to her tiny face that she was choking on her own blood and tissue. I scooped out the gory pulp with my fingers and then, knowing that the baby had no chance of surviving otherwise, I began mouth-to-wound resuscitation. I sealed my mouth over her devastated mouth and nose and began to breathe my life into her little lungs. And I prayed between breaths, "Please, little one, please live." The young cop next to me drove like Mario Andretti: without a moment's hesitation my mission to save this tiny child had become his.

We hurtled through dark alleys, down neon-lit boulevards as the siren pulsed and the flashing reds and blues reflected off the buildings. I continued to breathe life into the baby's lungs and in a few moments—or was it a lifetime?—I heard the most beautiful sound in the world . . . a baby crying. I had tempted her back from whatever dark place she had traveled to. I tasted her blood on my lips. In any other circumstances I would have been repelled by this gory intimacy, but at this moment I only felt an incredible surge of blessed joy. I believed she had come back for me. As I held that child and urged her to stay with me through my whispered entreaties, my silent pleas to God, I felt the pull of a bond that would never be torn asunder. My life and that of this tiny girl had collided and meshed in some prophetic way.

The trauma team was waiting at the hospital and I handed off my precious charge to those who would now shoulder the responsibility for her life. They hustled her away and I felt my heart pounding beneath my Kevlar vest. I tasted my tears before I even knew I was crying. I prayed as I silently watched the trauma team work their magic. Maybe those prayers were heard and answered: I looked up and saw the trauma team nurse approaching me . . . smiling. She said that the little girl was going to make it. She would need extensive cosmetic surgery in the future to hide the terrible scars that would be a constant reminder of this nightmare come true. I had a last glimpse of the tiny, fragile girl as the masked and scrub-clad figures huddled over her in the stark light. That image has stayed in my mind: the tragic reality of what had happened would never be clearer than at that moment.

As I walked out of the treatment area I heard an accented voice say, "That's him! That's the one!" I turned and saw the young couple whose nightmare I had shared. They ran toward me and thanked me in two different languages for saving their baby. It was only then that I learned that her name was Jackie. I had no words; I could only silently wrap my arms around the both of them. The mother looked up at me and, seeing her daughter's blood on my face, reached up and touched it almost wondrously with the tips of her fingers. I will never know what thoughts ran through her mind at that moment, I only know that as her fingers drifted away, her tears ran silently down her cheeks even as she tried to show her gratitude with a shaky smile. I could feel my own eyes start to burn and so I walked away and walked out of the hospital, back into the cool Las Vegas night, back to work.

BLUE & WHITE GRAVEYARD

BY CHARLES R. MARTEL

*Deputy Sheriff, Harris County Sheriff's Department,
Houston, Texas, twenty-five years.*

In the dead of night an errant breeze drifts across the
open lot adjacent to the railroad tracks. From a distance, a
train whistle echoes a mournful refrain . . .

Scattered about the weed-covered asphalt are the rem-
nants of once proud road warriors now left abandoned,
rusting, in various stages of disrepair . . . Impalas, Polaras,
Crown Vics . . . blue and whites broken and shattered
from round-the-clock shifts. Odometers marking a hundred thousand miles or more. Tire treads worn and flat.
Dented fenders, crumpled hoods, busted radiators . . . A
multi-band Motorola radio box jarred loose beneath the
dash. The spiral cord of a microphone hanging limp from
a twisted rear-view mirror. A crushed steering wheel bent
out of shape . . . The stale scent of human excrement
lingers, emanating from the cage-enclosed backseat.
Shards of broken glass embedded in the floorboards. A
bullet-riddled windshield, a blood-stained door . . .

The sirens are now silent. The overhead beacons no
longer flash. Their shop numbers faded, these once powerful police package specials have seen better days. But

only a few feet away, behind a Cyclone fence, a new fleet
of units glistens underneath the harsh glare of the fluores-
cent lights. A fresh coat of paint, blue and white, adorned
by a shield and the words RADIO PATROL. Ready for duty.
Ready to "S/O." Above the din of freeway traffic, the
glow of the city skyline awaits. They'll soon see action . . . robbery calls, traffic stops, "fast ones," silent
alarms, shootings and cuttings, major accidents, intoxicated males, family disturbances, assist the officer, officer
down . . . How long will they last? How long will it be before they, too, are put out to pasture, or are wrecked beyond repair? How long do they have before they join their
colleagues on the other side of the fence?

Does a strange parallel exist between the uniformed
occupants and their law enforcement machines? Are they
forever linked, bonded together by inextricable forces? Is
there an answer to these unfathomable questions . . . or
just the incessant sound of chirping crickets filling the
damp night air?

A LITTLE LESS THAN SMART

BY AL GIBSON

Las Vegas Metropolitan PD, Nevada.

One hot summer evening in Las Vegas I was on patrol on the infamous Boulder Highway known for its daily/weekly/monthly hotels, the kind of place that attracts dopers, thieves, and all kinds of lowlifes. As I was passing one of the many convenience stores that dot the highway a frantic store clerk flagged me down. "I was robbed, I was robbed!" he was yelling. Wow, I thought wryly, another robbery. That's only four tonight. As I was getting out of the patrol car the clerk was pointing at a young fat guy urinating on the store's Dumpster. "That's him!" he cried. Chubby saw me and without bothering to put away his pecker he began to run away. Well, since he had a pretty good head start and since I was laughing so hard, by the time I got around the corner he was gone. As I started to look for him in the housing project cluster where he had disappeared, I noticed a brand-new candy bar on the ground. Figuring Chubby could have dropped it, I employed my honed-with-experience investigative techniques (I watch *Columbo*) and bent down to touch the candy bar. "Ha! Evidence!" I said because it was still cold. Chubby *must* have dropped it because it was still over a hundred degrees outside and the candy bar hadn't even melted. I continued in the same direction and to my happy surprise I found another cold candy bar. This was getting good. I continued to follow a trail of candy bars that would have made Willy Wonka jealous. A total of seven candy bars in all over a distance of about one quarter of a mile. Then, finally, the search was over. I encountered my suspect crouched behind another Dumpster, stuffing his face with potato chips. After a brief struggle (he wouldn't drop the chips) I took him into custody.

Later, the clerk told me that he was surprised that the suspect had perpetrated such a crime. The clerk knew the suspect. In fact, he was a family friend. He had even had Thanksgiving dinner at the clerk's house. I considered these revelations and asked the clerk to give me all the details of the crime. It seems that the teenage suspect had entered the store, drank two beers, and had then proceeded to punch a woman at the ATM because she refused to take money out of her account for him. (Maybe she should have invited Chubby for Christmas dinner.) Then he had walked up to the clerk and demanded all the money from the register. The clerk refused so he punched the woman again and then stole the snacks. When he ran out of the store, the clerk ran after him and this was where I had entered the story.

I later ascertained that the thief felt no remorse for his crime and, in fact, slept all the way to the jail. I attributed this to post–sugar-high fatigue and withdrawals. And, yes, the evidence, all seven candy bars, melted before we got there.

YOUR HUSBAND—MY PARTNER
A LETTER TO LESA

BY RON CORBIN

*Police Officer/Instructor Pilot, Los Angeles PD,
retired, seven years.*

PROLOGUE

On Friday, June 11, 1976, at 12:50 P.M., twenty-nine-year-old LAPD Instructor Pilot Ron Corbin and LAPD Student Pilot Jeffrey Lindenberg, officers with, respectively, five and seven years on the job, were airborne in their Bell 47G-5 helicopter over the Hollywood Hills above the Los Angeles Zoo, just east of the Griffith Observatory. They were practicing off-site pinnacle landings on the mountaintop. Officer Lindenberg was at the controls on short final approach when the engine failed. Instructor Corbin was unable to recover and safely autorotate due to the low altitude and low airspeed at the time of incident. He desperately tried to salvage the crash by stretching the approach glidepath to a pad at the top of the mountain, but came four inches short of a safe landing. The helicopter fell backward off the cliff and dropped 162 feet down a 70-degree incline of rocky and brush-strewn hillside. The mission had just begun, so the aircraft was full of fuel and exploded, leaving a trail of fire. Other members of the Air Unit, who reported it to the LAFD Helicopter Unit, observed the resulting smoke. One of the FD helicopters was dispatched, thinking it was nothing more than a brush fire. Arriving upon the scene, two hikers who had run to the site and had Corbin on the ground, waved the FD helicopter down for an emergency medevac. Officer Lindenberg was not visible to the rescue unit. Aftermath: Officer Corbin received burns on 70 percent of his body (62 percent second- or third-degree) and was in the hospital for over two months. He was subjected to years of multiple reconstructive surgeries on his face, arms, legs, and torso. Officer Jeffrey Lindenberg, age thirty, was killed in the wreck and consumed in the resulting fire, leaving a grieving young widow, Lesa, and a seven-month-old daughter, Tina Michelle. The accident was ruled due to mechanical failure; there was nothing that either officer—pilot or student—could have done to change the tragic outcome.

This accident happened more than twenty-five years ago. Ron Corbin still bears the physical scars of the accident but one wonders if he still thinks about his partner, Jeff, who lost his life on that hillside so long ago. Oh, yes. The following letter is a dedication to all those who wear a badge and a uniform and who won't ever forget . . . not September 11, not a tragedy on a mountaintop, not any fellow officer's death, however it occurred. Cops may mourn privately but they don't forget.

Dear Lesa,

I'm fifty-five years old now, with another birthday approaching this June fifteenth. I don't have to remind you that this is just four days after the anniversary of Jeff's death. Even after all these years, I'm sure you and your daughter think of this every June, especially since it's so close to Father's Day. I want you to know that I, too, still can't celebrate my birthday without thinking back on that fateful day in 1976 when you lost a husband, and I lost a partner.

Lesa, you know I would have been at the funeral had I not been in the hospital. Those first couple weeks when I was in grave and critical condition are mostly a blur in my memory; as much probably from being sedated as to the extent of my injuries. Actually, before I became conscious enough to even be told that Jeff had been killed in the accident, the memorial services, the missing man formation fly-by, the playing of taps, and the twenty-one-gun salute had long passed.

I still remember, as if it was yesterday, when the news of his death was shared with me. When the doctor said he felt I was emotionally ready to receive the news, my wife Kathy—standing by my bedside with tears streaming down her cheeks—told me that Jeff had been killed in the crash. Her words numbed my mind. I remember that it was more shock than sorrow that hit me. I don't think I said anything back to her. I just lay there staring at the ceiling and thinking, "How is that possible? I should have been able to save him. Why him, God, and not me?"

I've never forgotten Jeff: his humor and wit, his desire to become a police pilot, or his love and devotion to you and his new baby girl. But I did come to grips with his death a long time ago. I believe most cops probably think their demise will likely come by a bullet, but there are many other inherent dangers to the profession: traffic accidents while in pursuit, stabbing by an emotionally disturbed person, a fall from a high-rise while trying to grab a suicidal jumper, death from a booby-trap bomb in a drug raid, crushed in a building collapse from a terrorist incident, and yes . . . even a training accident in a helicopter. The everyday danger of being a cop is understood only by other cops.

Lesa, I guess one of the reasons for writing this is that I need some final closure for me in another way. It had been months since the accident, so when I finally got out of the hospital, I wanted to see you. I wanted to express my sympathy and sorrow. Remember, I sent you a card saying that I would be glad to meet with you; to answer your questions and tell you everything I could remember about that day leading up to the crash. I wanted to cry on your shoulder and let you cry on mine.

You graciously replied to my note, but I was somewhat surprised that you didn't want to see me. It was a message of rejection that has kept me awake at nights, silently wondering . . . why? I thought, surely you would have questions that only I could answer. "Why did the engine quit when we were landing on that pinnacle in the mountains? Was Jeff a good pilot? Do you think he suffered?" So, yes, I was surprised when I received your reply stating that you preferred not to face me. This void has eaten at my heart for twenty-six years now.

It's difficult to explain the emptiness in my heart because I never got to talk with you. I wanted to explain how hard I tried to prevent the accident, and how close we came to walking away. To say there was a mechanical problem, and that in spite of what the department said, it was not pilot error and that Jeff did nothing wrong. I wanted to let you know that after climbing out of the wreckage with my helmet visor melted to my face and my clothing on fire, I mumbled Jeff's name to the hikers who came to my rescue; not heroically, but letting them know there was someone else for them to help. Lesa, I wanted to tell you how sorry I was for not being able to do more to save Jeff's life.

Kathy knows that I had a difficult time with your rebuff. I tried to understand your position; I tried to put myself in your frame of mind as a young widow with a new infant daughter and having to grasp the realization of suddenly being devoid of your soul mate. But the more I tried to understand your reasoning for not wanting to see me, the more I imagined there was more to what was really going through your mind.

Was it my burn scars that motivated you not to see me? I can understand that. Yes, maybe that was it. With 70 percent burns, I did portray a pretty grotesque specimen of a human. Or was it simply because you blamed me for Jeff's death? After all, I was the flight instructor. I was the experienced pilot with thousands of hours. I should have been able to prevent the accident. The more I dwelled on it, the more I came to the conclusion that it was probably a combination of these things. But whatever your reason, I respected your decision. And I thought that someday, when the time was right for you, you'd call me and then we could share our hugs and tears. But you never did.

I heard that you remarried—another policeman, no less. I'm happy that you were able to find someone else, someone you can love as much as you did Jeff. Although I've never seen her, I can imagine that your daughter is a beautiful young woman now. I mean, look at her parents.

In closing, Lesa, I just want to share a few more of my most personal thoughts, some of the things I would have shared with you had we been able to get together. I will always remember the good times Jeff and I had when we carpooled to work, and the laughter and joking that we shared with other pilots and police officers at the heliport. He had already proven to be an outstanding officer on the tough streets of LA, one of the top observers for the unit, and now he was progressing into a fine pilot, too. I didn't consider him just another student pilot. He was my police partner and a close friend. It was a pleasure teaching him some of the flying skills I had obtained.

In my flying career, I had previously experienced another engine failure, a cockpit fire, some combat damage, and myriad other in-flight emergencies. More fortunately, I survived two tours in Vietnam as an Army helicopter pilot, but my memories of this time end with having the names of twenty-seven of my pilot buddies inscribed on the Wall in Washington, D.C. When I joined the Los Angeles Police Department, I did so with the hope of becoming one of their helicopter pilots, and my dream was fulfilled in 1974. I looked upon my career as a pilot with LAPD's Air Support Division as one that would provide a higher degree of safety than that involved in combat flying. I never imagined, though, with all that I had been through, that I would have to face another death caused by a helicopter accident . . . especially someone who was as close to me as Jeff. His death only added to the tremendous amount of survivor's guilt I've experienced over the course of my lifetime.

It's hard for me to hear taps, or the sound of a bagpipe playing "Amazing Grace." I'm not ashamed to say that it brings tears. But I'll continue wiping away the tears if it means I never have to forget. Because I don't ever want to forget my army buddies or Jeff, I have a couple ways to serve as a daily reminder. First, every day at work I close out my computer with a sound file of taps and a volley of gunfire as a twenty-one-gun salute. It makes me think of those who wear a police or military uniform, and to remember that "all gave some, but some gave all."

Second, I have my dad's American flag, tri-folded and encased from his funeral, on display in my home. The three corners of the flag are a constant reminder for me; one corner representing his death, one corner representing my army friends who gave their lives in the service of their country, and one corner for Jeff—your husband, my partner.

With love . . . Ron

STAGING POINT FOR THE ALIEN INVASION

BY ROBERT BANKS

*Sergeant, Stanislaus County Sheriff's
Department/Patterson PD, California,
twelve years.*

In 1992, I was working for the Gustine Police Department in California's Central Valley. Gustine is a small community of about four thousand people and it was my first full-time job as a police officer at a POST-certified department.

During one week I received five calls from a male who was convinced there were invisible, and possibly illegal, space aliens in the attic of his home. Each time I responded I assured him, after the obvious drug influence evaluation, that there were no aliens in his house.

On the day of his sixth call I responded as usual and arrived to find the caller on his rooftop with a shovel removing the tiles from his roof. I called him down and asked him what he was doing. He told me that the aliens were still in his attic and he was going to get them no matter what.

They train you in the academy to always have a plan when you respond to calls and this time I was ready. I told him that I had discussed the alien problem with the proper state and federal agencies, being the community-oriented cop that I was, and had learned that the authorities were well aware of what was going on in Gustine. It seemed, for some reason, the aliens from Galaxy Alpha Beta had chosen Gustine as a staging area to kick off their invasion of earth and the enslavement of all mankind. They were only waiting to find the exact location of the staging area before taking action. As I had been working closely with representatives of Area 51, I told him, I was given a tool with which to combat the team of aliens who were here to pave the way for the others to follow. MPH Industries, the maker of fine handheld law enforcement radar, had been working with the federal government in the development of a new weapon to be used against the alien incursion. I told him that I had firsthand knowledge of the alien staging point and so was given a temporary commission as an officer with the Area 51 staff and had been provided with the weapon that would save the human race. He was captivated and dutifully followed me over to my patrol car and watched as I removed the instrument of the aliens' defeat, the MPH Industries radiation-emitting gun, which, of course, looked like a normal radar gun. We approached his house cautiously and, placing the end of the power cord into my Sam Brown belt, I began to destroy the alien invaders, aiming the gun at every crawl space, closet, and cubbyhole where the cunning and invisible aliens might be hiding. The caller assisted me in this task by pointing out all the areas in his home where he knew firsthand the aliens were holed up.

After about five minutes the special anti-alien radiation-emitting weapon had done its work and the aliens, I'm happy to say, had been destroyed. Weeping with gratitude, the caller thanked me for saving him from the aliens and from assimilation into their ranks. I, likewise, thanked him on behalf of a grateful nation for the assistance he had provided and made it clear to him that he had saved mankind from certain enslavement.

After my wholesale destruction of the alien invaders I never received a return call of any kind from this gentleman and I'm sure he tells the story to this day of how he, with the help of a concerned cop, saved humanity.

BERT & ERNIE

BY DAVID A. ROGERS

Public Safety Officer, Sunnyvale Department of Public Safety, retired after twenty-seven years.

My life was changed early in my career when my best friend was killed fighting a fire. I have counseled numerous friends and relatives who have suffered the loss of a loved one. I compare the loss to a book. Immediately after the loss, the book is open on the desk in front of you and you are wildly turning the pages. Then, with time, you slow down and start to read. With more time the book is closed and pushed to the top of the desk, occasionally to be opened and read. Then, finally, the book is placed on a shelf in your mind, taken down from time to time when events trigger a memory, sometimes when you least expect it . . .

Chuck Fraker and I became friends while in the Santa Clara County Regional Police Academy in 1974. I had been a cadet for one and a half years with the Sunnyvale Department of Public Safety, a combined police and fire department in Santa Clara County, and I was sworn in as an officer on my twenty-first birthday, in the eighth week of the ten-week course. Chuck was a reserve police officer in the City of Santa Clara. He wanted to work in Santa Clara, but Sunnyvale was hiring.

During the next two years, Chuck and I worked the same shifts and we were both on the pistol team and softball team. We soon became the best of friends. Chuck was married to Michelle, and they had two daughters. I married not long after and our wives also became friends. The four of us played pinochle and had dinner together at least once a week, usually at their house because of the children's bedtimes. We were together so much, in fact, that a coworker nicknamed us "Bert & Ernie."

Chuck and I were working the day shift, 0630–1430, with Friday and Saturday off. We carpooled and the days that I drove I would wait in the kitchen, having coffee as he'd go down the hall to kiss his sleeping wife good-bye.

On Sunday morning, August 1, 1976, I went to his house to pick him up at about 0600, as I thought it was my turn to drive. Unfortunately, he thought it was his turn. I saw his car was gone so I waited. He soon came back and we had a good laugh. For some reason, and for the first and only time, Michelle got up that morning and had coffee and pumpkin pie with us.

We arrived at the department, attended briefing, and went to our cars. We passed Dispatcher Ed Mendenhall coming in. Chuck said, "Hey Ed, how about cooking us up a fire today?" and we all laughed and went to work. Chuck and I were in separate cars that day, both working Beat 1, Northeast Sunnyvale.

The morning passed uneventfully—a quiet Sunday. But in the afternoon, a child was playing with matches in one of two upstairs bedrooms in an apartment in West Central Sunnyvale. His mother was taking a bath when she smelled smoke. She saw the bed on fire, so she closed the door to the bedroom and fled the apartment with her children and called the Fire Department. Engine 1, Truck 1, and Engine 3 responded, as well as six patrol officers, myself and Chuck included. The protocol was for the first arriving officers to pull the hoses and advance them and begin firefighting activities without any breathing apparatus on. I'd already fought many fires with my face close to the nozzle looking for cool, fresh air. Then, officers arriving later would put on breathing apparatus and relieve them.

This fire was no exception. Chuck arrived before me and made entry with another officer. The smoke was heavy, banked halfway down the stairs. It is not clear to me whether they had a hose line, but they were not wearing breathing apparatus. The officer with Chuck told him it was too hot and that they were leaving. He turned and went down the stairs, assuming Chuck was behind him. But he wasn't.

Chuck either pushed the bedroom door open or opened the nozzle, blowing the door open. Either way, the sudden introduction of oxygen into the room made the fire flare up violently, causing a backdraft condition. Chuck was standing in or near the doorway and took the brunt of the flames, involuntarily gasping. His lungs were seared shut, but he was conscious for a short time.

Smudge marks were found on the soot-covered walls where Chuck had tried to feel his way out of the apartment. The coroner said that he would have been in a state of unspeakable agony at that time. Chuck made it to the second bedroom, next to a bed below a window, and collapsed.

I arrived at the scene and was directed to put on a breathing apparatus, but then was told to extend a hose to protect other buildings. As I was doing so I witnessed a commotion as two public safety officers carried a person out of the burning apartment building. I initially thought, "My God . . . someone was in there!" then "Hey, he's got a turnout coat on—he's one of us!" and then "My God— it's Chuck!" He had been inside for twenty minutes. He wasn't breathing. Two officers began CPR, and I ran to

Truck 1 to get the resuscitator, then took over CPR for one of the officers. When the ambulance arrived, I went with Chuck.

It was the middle of summer and hot. I remember that a drop of sweat would drip off my nose with each chest compression I did. I remember thinking, "He's okay, he's okay," and saying it to myself over and over.

I was exhausted when we arrived at El Camino Hospital Emergency Room. I stayed in the nurse's lounge while they worked on him. A short time later a nurse—who I found out later was a Mountain View police officer's wife—came over to me, clearly upset. She said she was sorry. They had done all they could but Chuck was dead.

I know I was supposed to call someone; I wanted to go get Michelle but I didn't want to tell her what had happened over the phone. Michelle's father was a retired Santa Clara Police Department sergeant, but I didn't know his number. I left the hospital to pick up my wife and go over to Chuck's house. But Michelle was already gone; she'd gotten a call from someone saying that Chuck had been hurt and she'd left for the hospital, leaving her house full of people who were there for a Tupperware party.

When we returned to the hospital, Michelle was already there. I told her what had happened. She was in shock and wanted to see him. I remember going into the room and seeing his sheet-covered body before the doctor folded the sheet back. Michelle just wailed, "Oh, Chuck." There is nothing like the sound of the human voice in utter anguish. The needle mark was still there from the adrenaline injection they'd given him to try to restart his heart. He had small burns on his chin and nose and there were patches on his hands where the skin was missing.

The next week was a blur. I served as liaison to the family and department. There were no general orders or protocol for this. I went with Michelle's father to make funeral arrangements, to pick out a plot and a casket, and to arrange for the church services. At one point, the mortuary called to say there was a problem. I went down there and they took me into the prep room. It seems that the burns on Chuck's face were weeping through the make-up. "See this?" the mortician said, sticking a cotton swab in Chuck's mouth and lifting up the offending tissue for me to get a better look. I just stood there staring at the coroner's wide sutures and at the corrupted body of my friend. I told the mortician to do his best and left. I was twenty-three years old; Chuck had been twenty-five.

The viewing the night before the funeral was very tough. I stood the entire time on honor guard duty at the head of my best friend's casket. His youngest child, three-year-old Angie, oblivious to what had happened, ran up to me and said, "Hi, Uncle Dave!" I could not hold back the tears.

The next day was the funeral. I asked Michelle if she wanted Chuck's badge. No, she said—it meant so much to him that she wanted him to have it with him. So I pinned it to his chest on his dress uniform jacket before the service. I presented the folded flag to Michelle because she didn't want to receive it from a stranger. That was twenty-six years ago.

In 1994, we built a second home in Amador County, intending to use it as our retirement home. I also became an Amador County reserve deputy sheriff in order to get to know the county, the people, and to become involved in the community. They conducted the usual background, physical, and psych exams. One of the psych questions was, "What was the hardest thing you've ever done?" I answered immediately, "Burying my best friend."

I anguished for a long time afterwards—did I do the compressions right? Did I get the oxygen exchange right?

Did I overlook something? Could I have done something more? But I was assured by the doctors that even if they, themselves, had been right there when Chuck was brought out of the building, it wouldn't have mattered.

This is what I've lived with for almost twenty-six years. I can remember the events of that day, all that was said, with absolute clarity. I probably still haven't dealt with all the emotions. As time passed, I found I couldn't attend other police and fire funerals or see them on television— they evoked memories that were too painful. September 11 was especially poignant and caused "the book" to be reviewed yet again. Thank you for giving me the opportunity to tell my story. It was helpful to me to put pen to paper.

THE SHOW-UP

BY GAVIN KEENAN

Sergeant, Ipswich PD, Ipswich, Massachusetts,
twenty-two years.

In the daily jargon of police work, a show-up is an identification procedure employed to quickly identify someone who has just committed a crime. Basically it works like this: when a victim reports a crime to the police and can provide information describing the suspect, the police can search the immediate area of the crime scene in order to locate and detain the suspect. Once the suspect is located and detained, the victim is brought to the scene in order to provide a positive identification. The goal of the police during this procedure is to hear the victim say, "That's the guy." However, this being America, and especially Massachusetts, legal safeguards must be observed in order to protect the suspect's rights. In the Commonwealth police officers are often admonished to limit the degree of "suggestiveness" present during these procedures. That is to say, the police aren't supposed to make the suspect look too guilty to the victim during the process. But, as is often the case with many judicial edicts handed down by black-robed idealists, this often is easier said than done.

Consider if you will the following scene: a person calls

the police and reports that a blond-haired male adolescent wearing a pink wife-beater shirt and brown BDUs just threw a rock through his window and ran away down the street. Based on this report, the cops search the immediate area for the youth and are rewarded by locating someone who matches the suspect's description walking in the neighborhood. He is detained and questioned. Of course he denies any connection to the incident, and in fact is quite indignant that the police would accuse him of such an act. After all, don't the police know who this youth's father is? As this give and take goes on, more police arrive in order to lend moral support to the investigating officer, and perhaps to be in on any pinch that may result. In order to solidify probable cause, one of the cops suggests that the witness be brought to the scene for a show-up. This done, the witness observes a blond-haired adolescent surrounded by uniformed police officers who are busy hurling accusations at the youth. Naturally, in such a "nonsuggestive" setting as this, the witness is easily able to make the hoped for "untainted" identification. Indeed, in order to reinforce the witness's identification, the police handcuff the blond smart-ass and toss him into a nearby cruiser. And all this is done with the witness looking on and taking it all in. Is this an effective procedure? Yes. Is it also a suggestive one? Yes again. However, as I was to learn one night, the confounding variations to the show-up process can make even routine police work memorable.

This particular evening I was on duty in my small town with three or four other street officers, one of who was Detective Charlie Hathaway. Charlie had been on the job a lot longer than I had, and although I was his senior in rank, Charlie and I always operated as equals. We had worked together for a long time and I counted on Charlie's judgment and knowledge of the job. When the occasional big thing happened on our shift, we would always collaborate on the best approach to the problem. Usually we tended to think in opposite ways, bouncing our opinions off each other until we arrived at a solution. This approach served us well, and often led to either a good pinch or a way out of a bad situation.

We began this evening shift in the usual way, taking reports from the officers going off duty, drinking coffee, and thoroughly discussing "the issues of the day." The weather was pleasant, and as it was early June, it would be light out well into the shift. We eventually left the station and made our way out onto the street to work. I drove my cruiser down to the local ballpark to see and be seen, as well as to watch the local high school game. They were enjoying a good season, and this evening's game was no exception. The Tigers were leading by two runs in the bottom of the eighth inning, and there was a good-sized crowd on hand to cheer them on. I was just settling in to do some true "community policing," when a call came over the police radio reporting a robbery at Tobias's Market.

Tobias's Market was one of the last mom-and-pop stores left in town. When I was a kid growing up here there were more than a dozen of these stores. Some, like Tobias's, were ethnic in nature and appealed mainly to either the large Polish or Greek populations that once existed in town. But as with all things, this changed over the years, and these populations were dispersed, intermarried, and eventually displaced—outnumbered by the large influx of new people that moved into town in the 1960s and 1970s. Tobias's Market was just one room on the ground floor of the Tobias home. It contained a few coolers for beer, wine, and some cold cuts; shelves for candy, cigarettes, and bread; and a large countertop with an old manual cash register. A doorway behind the counter led directly into the Tobias living room and when you entered the store you could often see Mr. Tobias sitting there watching TV. Suffice it to say the store was not routinely a beehive of commerce. But it was clean and Mr. Tobias always treated you well.

At the time of this incident Mr. Tobias was in his late seventies, and although I don't think he needed to work, I do think that he did so to keep himself going. Mr. Tobias was a tall, kindly gentleman with horn-rimmed glasses. He always sported a white apron just like Pete the butcher on the old TV commercial. Several times a day he could be seen sweeping the sidewalk in front of the store, and he kept posters in the store windows advertising FRESH KIELBASA and GENUINE POLISH HAM. But Mr. Tobias wasn't as sharp as he used to be and, as I was about to learn, not the most observant guy around.

When the report of the robbery went out over the air I was only about a minute away. When I pulled up near the store I saw Charlie's unmarked cruiser parked on the street as well as that of another officer. I then made my way into the store. I saw Charlie talking with Mr. Tobias and I listened to learn what had occurred. As I looked around the store, I could see nothing out of place or obviously disturbed. Mr. Tobias was telling Charlie that he thought that he had been robbed. He went on to explain that about ten minutes before, a man came into the store and asked for some cigarettes. As he rang up the sale, Mr. Tobias said that the man placed his hand in his pocket, told Mr. Tobias that he had a gun, and demanded all of the money in the register. Mr. Tobias said that he gave the man what was in the cash drawer and the man then left the store. However, most of the day's receipts were stashed in an egg carton under the counter so Mr. Tobias wasn't sure how much had been taken. On top of this he could only give us a vague description of the robber:

white male, medium height, mid-twenties, dark hair. He didn't see if the guy had driven off in a vehicle and he couldn't tell us what the guy had been wearing.

What struck Charlie and me as strange about the whole thing was that Mr. Tobias was so unsure of certain things. He couldn't tell us what the man had said, didn't know how much money was missing (in fact there was still cash in the drawer), and couldn't say in which direction the man had run even though the store windows looked right out onto the street. We were beginning to wonder if what he was telling us had actually happened. Robberies were and are a rare thing in our town, although imagined incidents were not so rare. But just to cover ourselves, we had an area broadcast of the incident put out over the air. Once that was done, Charlie and I scratched our heads and wondered what to do next.

As we talked things over, I found myself becoming increasingly convinced that Mr. Tobias was confused and had perhaps imagined the whole thing. Charlie was not so skeptical, and kept probing Mr. Tobias for more details. As he did this, Mr. Tobias sank into deeper confusion, and was clearly losing the thread of events. At one point I asked Mr. Tobias if it was possible that what he had told us hadn't really taken place. I was understandably not thrilled when he replied that he wasn't sure. As the minutes passed, I was clearly entering the conundrum stage. I didn't want to completely discount the report as unfounded, but on the other hand I didn't want an unsolved crime on our hands that may not have occurred. I was in desperate need of an exit strategy.

Sometimes God can be good to confused and anxious cops. As I was about to bring our investigation to a undetermined end, a report came over the air from an adjoining town that the police had just arrested someone who had robbed a drugstore there. When our desk officer called over to get some details, we learned that a young white male had walked into a drugstore, stated to the clerk that he had a gun, and demanded Percocets. After he left the store, the clerk called the police who quickly found and arrested the guy who, by the way, was discovered to be unarmed.

Well this was great news to me, and before you could say crime spree, Charlie was on his way there to get a good look-see at the suspect. As for me, I drove Mr. Tobias over in hopes that he would be able to identify this guy as the person who robbed him. When we arrived at the neighboring PD, I had Mr. Tobias wait in the cruiser while I checked things out inside. I spoke to Charlie, who told me that the prisoner fit the description of our suspect, and even better than that, he was cooperating. We both felt that now was the perfect time for a show-up. I went back to the cruiser to fetch Mr. Tobias. Charlie went back inside the PD to sanitize the viewing area and the suspect as much as possible.

I led Mr. Tobias to the booking area where the prisoner was located. This was a room about twenty feet square containing desks, chairs, radios, bulletin boards with wanted posters—in short, all of the paraphernalia that you would expect at a small-town PD. There were at least five uniformed cops in the room as well as Charlie and myself. To be perfectly honest, this was a big deal for all of us. We don't catch robbers every day around here. And speaking of the robber, in the middle of this sea of blue uniforms sat a small, dark-haired, scared guy who for all the world looked like he desperately needed some of the Percocets that he had been trying to steal.

As Mr. Tobias and I entered the booking room, I could sense his nervousness. I asked him to look around the room and tell me if he had seen anyone there in his store earlier that evening. Of course he replied that Charlie and

I had been there but he did not recognize anyone else. Growing frustrated, I asked him if he was sure. He said that he didn't know. With frustration morphing to chagrin, I said to him, "What about that guy?" as I pointed to the spaced-out doper sitting in the chair with his head in his hands. "No, sorry," replied Mr. T, "I can't help you."

As I was about to press the point again, America's Most Wanted sat up in his chair, looked right at Mr. Tobias, and said, "Hey, that's the guy I tried to rob. I'm really sorry about that, I didn't mean to scare you." Before Mr. Tobias could argue the point, I thanked him for his time and had him brought home. Our suspect was arrested based on his "admission," a new legal theory of ass-backwards identification was established, and justice, I guess, was served.

THE EMOTIONAL SWITCH

by Rocky Warren

Sergeant, Placer County Sheriff's Department, California.

Jerry pushed open the door with his left hand, and the muzzle of the .45 in his right led the way into the room. Most people don't know that you can sometimes smell spilled blood before you can see it. That brassy, slightly corrupt smell was full in his nostrils now and the uniformed deputy winced slightly. The gun swept the tiny mudroom entry of the small farmhouse. The sights of the gun lay extended just below Jerry's sight line, ready to pop up in a fraction of a second at the slightest hint of need. The reporting party said there were two dead people in the house, and it smelled like they were right.

Edging to the side of the open door to the living room, Jerry caught sight of a pair of legs belonging to a body lying on the living room floor. Nope. Revise that. It's two pairs of legs. From their size and shape, Jerry knew that a woman and a small child lay in the center of the living room. As he moved through the doorway he could better make out the details. She was maybe in her late twenties or early thirties and lay on her side with her back toward him. The body of a girl was sprawled nearby on her back with her hand nearly touching the hand of her mother.

Jerry moved toward the bodies across a minefield of evidence. He was careful to move soundlessly and he did not step in the blood, bone fragments or cartridge cases scattered across the room. He kept his gun pointed toward the bedroom doors, covering the maximum point of danger.

When he was close enough, Jerry squatted down and touched the neck of the woman. He sighed when he touched the carotid artery and found no pulse. Not that he'd expected anything different. He began to reach toward the child to try the same thing but his hand stopped and then slowly drew back almost of its own volition. From his new vantage point, Jerry could see under the front bangs of her hairdo, and saw that the tiny girl had been shot in the forehead. An instantly fatal wound.

He heard the sound of a distant siren. The ambulance was still a long way off. Jerry keyed the radio mike and asked dispatch to stage the ambulance and asked that the medical technicians not come into the house. He wasn't sure yet if the suspect was gone, so the murder scene wasn't secure yet. He told dispatch that there were two "eleven forty-fours," two bodies in the house. Dispatch acknowledged, and he heard the return radio traffic from detectives who were already on their way to the scene.

Jerry moved through the rest of the house like a wraith, alert for a surprise. Wondering if the suspect would pop up out of nowhere, ready and willing to kill again. But he didn't find anyone. He then went back and checked the less likely places. Cupboards, dryers and small cubbyholes got a flashlight and the muzzle of a .45 poked into them. Still no one. By the time he finished the building search he was completely wrung out and dripping with sweat.

He had to steel himself to go back into the front room where the bodies lay. As he passed the woman, he glanced down at her again but this time his attention was riveted on her abdomen. He stopped and felt the tension arc across his shoulders. He squatted again and looked closely, taking in the swelling beneath a maternity top. Despite the gory mess from the bullet wounds to her abdomen, he could see she was in the latter stages of pregnancy. He shut his eyes and felt a momentary stab of pain. There were three murder victims in the room, not two.

The rest of the day was a blur. Jerry briefed the detectives, filled out forms, did coroner's duties, kept an entry and exit log of the crime scene, performed crowd control, contained the press, and attended to all the endless details. The front drive and the road to the farmhouse were packed solid with unmarked police cars, curious bystanders, and the media. To Jerry, the whole scene seemed surreal. Despite the bright day, the sunlight seemed to be a little dull, as if an eclipse had just reached its midpoint. There's a pall that hangs over a murder scene. There's also a pervasive sense of duty and responsibility. A feeling of loss, the recognition of theft. The ultimate theft, the theft of life. There were two voices that wouldn't be heard from again after this day. Three lives ended violently and it became the job of the police to find out who entered this house with a rifle and killed a woman, her unborn child, and her five-year-old daughter.

When the two coroner's stretchers were wheeled from the house all activity stopped. Hardened, cynical men and women who've seen more than their share stood fixed in place. The tiny form on the second gurney was mute but spoke volumes about tragedy and loss. When the doors of the coroner's van clunked shut, the silent detectives went back to their duties even more determined than they had been before.

Elsewhere, homicide detectives who hadn't even been to the murder scene were doing their duty. The ex-husband of the female victim had been notified of the death of the woman and child. The five-year-old girl was his daughter with the woman. His grief seemed huge, but the expression of it was suspiciously dry-eyed. His alibi was pathetic and it took only a few minutes for detectives to lock the ex-husband into a pattern of deception. He had to keep making up more lies to patch the leaks from which his first lies had sprung. He was now a clear suspect. When asked to describe his relationship with his ex-wife, he said they'd been separated for some time and she'd been dating. When he learned that she was pregnant with another man's child, he couldn't stand it. For that, he said, she had to die.

He had gone to her house and lain in wait, concealed in a barn on the property. He had smoked several cigarettes to pass the time. When his ex-wife and daughter came home and went inside he had hoisted up his .30 caliber M-1 rifle and went in after them. He stole the life of the woman he claimed to love by shooting her repeatedly in the abdomen, killing both her and her unborn baby. When he realized his little daughter was a witness and probably wouldn't be able to keep from talking about what had happened, he shot her once in the forehead and ended the possibility of her testifying against her father. Against her killer.

The man, the ex-husband and "father," was convicted of a triple murder. The sentence was life. Life without possibility of parole.

The locker room is dark in the late evening, and I leave it that way. I take off my uniform, my badge, my bullet-proof vest, and my gun belt. There's a place for every-thing in my locker. I slap the steel locker door with more than a little frustration, and it clangs shut with a metallic shudder. Graveyard shift isn't here yet, so I don't have to listen to their hooting and hollering about the stops and capers of last night. I also won't have to field questions about the ugly coroner's case I had today. Car crashes chew up small kids just as badly as they do adults and some drivers pull really stupid stunts. The case wasn't as bad as Jerry's triple-murder last month, but it still wrenches me to investigate the death of a child.

I take my time showering and changing into street clothes. Soaping up and rinsing several times still doesn't remove the grimy, weary feeling. From long, hard experience, I know the feeling will be with me for a few days no matter how much I might want it otherwise.

On the way home in my personal car, I drive the road but see very little of it consciously. In my mind there are a host of people. The faces left over from car wrecks, construction accidents, plane crashes, fires, natural deaths, suicides, and murders. There are new faces present on the roll call tonight. It'll take me a few days to a week before the faces from the nasty coroner's case recede into the background. For some reason, Jerry's sad trio of victims is present in my mind's eye—it's as if we all share the same burden of recall no matter who caught the actual case.

The welcome sight of my driveway flares as headlights slide across the gravel. The word has made it home ahead of me. My wife is at the door, and I get a huge hug from her. After rocking side-to-side and luxuriating in her arms for a moment, I let her go and step through into the hallway of our home. My wife follows; she knows what's coming. She's seen it before. When I handled the last bad one. When I got into my shootings.

I look in on my sleeping children. They stir lightly in their dreams as I brush my lips across their night-sweaty foreheads. There are tears that fall unseen and unremarked upon in the darkness.

The emotional switch that's been in the off position all day has only now been switched back on. And it gets harder to turn it on all the time.

God, please keep little children safe. Keep my family and community safe.

But if there's anything I can do for those who are in danger, who are afraid, let them call me and I will be there.

My phone number is 911.

THE McBUNGLER

BY MELINDA WALKER

*Sergeant, Washington County Sheriff's Department,
Texas, twenty years.*

The crook drove into the crowded McDonald's parking lot and worked his way through the heavy workday lunch-hour traffic to the rear of the restaurant. After parking his Ford Pinto beside the Dumpster near the rear delivery door (where his vehicle was less likely to be seen), the robber stuffed a pistol into his waistband under his shirttail and walked casually into the restaurant. He stood in line behind several customers and watched three teenage cashiers hurriedly ringing up orders while he contemplated the "motherload" he was about to make by knocking off the busiest lunch-hour restaurant in Houston.

When it was finally his turn to approach the next available cashier, the crook pulled up the blue bandanna tied around his neck to partially cover his face while simultaneously grabbing the pistol from his waistband. He pointed the pistol at the young male cashier whose eyes were suddenly the size of saucers as he stared, transfixed, at the gun barrel pointed at his face.

"Put the cash from your register into a to-go bag!" the crook shouted. The terrified cashier grabbed a large paper bag, opened his register and began stuffing wads of cash inside. The crook then waved the gun in the direction of the other two cashiers. "You too . . . both of you! Put your money into the bag. Hurry or you'll be short a cashier!"

The other two cashiers scrambled to open their registers and frantically began grabbing fistfuls of cash and stuffing it into the nearly full bag. Impatient, the crook snatched the paper bag out of the cashier's hands and then nearly trampled a small crowd of customers who had just entered the store as he fled out the door and ran toward his parked car.

"Shit!" the crook exclaimed as he rounded the corner. A bread delivery truck had blocked his Pinto in. Seeing no one through the open sliding door of the bread truck, the robber hopped into the driver's seat and searched for the ignition switch. He found it and turned the key. The engine growled but wouldn't turn over, though the sound caught the attention of the truck's driver, who was in the rear of the truck counting loaves of bread. The bread man, fearing he was about to be hijacked, grabbed a large aluminum bread tray and smacked the robber over the head.

The startled crook jumped from the bread truck and ran toward the drive-through lane, the bag of money swinging from one hand, his other hand wielding the pistol. The frantic crook spotted an unsuspecting lone female driver in a beige Volkswagen Beetle who was waiting to place her order at the drive-through window. He yanked her passenger door open and jumped inside.

"Get us out of here!" the crook yelled pointing the gun at the shocked young woman's face.

"What?" the woman exclaimed in disbelief.

"Just drive, lady!" the robber ordered.

The VW burned rubber and squealed out of the parking lot onto Westheimer Street, one of the busiest streets in Houston. The woman shifted into high gear and sped off, weaving in and out of traffic.

"Where to?" the woman asked. The crook hesitated. *"Where to!"* she demanded.

"Take the next right!" the crook instructed.

"What?"

"The next right, take the next right!"

The woman took an immediate right turn, following the car ahead of them into the security gates of an apartment complex.

"Not *this* right—I meant at the next street! Get us out of here!" the crook shouted, waving the pistol in the air.

The woman was shaking so badly by now that she could barely hold the clutch in long enough to change gears. She sped around the rear parking lot of the apartment complex and toward the exit gate. She slowed to a stop and reached out of the window to press the button to open the security gate. Nothing happened.

"Hit the button again!" the robber yelled. The woman was in tears by now but she pressed the button several times. Still nothing. The crook erupted into a fit of cursing and scared the woman so badly she panicked and jumped out of the car and ran toward the apartments. The crook, cursing loudly the entire way, jumped out of the car and ran around to the driver's side. He climbed in and tried to shift gears, only he had never driven a standard transmission before. The VW Beetle lurched forward then the engine died. By now the shrill screaming of multiple sirens filled the air.

"Dammit!" the frustrated crook yelled as he slammed his fist against the steering wheel. Desperate now, he grabbed the paper bag and evacuated the VW. He stuffed the gun into his waistband and began climbing the wrought-iron security fence but just as he reached the top, the moneybag got caught on a pointed fence cap and ripped wide open. The police sirens were now very loud. The robber scrambled over the fence and ran toward a nearby residential area.

By now the Houston police dispatchers were receiving dozens of calls and police cars flooded the vicinity. We closed in on the abandoned VW and began searching the residential area. We immediately found the "money trail" that led to the wooden privacy fence of a backyard.

The crook had managed to scale the wooden privacy fences of two backyards and was just topping the fence of the third yard when the pistol fell from his waistband. At the fourth yard, just as he topped the fence and dropped to the ground, he was met by a large, snarling Rottweiler. "Oh, shit!" the crook yelled as he reached for his pistol. Finding he was no longer armed, he jumped back onto the fence and began frantically scrambling to get back up but the Rottweiler lunged teeth first and latched onto the crook's right leg. The crook let loose an earsplitting, bloodcurdling scream and clung to the top of the fence while trying to shake the dog loose.

Now we were receiving numerous calls about a suspicious male jumping the backyard fences of several homes. I joined several officers following the money trail. We had just topped the third fence when we heard the scream. As we raced toward the sound we saw the crook hanging by both hands on the fence, the depleted McDonald's bag still clutched in one hand, a snarling Rottweiler attached to his leg.

Not surprisingly, the robber was actually glad to see us and more than happy to surrender. And there you have the case that was appropriately dubbed "the McBungler."

DEATH ON THE BORDER

by John Malone

*U.S. Border Patrol Agent; Ajo Station, Tucson Sector,
Western Region, five years.*

*There are roughly nine thousand Border Patrol agents try-
ing to protect our borders from the illegal entry of aliens,
terrorists, and drugs. We have a very small voice in Congress and most people have no clue what we do, or under
what conditions.*

Yesterday, a federal officer lost his life on the border in
Arizona. I was working when I heard the radio call announcing a "lookout" for a vehicle loaded with weapons
that was going to be driven across the border. A little
while later, while I was processing some aliens for "Vol-
untary Removal," I heard the Ajo Border Patrol agent
talking to the National Park Service ranger about working
some pedestrian-activated sensor traffic several miles
north of the international border. The Ajo agent is fairly
new and had been here less than two years. The park
ranger became permanent at Organ Pipe National Monument about two years ago and before that he had been
seasonal.

Some time after that, I heard one of the helicopter pilots from our neighboring sector in Yuma indicate that he

was involved in some activity near Lukeville. I began to realize that the Border Patrol agent, the park ranger, and the pilot were all working the vehicle traffic near Lukeville and not the pedestrian traffic from the sensor activations. It was a little hard to follow but I didn't have a good feeling about what was developing.

The Ajo station where I work is actually in Why, some thirty miles north of the border. Lukeville is the port of entry (POE) at the terminus of (AZ) State Route 85 on the border with Mexico. In this area, there is a road that parallels the border fence both east and west of the POE. It is one of the very few dirt roads in the area. The objective of the alien and dope smugglers is to get to the highway. Once there, the next step is to blend in with traffic and avoid the "temporary" checkpoint set up five or so miles south of the station in Why. This area is sparsely vegetated and consists of rocky hills and small mountains. These small mountains and the valleys and washes cause radio signal strength to be weak or nonexistent in some areas.

As best I could tell from listening to radio traffic, the situation in the field was worsening. The helicopter pilot was trying to direct the agents to the vehicle, now stopped, and its occupants. The pilot identified at least two bad guys and indicated that one of them had a "long arm" rifle. There were Mexican officials south of the illegal vehicle. I know this because the pilot used them as a reference point to guide the agents. The pilot's radio transmissions were distorted by static and helicopter whine so it was difficult to understand what he was saying sometimes. I don't remember if I heard any of the agents on the ground use the radio, but at one point, an agent not involved in the incident asked for all radio traffic to cease except for that of those involved in the incident. This started a dialogue between that agent and the dispatch that lasted a minute or two.

At about 12:30 P.M., I loaded up my illegal aliens for their return trip south and was starting to leave the station when I heard the pilot say, "Officer down!" I had to force myself to continue what I started in the vehicle I was in. I knew it would take too long to unload my aliens, lock them in a cell, try and find another law enforcement vehicle, and start south. I drove much faster than I should have in my unmarked vehicle—a '97 Ford van with almost 200,000 miles and full of passengers. On the way, I was passed by at least five other Border Patrol units running code (lights and siren). About five or six miles north of the POE, I passed the Border Patrol agent who was driving the injured officer, a park ranger who had been shot, north to rendezvous with an ambulance. And by then, five or six law enforcement vehicles were coming off the border road. I finally arrived at the POE twenty minutes later and discharged my passengers. Then I went to see if I could help.

When I arrived at the scene I found several officers performing lifesaving measures on the wounded bad guy. It was clear that I wasn't needed there so I drove north to assist with traffic control near the air evacuation site. I came upon the ambulance where it had stopped, twelve miles north, and the first person I saw was the Ajo Border Patrol agent who had been with the park ranger when the shoot-out had occurred. He was directing traffic on the two-lane road with a Customs special agent, but the look on his face was pure emotional anguish. I parked my van and set out to do what I could.

I could see that in the ambulance there were at least two paramedics working on the ranger. There were several more Border Patrol agents around the ambulance so I went over to talk to the Border Patrol agent who had been with the park ranger. He was terribly and understandably distraught. He wanted to believe that he had done all that he could. I stood with him and listened to him and reassured him that he had. Everyone kept looking toward the ambulance, wondering what was happening inside. Finally, I walked over and shouted through the open ambulance doors for the park ranger to "hang on." I didn't want to be a straphanger; I just wanted to offer some encouragement. Then I went back to the Border Patrol agent and listened and tried to reassure him again as we waited.

I don't remember what time I arrived. I know that we radioed to have both north and southbound traffic stopped. I know that one agent called our dispatch on several occasions to ask about the ETA of the air evac. More than once, he asked to confirm that there was more than one helicopter en route and that they were going to two different locations. At least one of the calls was to inquire about the ETA after the previous ETA had passed. At some point I noticed that one of the people who went to the ambulance and climbed in was another park ranger who I knew named Bo. When he exited the ambulance and walked in my general direction, I walked up to him, hugged him, and tried to say something encouraging. He just stared down the road and said he thought it was too late. Then, finally, flying up from the south, from the direction of the POE, came the air evac helicopter.

Bo and I hurried over to the ambulance so that we would be ready to help load up the injured ranger. We were standing there when it was decided that the helicopter wasn't going to take him anywhere. We were there when the doctor on the other end of the ambulance frequency called the time of death: 2:40 P.M. I watched as Lonnie, the EMS director and OIC at the scene, and Bo broke down and cried. It seemed like it was just the three of us standing there next to the body of the dead ranger. They both talked to him and stroked his arm, touched his forehead. I put my hand on Bo's back and just held it there. I watched as the paramedics unhooked all of the IVs and monitors and removed the trauma pressure pants. I stood by as they covered him with a blanket and pulled it up to cover his face.

I couldn't stay there any longer. I took the Border Patrol agent who had been with the ranger when he was shot back down to the POE.

When we arrived, we saw that the bad guy was dead. The dead ranger's buddy, who had been trying to save the bad guy's life, was sitting with a group of law enforcement officers. As I looked around, I saw Customs and Immigration inspectors (who work at the POE), Customs special agents, Border Patrol agents, county deputies, an Air Force K-9 handler temporarily detailed to the POE, and a couple of AZ DOT officers who also work at the POE. It didn't surprise me. While there may be some chest-thumping and service rivalry, when one law enforcement officer needs help there is never any hesitation. All of us know there are times when someone from another agency will be our only backup because our agency backup is miles away.

I want to tell a little about the dead ranger and how I knew him. I won't use his name because as I am writing this, his parents don't know yet that he's dead. I had the pleasure of meeting them one time and I would hate to know that they found out by reading this instead of being properly and respectfully notified of what had happened. It will be difficult enough even then.

I first met the ranger a few years ago when he first showed up at Organ Pipe as a temporary seasonal ranger. What I saw then, and what I remember most about him, was his smile. He always had one. I don't think that I ever

saw him frown or heard him talk negatively. The ranger
was young and eager like most new officers. He had been
a seasonal temp for several years before in other parks
and he really wanted to learn the job. He wanted to learn
the area, and he wanted to catch dope smugglers.

Christmas came about three months after he got here. I
remember that two other Border Patrol agents and I were
working swing shift (two P.M.–twelve A.M.) Christmas
Eve/Christmas Day near the POE. Sometime during the
shift, he came down and talked to us for awhile. The
ranger station and the housing area that he lived in was
about five miles north of the POE. He told us that his
family (mom, dad, and sister) was visiting him and he invited us up for Christmas dinner. Sometime during the
night, we went up and met his family and had dinner with
them. We spent an hour or so visiting and for me, that
night embodied the true spirit of Christmas. We were
more strangers than friends and yet that night I felt as if I
was with family. They welcomed us and shared their
food; I will never forget their warmth and generosity.

Over the last year or so I didn't see him very much.
My varied assignments had me working in other areas so
I wasn't working in the park where he was stationed.
When I did see him, whether on or off duty, we would
play catch up. He even joked about the fact that he had
me over for Christmas dinner and then I hadn't been
back. About two months ago, I ran into him and we spent
a little time really talking about what was going on in our
lives. That was the last time I saw him until today.

That's what happened. That's a little bit about him. I
wrote this to try and describe how one officer's death affected me. I wrote it to help me grieve. And, I also wrote
it to point out a few things that are wrong with this job
and the approach that our management and government
officials are taking with the border issues. A National

Park Service ranger died assisting a Border Patrol agent with his job. We are undermanned, our technology (communications, vehicles, weapons, uniforms, etc.) is outdated and ineffective, our national border policies are too political, the Ninth Circuit Court of Appeals is out of touch with reality, the court dockets are so full that we can't prosecute those that need to be, and the smugglers are getting more aggressive. I have yet to see the results of any other shooting incident investigation and our management has never officially—through e-mail—notified us of these events which we all know occurred. How are we, the agents, supposed to learn from these situations? It's almost as if they never happened.

In the five years that I have been at this station, I don't recall a single incident where a Border Patrol agent was shot at until a couple of months ago. That incident involved the Mexican military shooting at the vehicle of a Border Patrol agent who was doing his job on our side of the border. Since then, BP agents were shot at twice in one week in two different incidents. What is clear is that the trend of shooting incidents in our area has increased dramatically and it can only get worse in the future.

Yesterday I saw my first dead person and it was someone I knew and worked with.

LIEUTENANT DAD

BY O'NEIL DE NOUX

New Orleans PD.

My first day as a patrolman, as I sat in the passenger seat of my police car, I watched the people stare as we drove past. I was so self-conscious of the silver badge, the navy blue police uniform, my stainless steel .357 Magnum in its leather holster on my right hip, that I didn't need a car to sail down Jefferson Highway on that balmy spring morning. I bounced in my seat as my veteran partner told me, "Calm down, rookie."

"I'm so relieved to be here," I told him. You see, I didn't think I'd ever become a cop, even with my big brother a cop, two cousins on different forces, and my father a lieutenant, commanding the Crime Scene Division. At 5' 6", I was too small in 1976. The height requirement was 5' 8" until that Bicentennial year when they let women become police officers. The height requirement vanished and I headed for the police academy.

"Calm down, rookie," my partner told me again as I tried my best to find a traffic offender or suspicious person to check out. Three hours into our shift we finally received our first call, a bank alarm going off. It was nine

A.M., my partner reminded me. "Probably an employee opening the door."

I bounced in my seat until we arrived. Getting out first, I hurried to the bank door, peeked in like we were taught in the academy, and then slipped into the bank, where two women and a man stood in the lobby. The younger and prettier of the women spotted me, smiled and walked up.

"Sorry. False alarm. I set it off when I came in." She had long blond hair and wide blue eyes and a very, very nice figure. Tilting her head to the side, she examined my new uniform, silver badge and all, stopping her gaze when she saw my nameplate. She looked up and announced, loudly, "You're his son!"

Turning to the others in the lobby, she said, "Just like he said. His son's here to take the report."

My partner stepped around me and confirmed what I already suspected. My father, the lieutenant, had beaten us to our call, checked out the bank, and told them his little boy would be around to write the report.

The three cups of coffee I'd drank that morning turned acidic in my stomach as I filled out the false alarm report. My partner didn't help. He thought it was funny. And he laughed even louder when my old man beat us to another call, a disturbing-the-peace call, and managed to settle the matter before we arrived, assuring the arguing parties as he departed that his son would be there to write the report.

Calling us on the private police channel, my father gloated to my partner, saying, "I gotta take care of my li'l boy."

This brought me back to my first day at the police academy, sitting in class, waiting for the instructor to come in. The back door of the classroom opened and my father peeked in.

"I'm Lieutenant De Noux," he announced. "Is my son in here? He'll be the short one."

Someone pointed me out as my father stepped in carrying a clothes hanger with my four-year-old nephew's suit and said, "Son, I just picked up your suit from the cleaners for you."

The whole place erupted in laughter and I was known as "short one" for my entire stint at the academy. Didn't matter that I graduated first in my class, was class president and came in second on the pistol range. I was the short one.

My first week on the road was a hellish nightmare of following my disappearing-act father from call to call, while my partner cackled at me.

Thankfully, the second week I was transferred to the midnight watch to be attached to my permanent training partner. Needless to say, my father worked days, so I lost my shadow and learned so much from my training partner that I was a seasoned veteran by the time we rotated back to the day watch.

In suburban New Orleans, nights were hopping back at the end of the 1970s. We were the dark blue knights tooling around in our police cars, nabbing armed robbers, snaring rapists, catching speeding cars in long chases, catching good-looking girls skinny-dipping in apartment complex pools. We just watched them scoop up their clothes and run off. No way a half-French, half-Sicilian southern boy would arrest a naked lady. I watched, however.

The first morning back on the day watch was a typically boring Tuesday. My training partner and I sat in our police car in the middle of a parking lot across Jefferson Highway from a strip mall. Shortly before nine, I heard my father's voice on the police radio, notifying headquarters he was 10-8 (in-service as he left the crime lab on Metairie Road about five miles away).

As my partner and I sipped the good coffee we'd gotten from Morning Call Coffee Stand (steamy coffee-and-chicory concoction of café-au-lait) a bank alarm went off at the bank in the strip mall right across the street.

We were there in six seconds. Just as we were pulling up my father announced to headquarters he was at the bank. We looked around. No Lieutenant De Noux. My partner and I checked out the bank. Again, a false alarm.

As we pulled away in our car, I did it. I rid myself of my father beating us to our calls. I told headquarters it was a false alarm and asked my father to go to the private channel, knowing everyone else would follow to listen.

When he came on, I asked him where he was.

"What do you mean?"

"We were in sight of the bank before the alarm went off. Where were you?"

"I was there."

"You were at the wrong bank weren't you?"

"Negative," he snapped back.

"You were at the bank on Metairie Road. Admit it."

"I was not. I was on Jefferson Highway."

"Yeah. Where were you? In a tree?"

Six separate voices cut in laughing. For the next several days, every time my father told headquarters something on the radio, someone would cut in advising, "Watch out for that tree!"

And that was the last time the old man tried to show up his li'l boy.

THE GROCERY SCAM

BY JOSEPH KAISER, JR.

Suffolk County PD, retired after twenty years.

Patrolman Bobby Sisino had been assigned to our plain-clothes squad and was working the evening shift with me on a Saturday in early May of 1968. Although he had only been assigned to our squad for a short time, I considered him a great asset, someone I looked forward to working with. He was a few years younger than I was but he had the same drive and enthusiasm I felt I had. I figured our being teamed up would encourage both of us to work even harder.

The one gift that Bobby had that I lacked was a quick wit. He was one of those who could engage in verbal combat and never lose the battle. When I tried to mimic his ability I usually fell flat on my face. He was so deft at interrogation, in fact, that I would actually wait until we were partnered before confronting suspects over whom I needed the verbal upper hand. My strength lay in developing a case, in collecting and organizing each piece of the puzzle, and arriving at a proper conclusion. Together we made a great team.

As we were leaving the precinct that Saturday, we paused by the front door to listen to a conversation between one of the desk officers and a middle-aged white male. The man was an investigator employed by Whelan's Drug Stores and it seemed that one of their branch stores located in our precinct had had a large shortage of inventory for the past several months. He was seeking the help of the police in investigating this loss.

Bobby and I didn't need to discuss this; we knew each other well enough to know that it was the type of case we both found interesting. So we included ourselves in the conversation, questioned the investigator at length, and told him that we would visit the store the next day and see what we could find out. We would call him at his motel after visiting the store.

I arranged with Bobby to pick him up at his house the next day around ten A.M. and we would drive over to the store in my pickup truck. My truck was loaded with lawn mowers and gardening tools that I used in my part-time landscaping business, so I figured it would be a good cover. Our police department frowned on officers using their own vehicles when involved in police work but I often did it anyhow. At that time, unmarked police vehicles were stripped down four-door sedans with small hubcaps and a police radio antenna mounted on the rear trunk of the car. Anyone with half a brain knew these "unmarked cars" were police vehicles. Besides, Sunday was our only day off that weekend. We figured, why waste all that time driving to the precinct, checking out a car, and then have to return it if we struck out and made no arrest? We could make up some kind of story for the bosses if the question came up about us violating departmental procedures.

What the hell, we thought, let's just do it.

I picked up Bobby the next day and drove to the Whelan's Drug Store in the Mayfair Shopping Center in Commack. We arrived there about 11:30, both of us dressed in old clothes. We decided that Bobby would wait in the truck while I went into the store and looked around and if I saw nothing unusual then he would go in while I waited in the truck.

The store was fairly busy at that time of day. People had dropped in after church and were picking up their Sunday newspaper and the goodies for that afternoon's cookout. There were two ladies at two checkout registers serving customers, a young boy in his teens returning shopping carts from the parking lot, and an old man who must have been in his seventies stocking shelves and replenishing the piles of Sunday papers at the front of the store.

I went up and down each aisle a few times looking for something out of the ordinary but everything seemed in order. I even poked my head into the rear storage room. Still nothing. I was living that old cliché, "I don't know what I'm looking for, but I'll know it when I find it."

After about fifteen minutes of nothing I decided to leave in order to give Bobby a chance. I picked up some cigars and a newspaper and got into a line at one of the registers. Both registers were busy, each three deep with customers, all with shopping carts loaded to the brink with merchandise. As I stood in line I couldn't help but reflect on the fact that I hated shopping. I always have and I always will. When I need to buy something I go to the store, buy just that one thing and leave. I didn't like standing in line; I didn't like "comparison shopping."

As I was getting more and more impatient I couldn't help but notice all the stuff in the cart of the woman ahead of me. She had ten large bags of potato chips, a lot of makeup, and eight fifty-pound bags of charcoal. What in hell was she going to do with all that charcoal? Plus, I thought, her husband must really be rich to let her buy all that cosmetic crap. I wondered how much all of it was going to cost.

I guessed that it would maybe come to $100, maybe $150. That was a lot of money back in 1968, especially in this blue-collar section of Long Island. Since I was both bored and curious I listened as the checkout clerk finished adding up the cost of the merchandise.

"That will be $6.72, please," she told the woman.

My mouth dropped. So that's how they do it. Nice scam, I thought. I didn't do much of the shopping in my family so I was no expert on the subject, but I had to wonder how often a shopper would pay attention to the price total of the shopper in line ahead of him. Probably not very often. Most of the time shoppers are busy unloading merchandise onto the conveyor belt and not paying attention to other shoppers.

My turn came; I paid for my items and left the store. I saw the woman who had been ahead of me in the parking lot, loading up her blue 1962 Chevrolet station wagon with the merchandise she had just "purchased." I made a mental note of the license plate number as I walked over to Bobby.

"Well," Bobby said. "Find out anything?"

"Yeah. I found out that my wife and yours have been shopping in other stores when you wouldn't believe the bargains you can get at Whelan's."

Then I explained what I had observed and told Bobby to go in and check it out for himself. He returned ten minutes later shaking his head in disbelief.

"I saw the same thing you did, Joe," Bobby said, nodding at a pair of shoppers in the parking lot. "See those people loading up that white Ford sedan? They paid $8.37 for those three shopping carts full of food. What do you think we should do?"

We both looked back at the store, then at each other, then back at the store. Finally I shrugged and said, "I guess we'll just go back in and arrest everyone that's there, lock up the store, get the Whelan's store investigator over here, and work it out from there."

"Sounds good to me. Let's do it."

We reentered the store, took our badges out of our pockets, announced ourselves as police officers and told everyone in the store they were under arrest. We had no idea which customers were involved in these thefts and which weren't. We figured we would straighten that out at the precinct.

I rounded up the women working the checkout counters and the teenaged bagger and the customers in the checkout lanes while Bobby went to the rear storage area to arrest the old man handling the newspapers. I noticed that the old man was bent over and walking oddly.

"What's the matter with him?" I asked.

"When I told him he was under arrest, he shit himself."

"You've got to be kidding."

"Just wait till you get a whiff of him, then you'll know whether I'm kidding or not."

Bobby had not been kidding.

We contacted the investigator from Whelan's and he came to the store. He was pleased but shocked at how quickly we had closed the case. We pretended that our efficient and rapid execution of this case was routine and something we managed all the time.

We locked the store, posting the investigator at the door. He would check the identification of any persons who wanted to gain entrance. Then they, too, would be investigated in case they were also involved in the scam but hadn't been in the store at the time we made the arrests. I called the precinct for assistance and asked to speak to the watch commander. Lieutenant Meyers answered the phone.

I told him that Bobby Sisino and I were at Whelan's Drug Store in the Mayfair Shopping Center and that we'd just arrested not only everyone working there but also several customers as well and had closed up the store. I told him we needed about three or four sector cars and maybe the large prisoner van if it was available. I reassured him that it was not an emergency—everything was under control.

There was dead silence at the other end.

"Lieutenant? Lieutenant, are you there?"

"Kaiser," Lieutenant Meyers responded in a voice somewhat louder than his normal pitch. "What in the hell are you guys up to?! You're not even scheduled to work today! Have you and Bobby been out drinking all night or what?"

It took a while, but I managed to explain the situation in detail and Lieutenant Meyers eventually calmed down and sent me the transport I requested. The store employees who had been arrested cooperated by giving us the names and addresses of the others involved in the thefts and by identifying those customers in the store at the time of the arrests who had not been involved. Three civilian cars loaded with stolen merchandise were located in the front parking lot. They were impounded and taken to the precinct. We secured the crime scene and after about an hour we went to the precinct as well.

While at the precinct, those arrested continued to cooperate. They made phone calls to their friends and relatives who were also involved in the thefts, informing them that they had been arrested and suggesting that they turn themselves in, bringing with them what was left of their ill-gotten gains. Over the next few hours, several more surrendered, toting in bag after bag of stolen merchandise. Because Sunday is a quiet day, we were able to take a few sector cars off the road to help us with the paperwork. Even so, it was almost three P.M. before all the prisoners were processed and by then the precinct lobby was looking more and more like a supermarket.

So after the paperwork was finished there remained the problem of what to do with all the merchandise cluttering the lobby and stacked in the hallways. This evidence had to be inventoried and transported to the police property bureau where it would remain until each case was presented in court. The problem was that the property bureau was closed on Sunday.

I asked Lieutenant Meyers if he had any suggestions. He told me he had a key to the commander's office and he supposed that we could store the items in there provided I promised to explain the situation to the commander first thing tomorrow. Well, by the time we got all the stuff in the commander's office, it reminded me of "Collyer's Mansion," the story of the Collyer brothers who were found in 1947 by the New York City police living in a decaying three-story brownstone cluttered with an estimated 136 tons of junk. Reportedly, stuff was piled from the floor to the ceiling, including fourteen grand pianos, two organs and a clavichord, human medical specimens in glass jars, the chassis of a Model T Ford, a library of thousands of books, an armory of weapons, the top of a carriage, and a primitive X-ray machine.

I was reflecting on this as I left the precinct and went off to spend the rest of the day with my family.

When I returned to work the next morning at 8:45 the grinning desk sergeant greeted me.

"The precinct commander wants to see you in his office and he is pissed."

"Really?" I responded. "I wonder why."

I headed toward my office, stopping briefly as was my habit to say hello to Mrs. Hankie, the precinct commander's secretary. Mrs. Hankie was an older woman, slight of build, with one of the sweetest personalities I've ever encountered. She enjoyed her job and one could sense she particularly enjoyed working with the many police officers she came in contact with each day. Many of us grew to think of her as another mother, someone who sincerely cared about us and who would go out of her way to help us in any way she could. I don't know how long she had worked in her position; she was one of those people who seemed to have always been there.

"Good morning, Mrs. Hankie, and how are you today?" I greeted her, as if everything was all right with the world.

She looked up at me and smiled.

"I'm fine, Joe, and how are you?"

"How I am seems to be in question right now. How's the boss?" I asked.

"Not too good right now, Joe. He wants to see you in his office."

I took a deep breath, turned and headed for the commander's office. Mrs. Hankie followed.

The precinct commander at the time was Inspector Marcelli. He was a short man, slightly on the heavy side, and had been in charge of the precinct for a few years. Although his assignment had been relatively short, he had a good deal of time on the job and had been the precinct commander at several other precincts before coming here. I found him fair and easy to work for. Usually we got along well.

"Good morning, Inspector, you wanted to see me?" I asked as Mrs. Hankie and I walked into his office.

"You're goddamned right I want to see you! What's all this shit doing in my office?!"

I tried to explain what had happened yesterday but he ranted and raved, waving his arms about and asking questions without giving me the chance to answer. What seemed to bother him the most was that someone had access to his office, that someone had violated the sanctity of his castle, his holy place of authority.

Mrs. Hankie and I stood silently, side by side, waiting for an opening.

"How the hell did you get in here?" he finally asked.

I started to tell him but he interrupted when he heard all he wanted to hear.

"Meyers has a key to my private office?! What the hell is he doing with a key to my private office?! How many other keys are floating around this place? I'm the commanding officer of this precinct! What do I have to do to get some privacy around here?!"

During this entire conversation, Inspector Marcelli stood in front of Mrs. Hankie and me, dressed in full uniform, an impressive figure, except that he looked like he was standing amid a bargain-basement rummage sale— Whelan's merchandise was piled to the ceiling, completely covering his desk, and stacked on every available surface. There were nonperishable food items, clothing, gardening tools, toys, cosmetics, over-the-counter analgesics, and stuffed animals. There were coloring books, slippers, bicycle tires, and greeting cards. There was enough candy for Halloween.

To add insult to injury, Inspector Marcelli's fly was wide open.

I must admit that I toyed with the idea of suggesting to him that if he really wanted some privacy, he could start by zipping up his fly. Mrs. Hankie must have read my mind because I could feel her poke me in the side with her elbow to keep me quiet.

Eventually, Inspector Marcelli calmed down and grudgingly accepted my explanation and the merchandise was removed from his office and sent to the property bureau. The defendants involved in the case all pled guilty in court, were fined, made restitution to the store, and were fired from Whelan's.

Inspector Marcelli had the locks changed on his office door. Bobby Sisino and I went back to hanging around the desk sergeant after shift in case something interesting walked through the door.

Life got back to normal.

THE POTENTIAL

by Mark Falcione

Detective, City of La Mesa PD, California, nine years.

It would be my honor to be able to contribute something to this worthy tribute. I would like to start off by saying thank you for your efforts and consideration for our fallen brothers and sisters. I hope that my simple story will find a place in this book.

The city of La Mesa borders the city of San Diego along the eastern border of San Diego, California. We are a city of about sixty thousand and our department has sixty-seven sworn police officers.

This is my story:

On January 7, 2000, I was working traffic enforcement in La Mesa, California. Traffic cops generally get a bad rap from just about everybody, cops included. A lot of what we do is sometimes regarded as "chicken-shit" by the "real cops" out there. As a dedicated traffic enforcement officer it can sometimes become difficult to maintain your motivation. Traffic citations are the number one source of citizen complaints in San Diego County. Couple that with the fact that nobody ever likes to get a ticket and you can see how it can become tiresome, day in and day out, listening to the high-pitch whining of traffic violators expressing their displeasure at my doing my job. The one thing that always kept me writing tickets was quite simple. It was "the potential." "The potential" in any one of these encounters when I was issuing a ticket and explaining to an agitated motorist how a burned-out taillight, or a bald tire, or how not wearing a seat belt, really could lead to injury or death. "The potential" to save a life was actually there. So you see, every time someone else saw a chicken-shit ticket, I saw "the potential."

Well, at about 1520 hours (3:20 P.M.), I saw a silver Plymouth Neon with two twenty-five-year-old white males in it driving westbound on La Mesa Boulevard. I noticed that the Neon's passenger was not wearing his seat belt as required by California law so I conducted a traffic stop on the vehicle in the 8700 block of La Mesa Boulevard.

I spoke with the passenger of the vehicle, Thomas O'Brien, who identified himself with a Colorado driver's license. When I told Thomas the reason for the traffic stop, Thomas told me that there was no seat belt law in Colorado. You see, Thomas and the Neon driver had just arrived in California and they had recently rented the car at an airport car rental agency. I asked them if they had passed any of those BUCKLE-UP, IT'S THE LAW seat belt signs erected all along the California highways as they were passing through San Diego. They told me they did not pass any of these signs, and that they were unaware of the seat belt law.

Now, normally I would just issue a verbal warning to out-of-state tourists, but there was something about these boys' attitude that told me they just weren't getting the message. I gave them my standard seat belt speech—how

I had investigated hundreds of injury accidents, and how seat belts are always the difference between minor injury and major injury accidents, and how wearing your seat belt, although not always comfortable or cool, really can save your life. I told them how they should always wear their seat belts, whether it was the law or not, because of "the potential." Well, Thomas wasn't impressed and he just said if I was going to write him a ticket, I should get to writing, because they had things to do in California.

While I was issuing Thomas his "passenger not wearing his seat belt" ticket, Section 27315(e) of the California Vehicle Code, Thomas asked me what would happen if he left California and didn't pay for the ticket. I explained that if he didn't take care of it, there would be an arrest warrant waiting for him on his next trip back to California; however, I told him he was still missing the point. I was writing the ticket in an effort to impress upon him "the potential" of not wearing his seat belt. Thomas remained unimpressed. Nevertheless, he signed the "promise to appear" section of the citation and I asked him to wear his seat belt while traveling in California. Thomas did put his seat belt on, and the two boys continued on their way. I drove off with the feeling that I had just wasted at least as much oxygen as I had ink on that contact.

I didn't think too much more about Thomas or this unremarkable traffic stop, until May 12, 2000. That was the day I received a letter in the mail at my station. I didn't recognize the name or the handwritten return address from the northern California city on the letter. When I opened it, I found two pieces of paper inside. Thomas's parents had sent the letter to me.

The first piece of paper was Thomas's copy of the seat belt ticket I had issued to him about four months prior.

The second piece of paper was a State of Colorado Certificate of Death. The name of the decedent? Thomas O'Brien.

As you might expect, quite a few things went swirling through my mind about this time. Suffice it to say, I was pretty taken aback. I read the details on the death certificate and saw that Thomas had died of a lacerated aorta due to blunt force trauma. Thomas was only twenty-five years old. In the injury description box it was noted that, "Victim was a passenger in car that left road, hitting a rock." A call to the Eagle County Coroner's Office told the rest of the story. It seems that Thomas and a "friend" were leaving a casino in Colorado after doing a little drinking. There was only one very large rock on the entire road leading from the casino and the driver managed to drive smack into that rock. As fate would have it, the driver was wearing his seat belt, and Thomas was not. Thomas's chest became embedded in the dashboard of the vehicle as a result while the driver walked away with relatively minor injuries.

I replay that traffic stop, over and over in my mind, trying to think if there was anything that I could have done differently, if there was anything that I could have said that would have changed the outcome of this tragic chain of events, but that answer has never come to me.

There is a hard lesson to be learned from this story, but it's a lesson that cries out to be told, a lesson that begs to be heard. Because you see, there is "the potential" in almost every traffic stop, in almost every law enforcement contact. There truly is "the potential" to save a life. There is "the potential" to prevent needless pain and suffering, not only for the victims, but for their grieving families as well. There is "the potential" to make a vital difference in people's lives.

Police officers see, hear, and experience the most horrible things that occur on our planet; I just wish that everyone would realize that when a police officer takes the time to give someone some advice he's probably not doing so to hear himself talk but because he, too, realizes "the potential."

THE CHRISTMAS GIFT

BY WILLIAM SEYFRIED

Sergeant, Glendale PD, Arizona, retired.

It was Christmas Eve in 1981, and I reluctantly left for work on the midnight-to-eight-A.M. shift after opening gifts with my family. As anyone who has ever worked on major holidays knows, it is a time that can really make you question your career choice.

The shift started off quietly, and as we were at departmental minimum staffing, those working were relieved. As I drove my beat area feeling sorry for myself I was brought back to reality by the blast of the "hot tone" over the radio, signifying emergency radio traffic.

The call was a family fight, and the husband was reportedly drunk. On arrival, my backup unit and I entered a small home, typical of those in that barrio. We found an intoxicated male with an attitude, his sobbing wife, and several crying children.

He had pushed his wife around and called her and the kids names, but since this was pre–domestic-violence-law times, nothing could be done without the wife signing an assault complaint. She declined, but requested that we ask her husband to leave for the remainder of the night. We did, and he complied, but he kept up a stream of verbal abuse directed toward her all the way out the door.

Before we left, the oldest boy, about ten years old, proudly showed me his one and only Christmas gift. It was an LA Dodgers' batting helmet. He explained that each of the kids received one gift and that the box of grapefruit under the Christmas tree was to be shared by the entire family. He said he really wanted a bike to replace the one that had been stolen but that his parents were too poor to do that.

I left the call and went to others like it, all the while thinking of that kid. A couple of hours later, another "hot tone" had us responding back to his house.

We found that the dad had returned, enraged with the family for calling us out the first time. So he came back when we were gone and proceeded to break every window in the house using, you guessed it, the box of grapefruit. Of course, the "macho man" didn't stick around to greet us, which added to my frustration. The wife was surrounded by her kids and they all were crying. I left there feeling as low as it gets, and couldn't wait to get home.

When I got off work and walked into my house that Christmas morning, I looked around at all the gifts my kids had received, including my son's new bicycle, and I thought again of Henry, the ten-year-old. I sat with my wife and we discussed the shift and the call to Henry's house in particular and then I finally went to bed.

When I woke up I knew what I needed to do. My son's old bike was still in the garage, and though it was beat up, it was still a good bike. My son, who was eight years old, helped me to clean, polish and service the bike and my wife provided a red bow.

I drove to Henry's house with my son and the bike and explained to Henry's mother what I wanted to do. She was reluctant to accept the bike, saying that her husband might be mad. I explained that if he had a problem with it I would gladly give him several personal reasons for not making any more trouble for himself than he already was in. So though Henry had gone to relatives for the day, she agreed to accept it, and my son and I wheeled it up onto the porch.

Over the years I saw Henry grow into a nice young man who avoided gangs, drugs, and the perils of the barrio. As for my family and me, it was the gift we gave rather than the ones we received that made that particular Christmas all the more meaningful.

JIMMY

BY PONZIO OLIVERIO

Deputy Sheriff, San Diego County, California.

A few years ago when I was working the wonderfully quaint little beach town known as Imperial Beach, we had a residential burglary series that was giving us fits. Eventually we developed information which led us to a suspect I'll call Jimmy. Unfortunately, while we were convinced of Jimmy's complicity in the crimes we did not have enough evidence for an arrest or conviction, since Jimmy did not leave any clues at his crime scenes. But we knew Jimmy considered himself smarter than us and we knew he wouldn't be able to resist flaunting his superior intelligence in our faces. So, when we asked Jimmy to come to the station so we could talk about these burglaries and eliminate him as a suspect, Jimmy jumped at the chance to get a laugh at our expense.

When Jimmy arrived he was his usual charming self and he told us he wanted to help in any way he could. He even offered to talk to people he knew in town who might know something about the burglaries. Now, we were secretly videotaping this interview and at a psychologically advantageous moment we placed in front of Jimmy several items which had been stolen and recovered from one of the recent burglaries. We asked Jimmy how, if he had nothing to do with the burglaries, we had lifted several of his fingerprints from the items. This was a complete fabrication on our part, as we did not have Jimmy's fingerprints on anything. But Jimmy looked a little worried and gave a few weak excuses for how his prints might have gotten on the items. We kept pressing him and the charm started to deflate as Jimmy got more and more nervous.

Then, suddenly, he relaxed and a huge, smug grin spread across his face as he said, "You guys are pulling my leg! You don't have my prints on anything." One of the detectives leaned over the table and said, oh yes, we did, we'd found his prints all over the place. But Jimmy just kept grinning and shaking his head like he knew something we didn't. So then the detective asked, "You seem awfully sure of yourself, Jimmy, how can you be so sure we don't have your prints?" Jimmy looked at us and explained, as though he were talking to people who were just too stupid to understand, "I *know* you don't have my prints because I wore gloves when I pulled that job!"

Now the smug grins were on our faces and Jimmy's expression, as the realization of what he had just admitted dawned on him, was a sight I will always treasure. We don't only catch the dumb ones; sometimes we catch the smart ones, too, like Jimmy.

STANDOFF

BY GINA GALLO

Chicago PD.

I should have seen this coming. After the last eight hours on the midnight shift, I knew there was something beyond the normal street protocol, a particular kind of summer madness triggered by the past week of searing temperatures. When we hit the street at midnight, the mercury still hovered near one hundred degrees, somewhere between godawful and hellfire. The kind of heat that causes night fever, when the law of the streets is: "Anything bad that can happen will . . . and that's only the beginning."

For eight sweltering hours we saw them all, the predators and prey, shrieking victims and smoking guns that populate this grim landscape, lurking in the shadows or hovering in the dark. While our squad cars raced by to the next job, the next bloody scenario, they watched us. Winos, junkies, lizard-eyed pimps and their sweating whores lolled in doorways, waiting for the parade of street carrion that brought the next trick and the next high. Those eight hours brought it all—crimes of passion, of opportunity, of being just too damn hot not to kill somebody. Whatever the motive, the outcome was the same. More bodies, either seeping life or reeking booze, to be handcuffed or bagged and tagged, depending on their status.

The breaking dawn brought no relief, only the challenge of another day to survive on these steeping streets. For us, it meant a slight reprieve. Time when we could leave the nightmare behind, go home to our own life or what passed for it, and try to forget what we'd seen and where we'd been. Until the witching hour on the next night when we'd pin on our badges, hit the same streets and wonder if we'd ever left at all.

But this time, it was different. After eight hours of answering calls among what looked like the first string of Hell's third circle, I couldn't wait to get home. I had just walked into my house when the call came from my unit sergeant, advising me to report immediately to a hostage situation at a South Side location.

Hostage situation? I'm not a negotiator, and my assigned unit works the inner city West Side, not even close to the South. But the sergeant's brittle tone left no room for argument. Our whole unit was being deployed, he told me. I was to report immediately in full uniform and riot gear.

Which is how we got here, thirty cops positioned around the motel where a gunman is barricaded inside. He holds his wife hostage, brought her here handcuffed and gagged and vulnerable to whatever comes next. We don't find out until later about the crime scene he left behind. Or how he'd kissed each of his three sleeping children before delivering the center-mass gunshots that ended their lives.

So far, communications have been difficult. Between the phone line's static and his weepy rants, the shooter's only clear message is that there are no options, no possible ways to undo what he's done. His words are slurred, half sobs, half hysterical pleading. He'll kill her, and himself . . . and anybody who tries to stop him from escaping this miserable life. It's all about the stress, he tells us. He can't take anymore goddamn stress.

Minutes drag by like centuries. Positioned strategically around the motel, we wait, wondering when or if orders will be given to make the breach. Heat shimmers in dizzying waves from the pavement, hard to take under the best circumstances. Nearly impossible when fear, fatigue and tension sweat us as much as the blistering sun that glints relentlessly off the assembled squads.

Communications become more sporadic. He's tiring, our sergeant tells us. Or possibly drunk or high enough that his words are slurring more, harder to decipher. A dangerous sign since fatigue can trigger desperate acts. Shouldn't be long before the lieutenant gives the signal to— But wait. Another communication, this time from the shooter, and he's got a request. He wants one police officer in his motel room, just one person he can talk to. What he doesn't request is that the person is unarmed. The way his voice is wavering, he either hasn't thought of it or doesn't care.

"Too risky," the sergeant says. "It's an ambush."

"Remember his wife," the lieutenant replies. "This could be her only chance." And points to me, the selected emissary, and gestures toward the motel.

"You know how to talk to people," he tells me. "Just take it slow. You got your Kevlar vest on, your gun, and a team of guys will bust in twenty seconds behind you. You can do this."

I can't. My heartbeat is slamming in my ears and my knees have turned to jelly.

Fear becomes a black vortex that sucks me in, spins me through a series of nightmare images: my babies growing up without a mother, those other babies gunned down in their beds, my own bloody body ripped apart in the shoot-out.

"You don't have to go," the sergeant tells me, even as he adjusts my safety vest. "You can just say no."

I can. But I don't. In what feels like a dream sequence, I walk the forty steps to the motel door—forty, because I count them, wondering whose legs are carrying me since my body is numb. I turn and run a hundred times, a thousand, but somehow I'm still moving forward, toward that door and whatever comes after.

He's waiting for me. Cracks the door just fractionally, observes my hollow stare and the weapon at my side, and allows me the narrowest passage. Inside, the room is dark, reeking of sweat and fear and the sobbing wife's soiled garments. Her gag is still in place, cinched tight below eyes glazed with terror. For the briefest moment, her face melts into hope, or recognition. The look she gives me is unmistakable. I'm the only one who can help her. It's up to me to make it right. A preposterous notion, I think. How can I save anyone when my body is frozen?

The only things that move are my eyes as I watch the gunman. Resuming his place besides the moaning woman, he returns my stare. His eyes are spidered red, courtesy of the whiskey bottles that litter the floor, but somehow I know he's not drunk. The set of his mouth is too deliberate, his hand too steady on the butt of his gun. The Smith & Wesson .357 Magnum is a familiar weapon—a long sleek expanse of blue steel that's now aimed at her head.

"I'm going to kill her," he tells me. "And then I'm going to kill myself. Unless you kill me first."

A number of expected responses crowd my brain. I could say he doesn't really want to do it, or that we can talk about it, or that he's making a big mistake—all bullshit phrases that would mean nothing. In this scenario, he knows exactly what he wants, knows he can make me give it to him. And slips a finger over the trigger ready to force my hand. He's waiting, so I ask him the only thing I need to know.

"Why me?"

"Why not you? Who better?"

I know what this is, have heard of it countless times. Suicide by cop. Staring at the upraised Smith & Wesson, I never thought I'd be involved in one like this: Suicide of cop by cop. And then I level my weapon at my partner's sweating face, and wonder who'll pull the trigger first.

DANNY

BY SHAUNA BRAGG

*Police Officer, San Bernardino PD, California;
formerly Pomona PD, eight years.*

I woke up on a Thursday morning, May 9, 1996, to the phone ringing. The night before had been a late one and the last thing I wanted to do was talk on the phone. It was my buddy Dan calling to see if I was still going to drive to his house, because we were supposed to have lunch together. The beer-tequila combo headache I had was telling me to say no, but there was an excitement in Dan's voice and I told him that I would be there.

Dan and I had known each other for about two years. We were police officers for the city of Pomona, California; we were beat partners, and we were friends. For Dan to acknowledge you as his friend was a major deal. He would tell me often that I reminded him of his sister. He was quiet and mostly kept to himself, so if Dan invited you to lunch you couldn't turn him down.

I dragged myself out of bed and drove to his house. When I got there Dan was in the best mood I had ever seen him in. He gave me a tour of his house and during the tour he showed me a closet in the spare bedroom. Now, I knew the guy liked leather jackets. We all have some things we go overboard with, but Dan had eighteen different leather jackets in this one closet. It was like this spare room was kept especially for them, as if they were his children. Crazy, yes, I know. At first I was a little frightened and then I began to laugh until the tears were falling from my eyes.

Then, out of the blue, he told me to pick one. I thought he had had a momentary lapse from reality. These were his babies. Dan continued to urge me to take one of his jackets and I didn't understand why. I finally took one that no longer fit him, because he wouldn't leave me alone. Then we went to lunch, talked about hanging out more often, laughed, talked about flying to Hong Kong, and laughed some more.

We drove back to Dan's house where I dropped him off so that he could get ready for jujitsu, which he practiced with some other guys from work. We said our good-byes, laughed some more, and I drove off feeling glad that I had answered the phone that morning. That was the last day I would talk to Dan.

Friday night, May 10, swing shift. Two other officers and I had the bright idea to dress in plain clothes and go hunt down prostitutes and johns. There were two squads working that night and as long as we got some arrests the sergeant didn't care what we did. At about ten o'clock, as we drove down the street, I saw Dan standing on a corner talking with some people. I rolled down my window planning to yell, "I love you, Danny!" to make him laugh. Every time I called him "Danny" he laughed. I always told my friends that I loved them, especially the men and women that I worked with, because we were like a family. But I didn't yell to him that night and to this day I don't know why. Something stopped me. I wish I had because that was the last time I saw Dan alive.

As our shift rolled to an end we parked in an empty lot to wait for the time to pass. Then the call came over the radio. Someone called 911 saying that one of our officers was down in the street in an industrial area. My partner drove at about 100 mph to get to the location, running red lights and almost crashing. We were only about a mile away, but it seemed like a hundred. The entire time I kept telling my partner that it was probably a security guard because citizens mistook us for security officers all the time. But I was wrong.

As we drove up the street I could see the police unit with the driver's door open, headlights on, and an officer lying on his back next to the door, not moving. As I got out of the car and walked to the fallen officer I completely lost it. There, lying on his back with a bullet to his face, was my friend Danny. A chill came over me. Even though I can't remember everything that happened after that moment, I can still smell the moist air and feel the slight breeze that was blowing that night. And I can still see the shock and tears in other officers' faces as they arrived at the scene.

Yet even in the midst of this horrific night the officers still did their jobs. Officers from all over the county arrived in what seemed like minutes and more were still on their way from as far south as San Diego. As I walked around in a daze, not believing that Dan was gone, an officer from another agency ran up to me, hugged me, and said, "Where do I go?" All I could do was point to the command post. I cried, and then I got angry. So to control my anger, I kicked a sergeant's unit, causing a large, deep indentation.

The crime scene was preserved, the evidence collected, and, after many hours, the body of my friend was finally picked up from the street.

A funeral fit for a true hero was given and the killer, after running like a coward, was apprehended and the trial held. Dan's mother and sister sat in the courtroom every day with their heads held high. When the verdict, "Guilty!" was read, there was a roar of applause as the murderer was escorted from the courtroom and the sound of one officer yelling, "Dead man walkin'!"

Any police officer who has been at the scene of a fallen officer, no matter what agency he or she may be from, knows that it is one of the worst things to have to deal with in this job. In the aftermath they send you to a shrink and give you some time off. Well, I was one of those people who needed to get back to work as soon as possible or I probably wouldn't be able to be a cop anymore. I needed to get back in the game. Since I was taking psychology in school that semester, I told the shrink what he needed to hear and he let me go back to work.

It was hard. I was in a depression for months, but I hid it well. Sometimes. For a long time, I couldn't drive down the street where Dan was killed. I was short-tempered with everyone and I crashed a police unit rolling code three to an officer calling for help at a shots fired call. Flashbacks are hell. Blacking out behind the wheel and almost driving through a wrought-iron fence wasn't a good thing. But I survived like we all do because we see it every day. I was glad that I had Dan's leather jacket and that I had two new friends, his mother and sister.

Dan had been born in Hong Kong. A police officer walking along the beach heard his cries and found him buried in the sand with the umbilical cord still attached. That police officer took him to an orphanage where his American parents later adopted him. It was only fitting that Dan became a police officer.

Dan taught me to take care of myself on the street, to stay strong and to be safe. Dan's death taught me that you can love this job and bring honor to the badge but you must never forget that you have a family at home waiting for you. You must never forget to laugh and enjoy life.

You must always respect the men and women you work with because you may not see each other tomorrow. And you must try to remember that you are a human being and remember to stay human.

I love you, Danny.

MY REMINDER

by Chris Bolton

Police Officer, Oakland PD, California, three years.

It's 0353 on a Tuesday and I am the only thing moving in sight. I creep along the city streets in my patrol car while shadows slowly dance on the pavement in the headlights' glow before me. I am looking for something but honestly hoping to find nothing, as I am not in the mood to be working. My mind is drifting to the unpaid bills sitting on my kitchen counter and the social engagement I'll have to tell my friends I can't attend, once again, as I have to work. The dispatcher drones over the radio saying nothing that concerns me, breaking the still and peaceful quiet.

It is cold outside, the onset of another crisp and windy Bay Area winter's day. I drive with the windows down to hear my surroundings as well as to see them. My chief complaint is that I've forgotten my gloves. I am happy that I've escaped any and all discernible paperwork over the previous seven hours and have a short three more to go. Then it will be back to my empty apartment, a frozen dinner for one, and the daily struggle to sleep as the sun peeks in through the corners of my bedroom window. I'm literally on autopilot. I have nothing to do but to drive in

silence with my thoughts not on my job as they should be.

A voice screams somewhere in the near distance. It is a female. A voice in distress. Fuck. Great. I stop.

"Wa gu da gee moowa!" This time it is louder, echoing off the corridor of apartments surrounding me. Chinese? Korean? Vietnamese? I crane my head out of the window to pinpoint the caller's position. Now my cheeks and ears are freezing. Silence for perhaps a full minute . . . and then, *"Wa gu da gee moowa!"*

On the second floor of an apartment to my left I see a figure staring at me from inside a dark interior. She is ancient. She is weeping. She is definitely Asian. I have found the mystery voice. As soon as we make eye contact she disappears from the window, letting the curtains fall in place. They drift in the slight chilled breeze. I'm hoping she will remain gone. Did I mention it was cold and I had forgotten my gloves? It would be fantastic if she remained gone.

"Wa gu da gee moowa!" She is back. Her eyes are pleading. She has the look of a crazy person and I assume this is the reason she is screaming. What other explanation could there be? Who yells the same sentence from an open window at four in the morning? It makes perfect sense—she is mentally ill. I try to talk to her, more concerned about her neighbors' sleep than I am about her well-being. I'm just not in the mood, and I'm confident that this can be quickly resolved in time for my breakfast.

"Do you speak English?" I yell as I shine my spotlight at her window. She ducks briefly away and then is framed again in the light. Frightening shadows bounce behind her from my directed beam. She is gaping at them and appears to be terrified.

"Police!" I say without a response in return. I try to communicate again, slowly sounding the syllables out as if for a small child, *"Poe-leeece."* She looks at me with no

sign of recognition or understanding. *"Why are you yelling? Is there anyone else home? Can you come down to the door?"*

No answer. I'm growing frustrated and impatient with each passing moment. *"Can you go away? Go back to bed?"* I command this sarcastically without feeling, and add, *"It's too early for this!"* I wave my spotlight erratically and gesture for her to disappear. I'm hoping that she can take the hint. *"Go away!"*

She groans loudly. She screams. It is a grave shriek, from her gut, loud and terrible. I can't believe that no one else can hear this and I expect to see lights flicker within the apartment. Her bellowing will surely awaken her concerned family members. But there are no lights. No others. Her groans begin to take the form of pure pain. She disappears again into the recesses of the apartment. I decide to park and step out into the night.

I hear and see nothing of her for the next five minutes as I unsuccessfully rap on the main apartment complex door for entry. She must have a caretaker, someone that can be awakened. Surely someone will let me in. I am about to give up since I have not heard a further disturbance, but just as I consider this option I again hear her shrieks from the second floor above.

"Wa gu da gee moowa!" The same cry, unfathomable and full of anguish. I find access to the main building; the door to what I believe is the woman's apartment swings open in response to my knock. She is at the threshold and immediately grabs at my hand in an effort to pull me to her. I have my weapon out now, and I am sorry that I haven't yet called for a cover unit. Something about this isn't right. I may have underestimated the situation. I am an idiot for having delayed; I rectify my uneasiness by calling for an additional officer. I enter the apartment and follow the small, frail figure ahead.

There is a long hallway that leads to a family room and kitchen; a single bedroom door is to the left. The entire space is no more than five hundred square feet. I see a Chinese calendar hanging on the entranceway hall, and I request a Chinese-speaking officer to interpret. The radio is silent for a full ten seconds and then: "1L14, is that Cantonese or Mandarin Chinese?" Jesus . . . forget it.

The woman, wearing an old and disheveled blue robe, points frantically into the bedroom, moans inaudibly in Chinese, and stands nervously to the side to let me pass. I estimate her age to be ninety years, at least.

Within the small bedroom is a twin bed and single dresser. A man is lying on the mattress, tucked in under warm covers. He is motionless and peaceful looking. He is also cold, stiff, and without a pulse. He is clearly dead. If I had estimated the woman's age at ninety then I would have to guess his age at one hundred and twenty years if I were being generous. There are no signs of foul play. I find no one else in the apartment, and after a quick search I recover at least ten heart and blood pressure medications, which at least give me the name of the man. I grow more annoyed and irritable as I think of the long process of paperwork and phone calls in my immediate future, but I am relieved to think that I may be getting off on time since the death appears to be natural. I lead the old woman, who I suspect is his wife, into the next room and motion for her to sit down. She whispers, "Wa gu da gee moowa . . ." and then trails off into silence.

I begin the task of piecing this all together. I find an address book and call the first name I find written in English with a local area code.

"Is this Lisa Chang?" I ask.

"Yes," she replies, confused and weary. "Who is this?"

I am severely uncomfortable, knowing that I will have to soon explain. I feign compassion and explain to a perfect stranger how it came to be that I am waking her over the phone at four in the morning. The old woman is silently sitting nearby, looking at me uncomprehendingly.

Eventually, family members arrive and the old woman appears relieved to be surrounded by familiar faces and is no longer distraught. She stands and walks toward the kitchen where she intends to begin to prepare tea. But as she passes the bedroom door, where her husband lies staring unseeing at the ceiling above, she yells in horror and stumbles to his bedside. She rambles on in Chinese and cries, pulling his pajama top gently in an attempt to wake him. Family members come to her aid and lead her away from the body. Her niece explains that the old woman is in the late stages of Alzheimer's and will need to be repeatedly told that her husband has passed away. She tells me the old woman is confused at why we are all here, in her home, disturbing her in the middle of the night. Her failing mind cannot hold on to the details. She does not remember finding her husband dead. "Wa gu da gee moowa," she says in sorrow as she is led away. I take the opportunity to ask a relative what this now familiar sentence translates to.

Coroners are called, sergeants are notified, and I place an order with the desired funeral parlor since it is indeed deemed to be a natural death. Heart attack. My paperwork is completed and I begin to gather my things to leave. The old woman is once again shuddering with grief as she sits among family watching these strangers in suits and uniforms package her husband's corpse. I slowly close the door, leaving the woman's face framed by her withered and tear-soaked hands. She stares at me as I depart, a shared moment I'll never forget, and I realize she deserved better from me. Guilt and self-disparagement are my only companions.

I am ashamed of how I initially treated the confused

and elderly woman at the window. How easily I might have just driven off into the darkness without another thought if she had only been silenced at my request. I would have left her to an eternity of discovering and re-discovering her husband's lifeless body. She looked to me, to the uniform I wear and the badge I pin on myself each day, for help and hope. I am awful. I am shallow and selfish. I am disappointed in myself. How could I have conceivably begun treating such a situation with such cold, detached, and dispassionate recourse? Surely I have seen and dealt with circumstances much worse but never before have I examined myself in such a way. What am I becoming when I am more concerned about having breakfast on time than with the terrible loss this woman has experienced? A thirty-seven-year-long marriage and eighty-two years of life had slipped away into the night, leaving behind a sorrowing and bereaved family. And leaving me as the last caretaker and guardian. But I had nearly failed in my responsibility. How could I understand then what I didn't know until now? Perhaps that is what I must learn: compassion can precede knowledge if you are willing to listen not only to what you understand, but also to what you don't.

As I walk from the apartment I am greeted by the rising sun, a reminder that each day is a new one and I can choose how to live each moment. Seabirds and pigeons are beginning their daily battle over specks of crumbs left in the street, scattering as the morning commuters pass by, oblivious that a life has been lost within the residence just above. The world goes on.

I light my morning cigarette, take a long awaited slow drag of pleasure, and walk slowly to my car. "Wa gu da gee moowa," I say under my breath to no one . . .

"I am all alone . . ."

THE LONELY YEARS

BY DON COSSEAN

NYPD, retired, twenty years.

My partner and I were doing a 4-12 one evening and received a call of a suicide. The address they gave us was in an apartment house right off Coney Island Avenue in Brooklyn. These apartments were in the better part of our precinct, the 61st. We took the call, both wondering what we were going to find. Would it be a self-inflicted gunshot victim? Would we find brains splattered all over the room? Or would we find a victim with his/her wrists slit lying in a pool of blood? One thing is for certain, in police work every call is a surprise.

We entered the walk-up apartment house, climbed the stairs to the third floor, found the apartment number . . . and found the door ajar. That was a little strange. We carefully entered the apartment. Then we heard a noise coming from down the hall. My partner said "Hello?" and there was an uncomfortable silence until we heard, "I'm in here, don't try to stop me!" The voice was female, elderly and wavering. My partner and I exchanged a look and then we cautiously approached the kitchen; when we reached it, we saw a little old lady kneeling in front of the oven with her head inside. There was no smell of gas but we could feel a little heat coming from the oven. It turned out that it was electric and she was in no danger at all. So we sat her down and asked her a few questions. It turned out that she was very lonely. She had a son in Manhattan, and though she spoke of him fondly, he seldom came to visit her and rarely called. She had no other family and her husband had died years ago. So she had called us. All she wanted was a little company. We didn't have another call so we sat there for about twenty minutes and chatted, had some tea with her, and when we left she was fine. The next week we got the same suicide call at the same address and we ended up having tea with the lonely little old lady much as we did the week before. Rather than have this occur a third time, my partner and I just decided to stop by at least once a week to say hi and to chat. It was only several months later that we found out she'd passed away.

My partner and I hoped we'd made those days at the end of her life a little less lonely. We'd seen it so many times—older people abandoned by their families, living in isolation, desperate for companionship, yet tossed aside like garbage once they'd outlived their usefulness. On the day that I heard about the little old lady's death, I made a vow that whether on or off the job, every time I would see a senior citizen, I would make it my business to make eye contact and smile, and no matter how trite it might sound, say, "Have a nice day!" because, with the grace of God, we will all grow old someday.

LAND OF OZ

BY DENNIS N. GRIFFIN

Sergeant, Madison County Sheriff's Department, NY;
Patrolman, Village of Chittenango, NY; seven years.

In the early 1980s I was working as a patrolman in the village of Chittenango, located in Madison County in central New York. L. Frank Baum, author of *The Wizard of Oz*, was born in Chittenango, so many of us jokingly referred to the village as the Land of Oz.

I was working the graveyard shift one Thanksgiving. I remember the night as being cold, clear, and absolutely dead. By three o'clock, other than periodic status checks from the county dispatch center, my unit number hadn't been called once. Fighting boredom, I decided to run some radar on Route 5, the main road running through the village. After nearly an hour without a car passing, I was having difficulty keeping my eyes open. I knew I desperately needed some action if I was going to stay awake until the end of my tour. A few minutes later, I had it.

I spotted the headlights first. The vehicle was heading east out of the village. As I watched it approach, I saw that it was moving erratically; twice it crossed the centerline. When the car first registered on the radar it was doing sixty in a 30 mph zone. By the time it passed my spot, the station wagon was accelerating and nudging seventy. This is a DWI for sure, I thought.

The fatigue gone, I pulled onto the highway and started after my prey, lights ablaze. To my relief and surprise, the target pulled over almost immediately. I called in the stop and then approached the vehicle. There came my next surprise. Instead of a lone intoxicated driver, I found the car occupied by a sober young couple. The man was behind the wheel and he was excited. He said that his wife was about to deliver their first child and he had to get her to the hospital in Oneida, which was a few miles down the road. As my flashlight beam came to rest on the wife there was no doubt that she was very, very pregnant.

I was debating whether or not he should be driving in his agitated condition, or if I could safely escort them to the hospital, when he asked, hopefully, "Maybe you can help her deliver if we can't make it in time. You cops know how to do those things, don't you?"

The thought of me delivering a baby proved to be a great motivator. "We're going to the hospital," I announced. "Get into my car." He assisted his wife into the patrol car while I locked his vehicle. I called in my situation and asked the dispatcher to advise the hospital that we were on the way. Then I started on the longest ten-minute ride of my life.

To the benefit of everyone involved, we made it to our destination while there were still only the three of us visible. The hospital had a crew awaiting our arrival at the emergency room entrance. After his wife was taken inside, the husband had to fill out some paperwork and while he was doing that, I parked the car and put the bite on a nurse for a couple of cups of coffee. I handed the expectant father a cup and then tried to assure him that everything was going to be okay. It was only a few minutes later that a nurse informed him that he was the father of a healthy baby boy.

It was Thanksgiving night in the Land of Oz and I'm happy to say that the parents, baby, and even the nervous officer made it through just fine. And, yes, I had absolutely no trouble staying wide awake for the rest of the night.

Not in My House . . . an Officer's Lament

by Dennis McGowan

*Suffern PD, New York, Detective Bureau
Commander, retired.*

It was a beautiful May morning and I was awakened at
seven A.M. by the giggles and laughter of my children,
Eddie, nine, and Laurette, eight. I knew why . . . our new-
born daughter my wife had delivered a few months earlier. Whenever the kids looked in on Veronica, she would
smile. They would talk to her about everything and nothing, and her smile would broaden to a big grin. That's
when they would laugh, then Veronica would laugh . . .
back-and-forth . . . happy kid stuff.

I was working the day tour in uniform for the Village
of Suffern Police Department. Suffern is one of the myriad bedroom communities of New York City, located in
Rockland County about twenty-three minutes' drive from
the city. The day tour was a switch. My normal rotation
was to work midnight to eight, but Bobby Larkin, a fellow
officer, had a personal appointment and he'd be working
my midnight tour. I hated midnights, so the switch was
okay with me. Larkin was a great guy. Every day, he'd
stop before work and pick up eight cups of coffee for the
rest of his squad. To keep up his tradition, I did the same.
Didn't want any resentment to develop from the cops on

his squad. Joked and laughed with the guys coming in off midnights and then I was off in the one-man patrol car. It was an unusually busy day of simple calls from "the cat's stuck" to a "locked myself out of the car." It's not that Suffern didn't have its share of homicides, burglaries, and drug busts . . . but those stories will stay hidden for another day.

For the most part my tour was going by quickly, but at about 11:45 A.M. my easy day began to change. The call from the dispatcher came over the radio as a Peeping Tom up on Revere in Bonaire. I was in the area and responded. The woman, a Mrs. L, was terrified. An old woman, she had been trying to get dressed and, apparently, she'd forgotten to lower her shade. She saw this man was looking in, watching her and laughing. She thought she was going to be attacked. I drove around until I saw a figure around the back of Number 29. I got out of the patrol car and walked through the shrubbery, my hand on my gun, which I had pulled half out of its holster. I shouted, "Police! Don't move."

His oddly proportioned figure should have told me there was something wrong. But not until he turned toward me did I realize the young man was mentally retarded. I reholstered my gun and strapped it, asking his name. "Ted-die," he said. I took him by the arm to lead him away, and heard a woman through the window call out, "Thank you, Officer. Thank you, Officer." I nodded and placed Ted-die in my unit. I would have gone in and spoken to her, reassured her a little bit, but I didn't want to leave Ted-die to roam off. His clothes were pretty well soiled, as if he'd been outside for a few days. I popped the trunk, took out the blanket, and placed it on the passenger seat. I drove Ted-die back to the station house, where Sergeant Lewis and I tried for two hours to ascertain Ted-die's address or even his last name. But it was to no avail. Sergeant Lewis decided then to call Health and Human Services. "We'll let them handle this," he said, and I was back in my unit. One more hour and I'd be on my way home.

Sergeant Lewis burst onto my radio: 4-7-4, domestic at 2483 Terhune Avenue, our main thoroughfare. I made a U-turn on Orange Avenue and right onto Terhune. Double-parked in front of 2483, reached into the backseat and grabbed my nightstick. I hung it on the handle of my gun as I walked up the stairs to Apartment 3. I heard shouting, loud shouting, repeated shouting, but it was only one voice. No one was responding to it. I knocked on the door and then, as if I had turned on a radio, blaring music filled the apartment house. I didn't like that. I thought whoever had done it was looking to hide something. I knocked again. "Police. Open up." No one answered. I stepped back looking to kick in the door, then remembered my lieutenant who had said, *Before you kick a door in, try the knob.* I did and the door opened. The sparse room held a dirty crib, an unmade bed, soda and beer cans, fast-food wrappers, a half-empty box of rice which had fallen onto the wooden table, and a baby in a diaper, lying still on the floor. A well-built male lunged at me from my left side. I half-turned and threw a right, connecting with his chin. He dropped to his knees. I pushed him over onto his back, stepped on his chest, cuffed his left hand, then dragged him to the cold radiator pipe and closed the right cuff around the pipe. He cursed me, screamed at me: "This is what the police do when I want to discipline my own kid?"

"What did you do?" I asked.

He calmly looked at me and said, "Threw him against the wall."

"That's not discipline, fella," I said, picking the child into my arms. I felt for a pulse and thought I found one.

So here I am running down the stairs with the baby in my arms, beginning CPR with a rhythm. One, two, three, four, five. Blow. Using my middle finger and forefinger, I compressed the child's chest, staying with the rhythm. One, two, three, four, five. Blow. I thought the pulse was stronger. Sweat poured from my forehead, but I had to ignore it. I got in my unit. The hospital was straight ahead, four hundred yards from me. My backup had arrived and saw what was going on. He waved me on. I pulled out, steering with my knees. One. Two. Three. Four. Five. Blow. This baby could be my Veronica. One. Two. Three. Four. Five. Blow. Sacred Heart School was ahead. I hope there're no kids out. My car was doing over sixty. All was clear.

I finally made the emergency room. The doctor leaned over me, checking out the baby in my arms as I continued CPR. One, two, three. "Officer, stop. The child is dead." "But I felt a pulse!" He slipped the baby from my arms into those of a nurse.

"You wanted to feel a pulse," he said, and led me to a curtained area. "Here, gargle with these." He handed me two quarts of hydrogen peroxide. "Don't leave here until they're finished." As I gargled, I kept relating the baby to my Veronica. First, a retarded young man living in his own world who couldn't tell me his name and now, the baby.

The doctor was back. "We'll be doing an autopsy. You want me to send you the results?"

"No thanks, Doc. Just send them to Sergeant Lewis." Dead is dead.

I was back in my unit, then into the station house. It was unusually quiet. My backup had retrieved the child's father and had him locked in the cell. I couldn't look at him and went down to my locker to go home. Two wrapped cigars with pink bands fell from my top shelf announcing *It's a Girl!* I was numb. A couple of guys came in. They didn't need to say any words. One put a hand on my back and the other patted my shoulder as they moved to their own lockers. There were no words. We all knew this disappointment. Today was just my turn. I changed and signed out, then called my wife to tell her I'd been held up on a call. "How are the kids?" "Great, they're waiting for you." "Be there soon." Drove the ten miles home sorting out what was going through my mind . . . the retarded child . . . and the baby on the floor. I couldn't bring this sorrow home. Couldn't tell my wife. Wouldn't tell my children. As my friend Edward Dee says, we live in the worst twenty minutes of someone else's life. So I leave it behind . . . where it happened . . . where it belongs . . . not in my house.

SHOTS FIRED

BY JACK COMEAUX

Sergeant, Rogers PD, Rogers, Texas.

A hot night in August 2000 in Ingleside, Texas, a town on the Gulf Coast just across the bay from Corpus Christi. I had been an officer for about nine years and was working the evening shift from three P.M. to eleven P.M. when, toward the end of the shift, we got a shots fired call in the area of the Best Western motel. My sergeant and a San Patricio County deputy responded along with me and we began checking the streets of the area bordering the motel. La Quinta Street is a rather affluent area and not known for problems. We spotlighted the area, made several checks of the neighborhood, and checked the streets around the motel with no results.

Since all seemed quiet, Sergeant J. D. Nelson and Deputy Charles Howell pulled up side-by-side on the opposite side of a convenience store next to the motel to discuss where they were going to eat. Meanwhile, I was thinking that the only place that had not been checked was an alley that was overgrown with weeds and salt grass directly behind the motel. The area was pitch black and accessible only on foot. I advised the sarge by radio that I would be checking the alley.

I entered the alleyway holding my flashlight in my left hand up and away from my body and my .40 caliber Smith & Wesson in my right hand. There was a narrow pathway used by the kids crossing from the residential area over to the store down the middle of the block. I started down the path while scanning the area with my light.

All of a sudden, about seventy-five feet in front of me and to my lower left, I heard two gunshots and simultaneously saw two bright flashes. I realized I was being shot at and ran to my left to seek cover in the weeds while I instinctively returned seven or eight rounds from my service weapon in the direction of the flashes. I took cover behind a tree and then saw a third flash and heard a third shot, then silence.

Sergeant Nelson and Deputy Howell came running into the area calling for me, but I didn't answer for fear of giving away my position. I signaled them with a quick flash of my light and pointed for them to GET DOWN. We held our position and called for extra officers to assist. Once the area was sealed off, Deputy Howell, who was armed with an AR-15, thought he saw an individual standing further back from us in the weeds. We made a semi-circle and began advancing but it was an illusion created by the surrounding unit's spotlights.

Sergeant Nelson stepped to his left and his foot touched something and he yelled, "Let me see your hands!" There on the ground was the suspect, dead, lying on his left side with a bullet wound to the front of the head. My heart jumped up in my throat and I got shaky. I thought that I had killed him.

The dead man was a twenty-five-year-old white male from Houston who had come to Ingleside to see an old girlfriend after being released that same day from Harris County Jail for DWI. He had a pocket full of bullets and some beer and had been drinking and shooting holes in the back wall of the motel. This was the origin of our shots fired call. Fortunately he didn't hit anyone. Looking at him, I realized I had seen him earlier on the pay phone at the convenience store. What I didn't know until afterward is that I had become an unknowing participant in a suicide-by-cop attempt. He fired at me, knowing who I was, and I returned fire but I had missed him. Undoubtedly frustrated that I didn't comply with his wishes, the suspect turned his gun on himself. He died from a self-inflicted gunshot wound from the .380 automatic he was holding in his hand. I came through it okay, but I'll never forget it, and the academy instructors were right: you do automatically revert back to your training in critical situations. I got a letter of commendation for my part in the situation and I know I am very lucky that this guy missed me twice at seventy-five feet in the dark. Especially since at the time I didn't have a vest on. Go figure.

EUGENE

BY TIM GARDNER

Police Officer, Berkeley PD, California, retired.

A couple of weeks before Christmas, and not long after the news that the DA had not charged a case where two of our officers had been shot at, I found myself cruising in the south end of town. I was about to hit up my beat partner to get a cup of coffee so we could vent our bitterness at the situation when my MDT emitted the familiar sound of an incoming call. I punched buttons on the MDT keyboard and scrolled through the pages of the call. "RP Eugene wants advice regarding his brother's seizures," I read from the dull blue-lit screen of the computer monitor. The information on the MDT further described the RP as a quadriplegic.

This sounded good to me as I wasn't interested in getting involved in any long, drawn-out matters, and I was pretty sure I could dispense some simple advice and be quickly on my way. I parked my patrol car on Channing Way, just west of the apartment. After rechecking the apartment number, I got out and walked up to the front entryway of the building. I examined the shiny steel intercom box with its indigo blue digital screen and then punched the apartment number into the keypad.

"Hello?" a raspy voice asked over the intercom. I bent close over the speaker, not wishing to alert the whole building to my presence.

"Hi, Berkeley Police. You called?"

"Yeah. Can you come around the carport? My door is the first one on your left as you make the corner."

I walked around the side and knocked on the door. I waited several seconds, then knocked again, louder this time, wondering how a quadriplegic would be able to answer the door. I made a motion to knock yet a third time when I heard the dead bolt being drawn back. The door opened slightly and I saw a tall, razor-thin black man dressed only in boxer shorts standing in the doorway.

"Yeah?" he said.

"Is Mr. Williams here?" I asked.

"Yeah, that's me. What do you need?" he asked.

"Eugene Williams. Um . . . that must be your brother, right?"

He just nodded.

"Eugene called. Apparently he's worried about you."

"He's in the back. You can go on in, if you wanna talk to him," he said and turned and walked away from the doorway, leaving me to decide on my own which way to go. I leaned inside the doorway and saw the brother disappear inside another darkened room. The whole interior of the apartment was dark and I wondered why he didn't turn on any lights. I stepped in and flashed my light around the walls until I located a light switch, reached over, and flicked it on. I started down the long hallway, first passing the room the brother had disappeared into.

I could see the ghostly dim light of a small black-and-white TV flashing quick images from within what I assumed was the brother's bedroom. Through the slightly opened door, I could just make him out lying on a narrow mattress. It was remarkable how quickly he had gotten back there.

"Down here, right?" I called to him.

"Yeah," he said, his voice sounding muffled and far-away. "Right at the end. Could you turn off the hall light when you go?"

"Sure."

I continued down the hallway toward the open door-way of another faintly lit room.

"In here, Officer," another voice said. I recognized the same raspy, gasping-for-air voice from the intercom. I walked through the doorway and stopped abruptly. An immense hospital-type bed that was raised to about even with my lower chest mostly blocked my way. A partially-covered black man was lying flat on his back on top of the bed. His head lay slightly over to the left and he had to look at me out of the corner of his eyes. It was obvious he couldn't turn his head much. He had a very fat torso, but the arms that lay across his chest were frail and skinny and appeared to be held in place by some sort of Velcro straps around his chest. Three or four electronic remote controls were also attached to the Velcro.

"Thanks for coming," he said, as I noticed a clear plastic tube running from his nose to a large green oxygen tank on the floor next to his bed. The entire room was cluttered with medical apparatus, dressings, and containers of all types. Amid them all, three video monitors glowed with neon light. They had multiple buttons and dials; I couldn't tell if any of them was even a standard television set.

"No problem at all. How can I help you?"

"It's my brother. He won't go to the doctor," Eugene said.

I was relieved. It was to be a simple advice matter after all. I'd just tell him I couldn't do anything about his brother. He was an adult and free to do as he wished, and no cop could make him go to a doctor. I'd write a two-line report and be back in-service and on my way.

I started with my standard "it's not a police issue" speech when I happened to look into Eugene's eyes. They weren't pleading with me, or revealing shame about his condition, nor were they particularly sad. They didn't reflect annoyance with me. They were just resigned, as if he had long ago accepted other people's unwillingness to get involved in his life.

I suddenly felt guilty about my urge to kiss off the call and clear out just so I could stay in-service. I had arrived callous and aloof and now I was overcome with a sense of shame; how couldn't I recognize that just a little concern from me might have gone a long way for a guy in his shape? I was probably the first new face he'd seen in months, and yet I had been all set to just waltz in, give my canned sermon about what the police can and can't do for citizens, and go 10-8. As I stood there in Eugene's room, my need to go hook up with the guys for a cup of coffee so that we could lament the injustice of a DA's charging tactics seemed suddenly very insignificant. Shit, I thought, Eugene probably had dreams about just sitting upright in his bed, let alone going out for a cup of coffee with a couple of friends.

"Why won't he go to the doctor?" I asked, hastily trying to disguise the look I had had of being about ready to bail out on him.

"Says he doesn't need to. Says they can't do anything for him."

"What's wrong with him?"

"He's got some kind of seizures and I'm worried that he might get hurt when he faints. See, years ago, he fell down and hit his head, and ever since, he's been getting these seizures."

"Are his seizures large, like where he goes into convulsions? Or are they small, more like he's just frozen and staring?"

"Well, I don't normally see what happens to him from in here. But I think he just faints because I can sometimes hear a loud bang and then some rustling. Then he won't answer me for a couple of minutes. That's how I can always tell he's having one. I've called the paramedics before, but I guess always too late because by the time they get here, he's fine."

"Sounds like he might have some form of epilepsy. Has he ever seen a doctor?"

"Not since he fell that first time." Eugene was imparting all his information without moving any muscle below his chin. The only other movement in his entire body, other than from his lips and his eyes, came from the very shallow rise and fall of his chest as he continued breathing, connected as he was to the oxygen tank.

"So you're worried about him?"

"Yeah. I know you can't do anything, but I'm worried he might get hurt."

"I'll tell you what. I'll go talk to him, let him know that you're worried about him. I'll let him know how important it is for him to go to the doctor, okay?"

"That'd be great, Officer. He just won't listen to me."

I took another look around Eugene's room as I made ready to leave, and noticed several framed pictures of people who were probably family members. There was also a collection of videotapes beneath one of the larger of the monitors that hung near the ceiling. I recognized several popular titles: *A Fish Called Wanda, The Client, The Firm*. And then I saw five or six brightly colored boxes with strange titles like *Fleshdance, The Sextasy,* etc. It was obvious they were porno tapes and I realized that they were an important part of his personal video collection. I was suddenly and deeply struck by how screwed up, how stark and isolated Eugene's life really was. Depending on how long he had been paralyzed, these porno tapes could represent his only possible conception of what sex was like. He had the normal sexual urges of every male on earth but absolutely no way in hell of indulging in them.

"How long have you been laid up like this?" I turned and asked him, drawing nearer and tapping the bed slightly.

"About twenty-seven years."

"How long have you been in this apartment?"

"About the same, I guess."

"Do you have someone who looks after you?"

"Oh yeah. I have an attendant. I wouldn't be able to get by without one."

"You ever get outside?"

"Sure. I have a wheelchair."

As I looked at his large, totally helpless bulk, I knew what an ordeal just getting him into a wheelchair must have been. Not to mention maneuvering it in the cramped confines of this room.

"Looks like you've got yourself pretty well set up in here though," I said, indicating his remote controls and all the medical hardware around the room.

His eyes looked briefly around and again met mine. "Yeah, I really do, you know."

I smiled at him. "Let me go talk to your brother. What's his name?"

"Larry."

"Okay. I'll go see what's up with Larry and I'll be right back."

"Okay. Thank you."

I walked back to Larry's room and knocked softly on the door frame.

"Come in."

I went in and found Larry still underneath his covers in his narrow bed. He had the volume on the TV turned down so low, it was just a low murmur of background noise in an otherwise silent apartment.

"Hey, Larry. Eugene asked me to talk to you. He says that you've been having seizures. Is that true?"

Larry finally turned and regarded me with impassive eyes. He was near Eugene's age but where Eugene was fat, Larry was very thin. He was also missing most of his front teeth and he had the overall crusty, ashen-faced complexion of a regular crack smoker. I briefly wondered at the depth of his depression that he couldn't be bothered to come to life when a cop came not only into his apartment, but also into the inner sanctum of his bedroom. Where Eugene couldn't get out of bed, Larry, for whatever reason, wouldn't.

"I guess sometimes I do," he said.

"You don't want to get help with them?"

"I just don't ever get down that way to the hospital. I'd go over there if I was ever down that way."

"Well, you know, Alta Bates isn't more than half a mile from here. They can give you medication to control those seizures."

Larry's tranquil features twisted up in sudden annoyance and he glanced up at me again briefly before returning his gaze to the TV. "Eugene don't have no reason to be so concerned about me. He's got plenty to worry about just for hisself."

"You know what, Larry?" I replied gently. "You are absolutely right. But all the same, he is worried about you. And he's called me because of it. Will you promise me that you will go to a doctor so I can relieve his mind? Then I can leave you both alone."

Larry continued to look at the small screen of the TV. "Yeah, I guess I'll go," he said finally.

"Thank you. You have a good night," I said, backing out of the room.

"Could you turn the light off when you go?" he said, turning to regard me one more time.

"Sure."

I walked back down the hallway and delivered the news to Eugene.

"He's hard to talk to, isn't he?" he said.

"Pretty stubborn guy and all that?" I asked, smiling slightly.

"He's always been that way. Larry—he always knows best."

I couldn't tell if Eugene had laughed back due to his labored breathing but his eyes looked brighter for a moment.

"Well, I gotta go. Call me back if he has another seizure."

"I will. Thank you, Officer."

I turned to leave and just as I did, I noticed a long tassel of green and red tinsel strung across the top of the doorway. I hadn't seen it the first time I had gone out, and it suddenly struck me that Christmas could be something meaningful and hopeful even to someone as totally confined and helpless as Eugene. I felt a little shallow and very insensitive. In my cynicism, bred already from the repetition of dealing with the extremes of human behavior and the sordid particulars of their lives, I had coldly assumed that, for those like Eugene, there was just about nothing to live for. I had simply concluded that he was just waiting to expire after his long, suffering existence.

As I made my way out of the apartment and got in my patrol car I realized that it wasn't too late to stop myself from getting hardened and losing my sense of compassion. It dawned on me that it had been almost two years— almost to the very day—that I had been sworn in as a police officer. And over the last two years, I had seen lots of situations, many of them with tragic outcomes. I had been made completely aware of the degrees to which people would go to get revenge, to get high, to get laid, to get off easy, and to get away with something—even to the point of telling outrageous lies about my own conduct. And, as a beat cop, I just tended to respond to calls for service, most of the time only scratching the surface of the reported problem. My solutions were simple and temporary, like arresting the primary aggressor in what may have been a long and twisted tale of abuse between a constantly battling alcoholic married couple, or incarcerating a drug-crazed son for beating up his mother after she wouldn't surrender her Social Security check for his fix.

Yet, right when I began to slide into that attitude of "nothing can surprise me because I have seen it all," the attitude of the cop who is on his way to being a seasoned vet, I got slapped awake. I had been given a chance—in a small way—to shine a light into the tunnel of repetitive darkness and deadly mystery that was the job. Driving away from the apartment, I realized Eugene had given me an opportunity to remember what I was really supposed to be doing as a cop. I had been brought up short while trying to kiss off a routine call for service. Realizing that fact, and having adjusted my attitude, maybe I had been able to give Eugene something a little more meaningful, a little more compassionate than what he had experienced before. I hoped that for the Christmas holiday someone would be around to take him out to celebrate. Maybe it would be a little more significant than that strand of green and red tinsel that hung from his door frame.

RETROSPECT

by Scott Partridge

Sergeant, Metro-Dade PD, Miami, Florida, sixteen years, retired.

It began as a routine day. I was working afternoons out of the old Station 5 on Bird Road as a squad sergeant. I had put my troops on the road and gone to a meeting at our headquarters building downtown. On my way back from the meeting, I stopped at a Chrysler dealership on Southwest Eighth Street to look at a car. I had my handheld radio with me, so I was just strolling around the showroom when a 3-41, an injured person call, went out. It was near shift change and all the troops were tied up on calls, so the dispatcher raised me.

"51-10."

"51-10," I responded.

"Be advised that I'm holding a 3-41 injured person, there are no units available in Area One so I'm sending a unit from Area Two."

This told me two things: one, that there was someone out there injured, possibly seriously; and two, the nearest responding car was a considerable distance away. As a road sergeant, I didn't necessarily have to respond to calls but in some cases I would back up the officers when we were short-handed. As strange as it sounds now, something told me it was important to take this call and I have found in my years of police work that it is essential to pay close attention to your sixth sense and your instincts. Most of the time they guide you better than reason ever could.

"51-10, show me responding from 82 and the Trail." I switched on the red lights and turned on the siren. The address was only a couple of miles away but any time you're running on an emergency signal the adrenaline kicks in and all of your senses come into play.

When I came on the police department, we wore helmets instead of hats, and it was mandatory to wear your helmet while running a three-signal. In the academy they told us that when you took the time to put your helmet on, it gave you the chance to gather your thoughts and to calm down. The closer you get to the call the faster you are going psychologically. Your palms start to sweat and you find yourself breathing more rapidly. I don't know whether it's the siren or the speed or the adrenaline, but whether it's your first or hundredth three-signal, it is an incredible rush. It must be a combination of the excitement, the anxiety of trying to locate the address, the stress of controlling the vehicle at high speeds, the unknown element of the call, and the ultimate realization that this is what it's all about.

It comes down to you against all the unknowns. What is happening? Where is it happening? Why is it happening? Can you handle it when you get there? Added to all these questions is one cold fact—someone's life may depend on your abilities. This is a critical occupation. Most of the time we can't start over again. This is for keeps.

All these things were going through my mind as I arrived in the area of the call. I finally located the street, and was heading for the house address when I saw a kid standing in the front yard of one of the houses. He was around twelve or thirteen and he was waving his arms and crying. As I turned off the car and hit the trunk release, I told myself to calm down and take it by the numbers. I'd been a cop a long time so how tough could this be? I grabbed the first-aid kit and followed the kid inside. He was almost hysterical and he kept saying, "It was an accident, it was an accident."

By this time, I'm on hyper-drive and I have so much adrenaline surging through my system that the whole scene seems surreal. I find a boy, about thirteen, lying on the floor. He's bleeding profusely. It's a head wound. He's been shot in the face. There's a 9mm Browning pistol near him. He's just a kid. He's in shock. He's lost a lot of blood. He's fading fast. I tell the other kid to get me some towels. I have to scream at him. He has accidentally shot his best friend, and he's going into shock, too.

Where the hell is Fire? Step them up, I need them now! We're going to lose this one! Try to stop the bleeding. Bandages, direct pressure. He's turning blue. I'm losing him! He's bleeding into his throat. He's drowning in his own blood. Get him on his side, clear the airway. Oh God, don't let me lose this kid, he's so young, he hasn't really even started his life.

Nothing else matters. There is no past, no future. There is only now. It's just me and this kid. He's within a millisecond of death, and I'm the only one who can possibly prevent it. I might as well be flying a fighter jet or slaying dragons in some far off world because nothing else matters but saving this kid's life—right here, right now.

It's an emotional roller coaster. First, there is fear. Fear that I will ultimately be unable to save this young kid. And, anger. Anger with some parent who made the mistake of leaving a loaded gun where these kids could find it. And sorrow for both of these young people who will have to bear the horror of this moment for the rest of their lives.

He coughs, and spits out some of the blood. I've got him breathing again. I manage to slow the bleeding with the towels.

I finally hear the sirens, and Rescue arrives a few minutes later. The kid is given a temporary airway and then he's transported to the hospital. I try to get some of the blood off my uniform and then sit with the other kid and calm him down until his parents arrive.

I leave the scene twenty minutes after I arrived, but it seems like twenty hours. About a block away from the house, I pull off the road and just sit there. I need a few moments to calm down. It will probably take many hours and a few strong drinks to really calm down but this will have to do for now.

That was many years ago but for years I didn't even know who the kid was. There were neither glowing letters of praise, nor awards of merit nor even a simple thanks. But that didn't matter. On that particular day, I faced another dragon and was once again victorious. I lived more in a matter of minutes than most people live in years. There is no exhilaration in the world like it. It's the ultimate personal test.

Today, there is a boy who will finish school, maybe go to his senior prom or play high school ball. He will grow to be a man; maybe he'll get married and raise children and grandchildren. He'll do these things because I was fortunate enough to be able to hold onto him long enough to get him professional medical attention. That is an accomplishment that I will treasure all the days of my life. There are very few occupations in this world in which you can say that your actions directly saved lives, but this is one of them. That's why I joined and that's what I miss the most.

KUNG FU CURT

BY ANDREW BORRELLO

*Lieutenant, San Gabriel PD, California,
thirteen years.*

During an extremely cold winter evening working graveyard shift, my three buddies and patrol partners, Tony,
Curtis, and Kevin, met me in an underground parking
garage. It was 0330, there were no calls, nobody on the
street except us, and we were bored . . . really bored.

Tony, Curt, and I were discussing things that cops usually discuss while Kevin (a.k.a. Uncle Kev) read the paper. Curt, a bodybuilder since his teens—twenty-nine-inch
waist, the bastard—suddenly looked at me and assumed a
somewhat dramatic kung fu stance. As he shifted his
weight from foot to foot back and forth while slightly
bobbing, he held his hands up Bruce Lee–style and yelled
a high-pitched "wheeeeaaaaaaa" which echoed throughout the garage.

Curt, with muscles flexed and in perfect form, spun his
body around to demonstrate his martial arts skills by exe-
cuting a perfect spinning back kick. What Curt didn't
know is that he was standing on small pieces of broken vehicle glass . . . not a good thing. As Curt snapped his leg
around his anchored boot shot upward, placing poor Curt
about four feet off the concrete and perfectly horizontal.

Needless to say, gravity immediately took over and Curt fell to the earth with impressive velocity . . . *thump!* . . . right on his back. He attempted a quick recovery but found that the combination of having the wind knocked out of him and wearing all his equipment prevented him from getting up. What we witnessed was a grown man trying futilely to get up, but he could only get his feet and head off the ground. As he briefly struggled he looked as if he were having a spastic seizure of embarrassment.

Well, at this point, I noticed I could no longer breathe. As I dropped to my knees and then to my hands the last thing I saw through the tears that started running down my cheeks was Curt's humiliated, bright red face. I exploded with the hardest laughter of my adult life. Gasping for precious air, I looked up again only to see Tony and Uncle Kev on their hands and knees laughing their asses off. As Curt finally stood up—a proud and talented martial artist—and the pieces of broken vehicle glass fell from his uniform, the laughter roared throughout the garage until our jaws and stomachs ached with pain.

Despite Curt's embarrassment and our relentless recollection of that day I must admit that it truly was an incredible kick. Kung Fu Curt's unique execution of a single spinning back kick knocked three cops on their butts without even making contact. These are the little incidents that happen on slow nights on the job; this is the stuff that legends are made of.

OF LIFE

BY DAVID POMEROY

Detroit PD.

I've been a policeman for nine years and have spent all but one year of it on the streets. I have been involved in several shootings, one in which an officer was killed and three other officers were also shot. My partner, and friend, was critically injured and lost his eye and was paralyzed from a bullet to the head. In a nutshell, I've seen quite a bit. I've watched children and adults die. I've had many sleepless nights and still have nightmares from the various shootings. The story I want to share with you, however, has nothing to do with any of that. It happened a few weeks back and it is something I will never forget.

My partner, Tom, and I had just finished an arrest of a guy for armed robbery and were an hour from the end of our shift when a run came out for a thirteen-year-old boy who had hung himself in a bathroom. When we arrived, the little boy was lying on the bathroom floor, unconscious and without a pulse. Lying next to him was the dog chain that he had used to hang himself from a hook on the back of the bathroom door. Tom and I picked the boy up and carried him to our scout car to transport him, because EMS was ten minutes away. Another officer jumped in the backseat and began CPR. We got the kid to the hospital within five minutes and he had regained a pulse by the time we arrived there.

Tom and I sat in the triage room and watched the doctors work to bring that kid back. Within twenty minutes, they had the kid's heart beating on its own and I remember feeling like I had done something good. After they stabilized him, the doctor came up to us and told us that although he had a steady heartbeat, he had gone without oxygen for too long and would most likely be brain dead. Talk about having the wind knocked out of you. We checked on the kid a few days later and our worst fear was confirmed: he was on life support and in a permanent vegetative state. The follow-up investigation confirmed that it was an attempted suicide and not an accident. We later learned that the family had discontinued life support and the kid had died.

Now, it's only been a few weeks but it haunts me to think we saved that kid only to have him lie in a hospital bed with tubes inside him for the rest of his "life." The other thing that troubles me is what could be so bad in the life of thirteen-year-old that he would rather die. I remember playing baseball for hours on end when I was thirteen and loving every minute of my life. I can't imagine what this poor kid's life was like for him to want to die, but now we have to live with the fact that we didn't do him any favors by helping to bring him back.

SEASON'S GREETINGS

by Charles R. Martel

Deputy Sheriff, Harris County Sheriff's Department, Houston, Texas, twenty-five years.

Many years ago, during the Christmas holidays, there had been a rash of armed robberies that had occurred at local supermarkets throughout parts of Central Texas—Waco, Temple, Round Rock. One police department took decisive action to combat the situation. They assigned several officers to undercover stakeout teams that were set up in stores believed to be targeted by the robbers. These plainclothes tactical response units were commonly referred to as "shotgun squads." They'd wait outside a business and if a robbery were to occur, the officers would jump the bandits as they fled the scene. Armed with 12-gauge automatic shotguns loaded with deer slugs and double ought buck, the police hoped to deter suspects from committing such brazen holdups.

One night, a week before Christmas, two bandits wearing ski masks attempted to rob a Safeway store. One was armed with a .357 Magnum while the other carried a sawed-off shotgun in a leather sling beneath his overcoat. Both suspects forced customers and employees to lie facedown on the floor. They robbed the courtesy booth, stole money from the cash registers, pistol-whipped the store manager, threatened to kill a pregnant woman, and fired two shots into the ceiling. As they exited the front of the store brandishing their weapons, both hijackers were confronted by heavily armed police who had on-viewed the robbery from the parking lot outside. A blazing gun battle ensued and when the smoke finally cleared, there were two fewer bad guys in the world. Fortunately, no officers were injured or killed.

Later, when crime scene investigators were questioning witnesses, one detective asked a bystander what he had observed. The young man answered, "I didn't see nothin'. I was under a car but I heard it all!"

"What do you mean?" inquired the officer. "What did you hear?"

"I heard what the cops said when those two crooks came runnin' out the store wavin' their guns!"

"You mean you heard the officers yell, 'Freeze! Police!'?" asked the detective.

"No, not exactly," said the witness. "It was more like, 'Merry Christmas, assholes!' *Boom! Boom! Boom!*"

Following a thorough investigation the shooting was deemed "righteous" and presented to a grand jury. All officers were no-billed and everyone had a happy holiday season.

YES, IT IS PART OF THE JOB!

BY MICHAEL SUMMERS

Lieutenant, Burbank PD, Illinois.

On September 2, 2001, at ten P.M. I was working as the watch commander for the Burbank Police Department and as I completed roll call, I told the midnight guys to be careful and to hit the streets. Just as I did so, I heard my street sergeant on the radio requesting that I come to the scene of a domestic disturbance in which a male subject had locked himself in his garage and was threatening to blow himself up.

I raced to the scene and upon my arrival my sergeant told me that the man was distraught over his failing marriage and wanted to die. As I approached the garage I could hear a hissing noise coming from inside. I stood in front of the garage window and introduced myself to the man inside as Mike, and he told me his name was Jerry. Jerry had a distinct Polish accent but he spoke English well. From my position at the window, I could see that the hissing noise was coming from two large propane tanks in the garage. I asked Jerry to turn them off so that we could talk about his problems. Jerry was hesitant but he went and turned off the main valve and returned to the window. I could tell that Jerry had been drinking and I saw that he was holding a torch igniter and a cigarette lighter. We talked for fifteen minutes about Jerry's marital problems and I told him that I thought I could help him. I think Jerry started trusting me at this point because he handed me the torch igniter. My throat was getting sore from the heavy concentration of propane gas and I told Jerry to come out so that we could sit down with his wife and try to work things out. At this point, Jerry heard a noise coming from outside, at the back of the garage, and he immediately turned the main valve to the propane tanks back on. I knew if he used the cigarette lighter with the tanks open the explosion would be devastating to the surrounding neighborhood. I reassured Jerry that nobody was behind his garage and chided him for acting foolishly; I asked him to turn the gas back off. Once again, he complied. For the next fifteen minutes or so we spoke through the garage window, face to face, and Jerry talked angrily of his wife and asked me to bring her to the window to speak to him. I figured that Jerry had other plans than just talking to her so I told him that his wife had been evacuated from the area and if he came out he could speak with her for as long as he wanted. I kept him talking but then Jerry started to slowly turn the flint wheel of the lighter. When I told him to knock it off and to just give me the lighter he said, "Don't worry, it won't spark." But he did extend his arm toward me to hand me the lighter . . . when the garage exploded.

I recall being hit by a ball of flame and seeing the garage window go flying over my head, striking my right elbow as it passed. I was on fire and I began pulling my shirt off when my fellow officers came to my aid and helped put out the flames. I was hospitalized in intensive care for three days with burns to 18 percent of my body, mostly confined to my face, neck, and arms. I was extremely lucky to be alive. Jerry suffered burns over 30 percent of his body and survived.

When people ask me why I did what I did, I simply tell them that it is part of my job. They stare at me and say incredulously, "Part of your job is getting blown up?—that's ridiculous!" But in December of 1982 I raised my right hand and took an oath, like all police officers. There is nothing in the oath that says you are willing to die or be injured, but that risk exists every time you pin on your badge and every cop knows it. In most situations we are the first ones in and the last ones out.

On September 11, 2001, New York City police officers reported for work and by the end of the day many of them died doing their job because they too took the oath. I consider myself the luckiest man in the world; I did my job but lived to tell my story. People who think that a cop's job is to simply harass the public and write tickets and maybe grab a doughnut here and there . . . think again. Cops do countless great deeds every day and their actions largely go unnoticed. But in the very rare circumstance, when a cop crosses the line, that's what we hear about. I hope that the recent tragic events have changed that by showing just how perilous the job can be; I'm here to tell you that when a cop gets injured or killed while performing his or her duties it is simply an ugly part of the job.

DIRECTING TRAFFIC

BY STAN DAMAS

*San Francisco PD, California; retired after
twenty-five years.*

Much of police work is spent driving the streets of a city
in a patrol car. Family disputes, minor neighborhood ar-
guments, and traffic control take up most of your day.
Parking is always a problem and the most flagrant offender is a double-parked auto. Any person who leaves
his automobile in a lane of traffic, forcing others to maneuver around it at their peril, is thinking only of himself.

One afternoon my partner and I came upon a double-
parked pickup truck in front of an apartment house. The
driver was still seated in the vehicle and he seemed oblivious to the line of cars honking their horns behind him.
What nerve, I thought, as I pulled up behind the pickup
and walked up to the driver's window.

The startled driver quickly explained that he was helping a friend move and just one more trip was needed to
finish loading and then they would be on their way. As he
was speaking, I observed this friend exiting the apartment
house carrying a small television set. He set it in the rear
of the pickup next to a bunch of other household articles.
I told the driver to hurry up and then I stepped back to

wait for them to leave. But as the second fellow entered the truck, I heard him ask in a low voice, "Have you got the hot wire?"

I hurried over to my partner who was now directing the backed-up traffic around the police car. He noticed the look on my face and asked me why it was taking so much time to move the truck.

"The truck is stolen!" I said quietly. "These guys are burglars and the truck is full of stolen property." I explained how nervous the driver was and how the second man had requested a hot wire but my partner, a staunch defender of smoothly flowing traffic, was more concerned about the cars behind us. He continued to wave his arms and to direct traffic around the impediment—the stolen pickup full of loot.

I was getting frustrated. "Will you stop that!" I demanded and almost had to beg him to help me to identify the two guys and to check the ownership of the truck before they drove away. He finally consented, taking one sad last look at the traffic bottleneck and the faces of the drivers whose eyes were locked on him as a beacon of commuter hope.

We walked around the truck and questioned the two men and it only took a few minutes to verify that the truck was indeed stolen and the property had been removed from the apartment without the owner's permission. The two suspects were given bracelets and made guests of the city.

In my police report I left out one fact: how my partner had been directing traffic around a burglary in progress.

He was, after all, my partner.

SWEET SIXTEEN

BY JOHN SCHEMBRA

Sergeant, Pleasant Hill PD, California; retired after thirty years.

She had just turned sixteen last week and life couldn't be better. It had been a great summer, hanging out with her friends and taking trips with her family. She had been practicing her driving, preparing to take the driving test next week to get her license, and her mom had promised she could drive for their outing today.

They were going to lunch at the California Pizza Kitchen in Walnut Creek, her favorite restaurant, then to Sun Valley Mall in Concord to do some shopping for school clothes. It would be a good practice session for her driving because there would be some traffic, but not too much.

They left at eleven A.M. for lunch. She drove the ten miles to the restaurant, staying at the speed limit and being very careful, pulling into the parking lot twenty-five minutes later. She had trouble maneuvering the car into a parking place, having to go back and forth a couple of times until it was straight and in the middle of the space. They laughed over her difficulties but her mom made a mental note to have her practice when they got to the mall.

He left his house in Martinez at 10:30 A.M., driving his

pickup to Orinda to help a friend work on his car. It needed a brake job, and they were going to change the oil and radiator fluid at the same time. He drove slightly below the speed limit, making sure he obeyed all the laws. He couldn't afford to be stopped by the cops again. His license was suspended and he was on court probation for three prior drunk driving convictions. As part of his probation, he was not supposed to be driving at all, but he had been doing so since his release from jail three months ago.

He parked in front of his friend's house and walked up the driveway to the open garage. His friend had already started working on the car and had removed the front wheels. At that moment, his friend was sitting on a milk crate drinking a beer. As he came into the garage, the friend reached into a cooler next to him and tossed him a beer. Catching it, he popped the top and drank half of it in three large gulps, belching loudly. His friend laughed and fished another beer out of the cooler for himself. When they finished those, they began working on the car.

The mother and daughter left the restaurant at one P.M. The daughter was driving and she turned left onto North Main Street and drove the seven miles through Walnut Creek and Pleasant Hill to the mall. Her mother had her drive to a deserted part of the parking lot where she could practice before they parked near the mall entrance. Afterwards, they walked into the mall, laughing and talking more like best friends than mother and daughter.

It took the two men two and a half hours to complete the work on the car. During that time they finished the other seven beers in the cooler, the man with the suspended license drinking four of them. By the time they went into the house for something to eat he could feel the effects of the alcohol. Even with a buzz on, he had two more beers with his food.

After lunch, they sat in the kitchen for a while, talking and drinking even more beer, until 3:30 P.M. when he looked at his watch. He figured he had better get home before his wife, as she would be really pissed if she knew he had been driving. She was going to be mad enough when she saw he had been drinking. That, too, was a violation of his probation.

He finished his ninth beer and left the kitchen, walking to his truck parked at the curb. He got in and after several tries, got the key in the ignition and started the engine. Dropping the gear selector into drive, he accelerated quickly, spinning his tires as he pulled away. He turned right onto Mt. Diablo Boulevard, accelerating to 55 mph in the 35-mph zone, weaving in and out of the lanes as he passed slower vehicles. He turned westbound on Taylor Boulevard and sped up to 66 mph in the 45-mph zone, heading up toward Pleasant Hill.

The mother and daughter finished their shopping by 3:15 P.M. She treated herself and her mom to a smoothie that they drank while walking to the car. She pulled slowly out of the parking lot and turned onto Contra Costa Boulevard. They planned to take Taylor Boulevard over the hill into Lafayette. There wouldn't be too much traffic and once they passed Pleasant Hill Road there were few homes or businesses along the road and only a couple of stoplights. It was two lanes in each direction, divided by a four-inch concrete median. It would give her an opportunity to drive a bit faster than she was used to, preparing her for their freeway practice next week.

She turned eastbound on Taylor and drove at the 45-mph speed limit, passing the Pleasant Hill Police Department and proceeding over the hill and through the intersection with Pleasant Hill Road. She accelerated smoothly to 55 mph, the posted speed limit, and moved into the slow lane. She sang softly to the song on the radio as she drove up the hill.

His speed rose to 72 mph as he crested the hill and started down. He pulled into the right lane to pass the car in front of him, accelerating to 78 mph. As he rapidly caught up to the next car in the right lane, he misjudged how fast he was going. He suddenly realized he was closing too fast and yanked the steering wheel to the left, trying to go around the car. That much force at that speed caused the back of his pickup to slide to the right. He yanked the wheel the other way, overcorrecting the skid, causing his front tires to hit the low median at an angle. His truck went airborne for a short distance, knocking over a DIVIDED HIGHWAY sign on the median. When his truck landed in the opposing lane he lost all control and rocketed across both lanes toward the hillside.

From the corner of her eye, she saw a blur coming toward her. She barely had time to react before the truck hit her car at the left front headlight. In the first two hundredths of a second the airbag deployed, preventing her face from striking the steering wheel. It didn't matter, though, as the force from the truck drove the engine into the front seat area, crushing her chest and rupturing her internal organs. She died almost instantly, feeling nothing, no fear, and no pain.

Her mother was "luckier." She saw the truck coming and tried to brace herself, which broke both her legs. Her left leg was shattered when the engine was driven into the front compartment and her right leg snapped just above the knee. She cracked six ribs on her left side also. The worst injury happened when her left hand was almost severed at the wrist by the torn and twisted metal forced into the front seat compartment, and she had some internal injuries from striking the dashboard as it was pushed into her seat. She would live, though it would take several surgeries and almost two years before she completely healed. The doctors reattached her hand, though she would never be able to use it normally again and she would always walk with a slight limp. Though her physical injuries would heal she would never get over the loss of her daughter.

And him? When he struck the car, he slid forward on the seat, breaking his right leg. His face hit the steering wheel, breaking his nose and knocking out a couple of teeth. He would heal and be as good as new in six months.

The 911 lines all lit up with frantic callers. The two beat cars were dispatched and I, as the shift supervisor, automatically responded to the scene. I sped there with lights and siren on. From the sound of the dispatcher's voice, I knew this would be a bad one.

I was the second car to arrive and immediately ran to the closest vehicle, a pickup truck. The first arriving officer was already at the bent and twisted wreckage of the car, leaning in the passenger window. There was debris from the two vehicles scattered across the road. Pieces of metal and bits of glass covered the roadway and oil and radiator fluid made the footing slippery.

The driver of the truck was semiconscious and moaning, and I could see he was bleeding badly from his facial injuries. The interior of the truck reeked of alcohol. I grabbed a T-shirt from the front seat and pressed it to the driver's face to stem the flow of blood. When the second beat unit arrived, I had the officer take over and looked to see where the first officer was. I could see him leaning in the car, and, since I could hear the sirens of the approaching fire truck and ambulance, I walked to my patrol car, popped the trunk and started taking flares out.

"Sarge, you better come here," called the officer at the destroyed automobile. I felt a sense of dread when I heard that, but walked quickly to the car. As I came up to the driver's side, I could see the twisted metal and the engine in the compartment and the upper torso of a young girl. She looked to be sleeping though her face was ashen. There was no blood. She was leaning forward over the engine, which had crushed her against the seatback. I felt for a carotid pulse, knowing there would be none but hoping just the same. Her skin still was warm though the life had left her body. Fighting down the lump in my throat, I closed her eyes and turned away.

It took the fire department a half hour to cut away enough of the car to get her mother out so she could be taken to the hospital. She barely survived.

It took another hour and a half to remove the body of the driver, this young girl who had her whole life ahead of her, a life cut short by a drunk driver. She would never have another birthday. Sweet Sixteen was her last.

He was the first person in California tried and convicted for murder in a drunk driving case under a new law passed a few months earlier. He received twenty-five years to life, and would not be eligible for parole for eighteen years. Of all the cases I handled in my thirty years with the force, with all the brutality and death I have seen, this is the one that will haunt me the rest of my life.

FEAR IN CHILDREN

BY DAVE CROPP

Sergeant, Sacramento PD, California.

> *Men fear death as children fear to go in the*
> *dark; and as that natural fear in children is*
> *increased by tales, so is the other*
> —FRANCIS BACON, 1561–1626

At some point in the career of every cop, we realize that there would be no heroes without victims; no one to rescue without tragic cruelty at the other end; no celebration without solemn contemplation and prayer. Why such a trade-off? Maybe the world would be a better place if we didn't need heroes.

July 18, 1988, started out like every other day for my partner, Tim, and me—a hazy, hot Sacramento afternoon. But this day would end like no other. I remember some details vividly, others I don't recall. But what I do remember, I will never forget.

Tim and I were assigned to a Street Drug Enforcement car in North Sacramento—Del Paso Heights. We had gone through the 1979 Sacramento Police Department's (SPD) academy together. We were about the same age and got along well; in fact, we were very much alike with one exception: I was pragmatically more pessimistic—always calculating the worst-case scenario. Tim was a true optimist. With a silver tongue, the gift of gab, and a perpetually friendly smile, he could talk his way out of any crisis, whether an explosive domestic violence situation or an interview with Internal Affairs.

We drove an unmarked car but wore the standard SPD uniform. Our job was to post an in-your-face presence in high drug-trafficking areas. We were exempt from regular call assignments, meaning we could travel the streets of North Sacramento as we pleased. We would eat when we wanted to eat, patrol where we wanted to patrol, and chase whom we wanted to chase. Once it got dark, we could slip in and out of inner-city shadows, creep through fields, watch from the tops of nearby buildings or behind abandoned cars. On a typical night Tim and I would find ourselves in two or three foot chases, usually short foot chases—we lost most.

Overall, we caught our share of street dealers, guns and drugs. This was our gig. We were tough young cops and everything was fun and exciting. Getting drug dealers off the streets was about the most important thing a young cop could do, and I was proud to do it. But, like most young cops, we had a lot to learn.

Sacramento had recently been thrust into the national spotlight with a child abduction case. Four-year-old Candi Talarico had been abducted and missing for six weeks and was the focus of a nationwide manhunt. Everyone presumed the worst, or at least I did—after all, six weeks!

Our shift began at four P.M., the hottest part of the day. Tim and I logged on as unit "Tac-4" and we decided to get something to drink. Tim drove as always, talking about nothing in particular as always, while I tuned the old standard radio to our favorite music station. And so we were prepared for another exciting evening in North Sacramento: superficial dialogue, music blasting from a cheap car radio, police chases, drug and weapon seizures. We loved every minute of it!

When we emerged from the drive-through lane, large sodas in hand, the police radio suddenly commanded our attention.

"All units—a possible suspect in the Candi Talarico case is being detained in Elk Grove—further information is pending at this time."

I remember a dull sinking feeling in the pit of my stomach as I thought of my own two small children. I started shaking my head from side to side, trying to dispel the abhorrent thoughts from my mind as if by shaking my head I could forcefully cast the demonic images away.

"That poor little girl," I muttered, "I can't imagine what her parents must be going through. The thought of something like this happening to my kids makes me sick to my stomach."

I returned my attention to sipping my soda, and tried to focus on the adventures awaiting us in our night as North Sacramento drug enforcement officers. Then I realized that Tim hadn't uttered a word. I glanced to my left and saw that Tim was sitting tall and tense, staring straight ahead. He hadn't heard a word I'd said. Well, I thought dismissively, he doesn't have kids, so he doesn't understand.

But Tim did understand. Suddenly, Tim, as if possessed by internal forces, grabbed the mike and with a dry commanding voice said, "Tac-4, we'll be en route to Elk Grove to assist in the operation."

"Tac-4 check, I'll show you en route."

We jumped onto the freeway, pushing our little department clunker as fast as it could go all the way to the small rural town of Elk Grove. For the first time in our partner-

ship we didn't converse en route. We arrived twenty minutes later, but it felt like two.

The scene was an old, whitewashed, wood-sided
Methodist church surrounded by grand oak trees. There
were marked and unmarked police cars from a myriad of
agencies. There were federal, state, and local agents, uniformed and in plain clothes, all pursuing an assigned task
within a larger coordinated effort to find the missing girl.
While not personally privy to the investigative leads that
had identified our suspect, I overheard others talking
about the perpetrator. He was a handyman at the church,
apparently a deaf-mute. While the suspect was cooperating with the police, his inability to communicate with authorities had stymied the investigation.

I lost sight of Tim the minute we got out of our car.
Usually, in critical events such as this, partners stay together for pragmatic tactical reasons, but this situation
was different. I was in an odd state of perpetual numbness
and what I think of as an apathetic emotional purgatory—
I kept trying to dislodge those unwanted conceptual perceptions that surrounded the images of a little girl
missing for six long weeks. But my emotional state was
what was required for what happened next; it became my
strength rather than my deficit.

The car had identified the suspect's location: a dirty,
faded-blue Ford Escort, which had been parked in front
of the church for God knows how long. Two days prior,
the suspect's car had been associated with the Sacramento abduction of Muey Saefong, a four-year-old Laot-
ian girl. The similarities in modus operandi between the
two abductions preliminarily linked both cases. Now, so
close to solving both cases, investigators frantically
searched for the whereabouts of innocent little Muey Saefong and precious Candi Talarico. Dozens of officers
were scurrying around the scene searching for any and all

clues. As I walked among them, I momentarily felt the urge to return to North Sacramento and chase drug dealers and to leave the search for abducted children to those who were already here. But that urge passed and, as I hadn't been privy to any investigative information acquired thus far, I realized I needed to learn more.

I looked around for someone I recognized and my eyes fell upon a tall, lean plainclothes investigator sporting a tan coat and standing alone across the street. His straight brown hair was wet with perspiration and the intense look on his face told me he was extremely involved, both emotionally and professionally, in the investigation. I could tell by the expression on his face that he sensed the end was near. I started to walk over toward him but I stopped short, realizing with a chill that grabbed my spine just what it was he was focusing on. He was staring, emotionless, at the trunk of the suspect's car. No one else was focused in the same direction. No one else appeared to be thinking what he was thinking.

I was watching as he suddenly came alive and threw his clipboard to the pavement and darted toward the rear of the suspect's car. He had previously acquired the keys to the evil conveyance, and was nervously fumbling with each loose key, desperately trying to discover which one fit the locked trunk. Everyone's attention was now on the frantic investigator at the trunk of the suspect's car; we all were frozen in time and space, united in thought, in duty, and in hope. When he found the right key, he ripped open the trunk.

We all watched as this investigator, this hero in a rumpled suit, gently lifted little Muey Saefong from her mobile tomb. Her skin was discolored red, her jet-black hair was sopping wet with sweat, and her body limp and lifeless. Muey's little eyes were closed and her small head fell to one side; her mouth, hands and legs were ruthlessly subdued with gray duct tape. I stared in horror, feeling numb and useless. "Oh my God!" was all I could say.

Suddenly another officer grabbed me. "Come quickly!" he ordered.

"Yes sir!" I replied dutifully and followed though it was hard to tear my eyes away from the figure of the tiny child. He led me toward the steps of the church. Not sure where he was taking me or what he wanted me to do, I prayed for God to give me something useful to do. As I followed him, I heard someone shout that Muey Saefong was alive. Impossible, I thought, how long has that poor little child been in the back of the dark airless trunk—two hours, two days? It's a miracle indeed!

When I reached the shaded west porch area of the church, I was teamed up with another uniformed SPD officer—Gary, a veteran officer also assigned to the same North Sacramento sector, but on the team with the good days off. Our orders were simple: to search the church for Candi Talarico. Based upon the horrific picture of Muey Saefong still vivid in my mind, I pessimistically presumed the worst.

Unexpectedly, I found myself face-to-face with the suspect. His thick black hair and curly beard were dirty and unkempt. His hands were cuffed in front of him. He was small, thin, and unassuming. I was marginally aware that I should be feeling a sense of horror and the impulse to do something awful to this guy. But he's just a suspect at this point, not imposing or threatening in any way and I could not yet connect him emotionally to the tiny child pulled from the hellhole trunk of his car. My sense of duty persevered and I made inquisitive eye contact with the suspect, trying to learn something about him. His head tilted downward in a self-deprecating manner, his cold black eyes slowly reached up to meet mine. I was assessing him: What does he know that we don't? What is he thinking?

Then I noticed that the suspect was holding something in his dirt-encrusted hands—a piece of paper and a pencil. Sheepishly, he displayed his penmanship; it seemed tired and sloppy, revealing him to be uneducated, nervous, or scared. But the penciled words he'd written sent a chill rippling through my body: "I'll show you where she is." He glanced pointedly toward the entrance to the church and Gary and I followed his gaze.

The three of us entered the church—Gary and I, and the suspect. Everyone else was busy assisting with the revival efforts of Muey Saefong. The snapping of pictures by the press behind us sounded like a far off parade of applause and firecrackers. We followed the suspect to the back of the church. There was no one else inside.

The wood floors echoed with our every step, as if our presence had been expected, our fate predetermined. But only one of us knew the fate of our precious treasure. We followed him through a doorway, and down a short wooden flight of stairs. All my senses were engaged and I took note of the plain, unpretentiously crafted wood stair steps, and the smooth wooden handrail. Then more stairs descending to the cool dry basement floor below.

The natural light gradually diminished as we continued and I felt isolated in an austere quietness. When we reached the shadowy basement, I found myself staring at dozens of simple brown cardboard boxes of various shapes and sizes. Gary motioned for the suspect to sit down on the stairs, which he did.

Slowly, we started to look around for Candi. I wondered what Gary was thinking; his face was as intentionally blank as mine was. I'll never forget the many horrible images running through my mind as we searched the basement floor, or the way we quietly, almost reverently, called out for the invisible victim, "Caaandiii . . . Caaandiii." Would we find her hiding in some obscure corner, surrounded by cardboard boxes, crouched in a fetal position with her arms tightly wrapped around her legs? Would we find her alive? . . . or not?

To this day I can still recall every detail of the thoughts going through my mind during those moments. I can still smell the stale, dusty odor of the church basement. I can still see the eerie monolithic structure composed of the cardboard boxes; I can still remember that strange confluence of nightmare and reality. Stillness abounds; there were no sounds, no cries—nothing. No sign of anything out of the ordinary. I wondered what the crime scene would look like. I wondered how we could process the rescue without contaminating the crime scene.

As my eyes adjusted to the darkness, a curious sight distracted me to my left—a small hatch door atop a raised, rectangled wood structure. I had assumed we were standing on the bottom floor, but neither Gary nor I had realized that we were still three feet off the dirt floor bed. The hatch door appeared to be part of a small storage area no more than six feet by four feet wide; the hatch door itself was probably no more than twenty-four inches square.

I reached over and slowly opened the hatch door, half expecting something to reach out of the black hole and grab my hand. As I rested the hatch against the rear wall of the foundation, I felt my skin crawl and the hackles rise on the back of my neck. I bent down and cautiously peered inside but it was much too dark to see anything. I instinctively reached for my flashlight but then I realized that I had left it in the car. It was still daylight, a hot July afternoon—why would I need a flashlight? I noticed with embarrassment that Gary's flashlight was appropriately attached to his Sam Brown belt—the way it should be, the way I was taught to wear it. After that day, I would never forget my light again.

Pointing to the hatch door I quietly remarked, "Hey, Gary, check this out."

Gary had been focused on the shadowy areas between the cardboard boxes, carefully moving things aside, examining any possible hiding or storage space. He looked over at me, saw the hatch I was pointing at, and came over to stand by my side. We both looked for a few moments at the gaping hole, processing our private perceptions and expectations.

"Let me borrow your light, I left mine in the car," I almost whispered.

Without saying a word, Gary walked over to the hatch door and leaned over the dark hole, reaching back for his flashlight at the same time. Using one hand to brace himself and the other to hold the light, he placed his weight atop the wooden structure and his upper body disappeared down into the darkness of the recessed storage area. Nervously I glanced toward the suspect behind me. He was still there, shaking his head from side to side like he knew something too terrible to utter aloud. But then Gary's excited voice dispelled the chill of the moment.

"Candi? . . . Candi! It's the police, honey—it's okay."

I felt my heart leap in my throat and I yelled toward the top of the stairs to whoever was up there to hear, "She's alive! She's okay!"

Gary's back was taut with tension but his voice was gentle, soothing. "It's okay, honey, I'm the police. Follow my light . . . that's right . . . we'll take care of you."

I heard rapid footsteps on the hardwood floor above and repeated cries of "She's okay! . . . She's okay!" were echoing through the church as the rescuers relayed the news. What I couldn't see at that moment, but what I seem to recall vividly in my memories, was tiny Candi

Talarico cautiously inching her way along the dark dirt basement floor toward the welcoming beacon of light.

"That's a good girl, honey, keep coming, follow my light," encouraged Gary. He reached back and handed me the light so that he would be able to grab the child with both hands. I stood behind him and directed the light over his shoulder as far as I could reach, illuminating the dark abyss so that Gary wouldn't lose sight of Candi, so that she would have the light to guide her. It seemed like forever but it was only a few moments until Gary was able to grab the girl and pull her out of perpetual night. He raised her up, cradled her in his arms, holding on tight. She held on tight too.

I held my fingers loosely over the beam of light so as not to hurt her eyes while providing enough illumination so that I might check out her physical condition. For a few unforgettable seconds I found myself staring directly into the most beautiful pair of little blue eyes I had ever seen. I was astonished to see that Candi appeared physically healthy; her eyes were wide open and she was looking all around her. But then I noticed something that disturbed me: her facial expression presented somewhat of a flat affect, or revealed very little emotion. I wondered if this was the result of her terrible ordeal, if to mentally survive six weeks in captivity she had viewed all that was happening to her from a great emotional distance. I didn't know the answer then and I have wondered about it often over the years.

It seemed like Gary and I stood there with Candi for a long time but it was really only a minute or two. A million thoughts raced through my mind: What was she thinking? Was she scared? Was she happy to have been rescued? Did she have any clue what was happening? Those few moments, the time spent looking into those eyes, at her emotionless expression, lasted far longer emotionally than they did in reality.

Gary and I turned toward the stairs just SPD Sergeant Dave Wilson started down. Sergeant Wilson was a veteran cop and a large, strong man, with reddish blond hair, clean-shaven with soft comforting features. I still remember the diffused ray of sunlight that penetrated the stairwell as if Nature were celebrating the rescue and comforting the youngster. Sergeant Wilson took Candi in his arms, holding her as if nothing in this world would ever hurt that little child again. He turned and carried her the rest of the way upstairs to the church and outside to awaiting medical personnel.

As Sergeant Wilson stepped through the doors of the church with Candi, there was an explosion of camera flashes—every camera in Sacramento must have been trained on those church doors. The unforgettable image of this intensely focused and tough cop, his sleeves rolled back, his strong arms encircling and protecting little Candi Talarico, made every paper in town as well as headline news around the country.

Gary had taken the suspect back upstairs so I found myself emerging unhurriedly from the basement and wandering around toward the back of the church, trying to stay away from the reporters' cameras. I realized I hadn't seen my partner, Tim, since we had arrived. I felt emotionally numb and couldn't seem to put everything that had happened over the last hour into perspective, so I stepped outside the back doors and took a seat on a cool cement porch ledge. I didn't really hear or see anything other than the leaves in the great oak trees being rustled by the gentle afternoon breeze—part of me was still in that dim basement looking for something I was afraid I wouldn't find. I said a fervent prayer for Candi Talarico and Muey Saefong . . . Dear God, bless those little girls and their families.

A moment later I noticed that life around me had gone

on as if nothing out of the ordinary had ever occurred. Motorists drove by as usual, honking their horns needlessly, brakes screeching, tires squealing; pedestrians maneuvered for an opportunity to dart across traffic. I noticed lawn mowers buzzing in the distance—all this was evidence of the perpetual and sobering reality of life. It goes on no matter who lives or dies . . .

It was time to find my partner.

When I got to the front of the church, I found that the ambulance had rushed the two girls off to the hospital and most of the media had followed. The entire area was now a crime scene, taped off from onlookers. The only cameras that were flashing were those of the crime scene investigators. Procedure required that two CSI officers concurrently photograph each item of evidence just in case one camera doesn't work or the film doesn't develop.

I know from experience that detectives had already started to canvass the neighborhood, home by home, looking for information, witnesses, or clues. Every scrap of evidence would be identified, numbered, and recorded. Detailed diagrams would be prepared. The preliminary investigation lasted well into the evening, requiring the fire department to respond with a portable lighting arrangement.

I found out that Tim had been assigned to accompany our two young victims to the hospital in the ambulance. I spotted our unmarked police car in the distance and started toward it, still in my strange daze. My fingers actually burned on the chrome handle as I opened the door. I seemed to fall into the hot, dry seat. I started the motor and drove off. I have no memory of driving to the hospital, nothing other than parking near the emergency room entrance.

But as I climbed out of the car, I realized that my clothes were dusty and dirty. I had been sweating profusely down in the basement of the church, but it was only then that I became aware of it. There were charcoal streaks across my face and on the backs of my hands.

I noticed Tim seated on a cement bench next to the glass ER doors. He was leaning forward, his elbows resting on his knees, and he appeared to be lost in thought. I was making my way toward him when a local news reporter suddenly emerged from my periphery. She was holding a notepad and there was a camera guy behind her. She asked me if I had anything to say about the rescue of Candi Talarico and Muey Saefong.

"No," I said, "I just want to go home and hug my kids." That brief statement, which made the local evening news, may have seemed stoical, but it was nothing but pure emotion. It remains the most heartfelt official statement that's come out of my mouth in my twenty-three years as a cop.

Tim looked up; we made eye contact but said nothing. He went back to staring at the dried air bubbles in the cement walkway, while I stared at the glass ER doors.

"I'm going in to find out if I can see Candi."

"Okay," he said.

Entering the chaotic world of ER, I tracked an ER nurse whom I recognized and asked her if I might be able to see Candi. She went off to ask the doctor and returned a minute later.

"Come on," she said, "I'll show you where they are."

We walked together down the corridor and around the corner. I was oblivious to everything around me, even though the emergency room was bustling with injured and was fully engaged in a myriad of traumas.

I was led to a hospital room with two beds: Candi was sitting on one, Muey on the other, each with their respective mothers standing close by. They appeared to be engaged in conversation as I entered. I've interrupted, I thought, but was gratified when both mothers smiled appreciatively.

I was suddenly at a loss for words. A flood of emotion roared through me.

"Hi, honey," I mumbled to Candi, "I met you back at the church." I gave her a quick hug, thinking to myself that I shouldn't have mentioned the church—stupid!

"How are you doing?" I asked.

"Okay," she replied.

"Well, I just wanted to check up on you, I'm glad that you're okay—I have two little kids just about your age." I felt a hand placed softly on my back. It was Tim; he'd arrived and was standing next to me, sporting a half smile. I figured he'd know what to say, but he didn't. He just stood there with his half smile and listened without saying a word.

A small tear ran down my cheek, then another. "Well, I should go before I make a really big fool out of myself," I concluded as I wiped the tears away with the back of my hand.

Candi's mother and I exchanged hugs. I did the same with little Muey and her mother. "Good luck, sweetie," I said to Muey. The reply was an innocent, wide-eyed nod and a faint smile. I wasn't sure if they understood English or not—but the message was crystal clear: "Bye now!"

Tim and I left the small hospital room, walking solemnly through the hallway, then out of the ER and back to our hot stuffy car. Then back to work . . . as drug law enforcement officers in North Sacramento. I really don't remember the rest of our shift.

THE MORNING AFTER

BY PHIL DUNNIGAN

San Francisco PD, retired after thirty years.

How do you tell your family not to worry? That it's just a job, that you'll be careful and it's okay? Especially when you know you can't guarantee any of these statements and it is often not okay?

One time at work I had a problem and I carried the effects home with me. Everyone tries to work things out their own way. Some use physical means—sports, hobbies; some hoist a few wet ones with the boys. For me, it's writing an experience down so that maybe in retrospect I can learn something from what happened, good or bad.

Maybe I was writing so that those I cared about would understand and would not have to wear those silent, fearful frowns whenever I came home with a slight limp or something else I couldn't hide. Knowing what happened never seemed enough; understanding what happened seemed to help.

It's said that positioning is everything in life. The following was written from a position where my left ankle was raised in the air. The doctor claimed that this was the "healing position" for sprains of that type. No big thing.

A couple of days emulating a dying cockroach and I would be back hitting the bricks with the best of the city's finest.

It's also said that we create our own environment, that we're captains of our own fate, so to speak. If this is true, then it was really *me* and not that resisting teenage burglary suspect who put me into that position of appendage suspension. It's true, I could afford to be philosophical, as the doctor had given me two days at home to re-create an incident that only took a few moments on the street.

So there I was . . . at 4:15 in the morning with the most serious thought in my mind being breakfast. A window-smash burglary had been reported earlier. A routine matter, but this one was accompanied by a vague description of a fleeing suspect . . . vague being better than nothing.

What happened is as follows:

I'll make one more pass through the area and then head for the skillet.

There's somebody and he doesn't look right.

Clothing's close too.

He won't stop for me.

Looks my way and starts walking faster.

I get out.

Has no ID but plenty of vague answers.

He's told why he's being checked out (the burglary).

Now he stiffens and tries to back away.

Won't halt.

He's getting out of reach . . .

He's starting to go!

Got a hand on him.

Now we're both down.

He's on his stomach, I'm on his back.

He's quick, strong, resisting.

Can I hold him?

How good a suspect is he?

Can the witness ID him?

Is he a felon or just a wild-ass kid?

Can't let him up and he won't stay down.

Going to have to hit him.

But how hard?

Will the blow slow him down?

Will it show in court?

Do I have the right person?

DELIVERED: one quick medium rap on the back of the suspect's head.

RESULT: He pauses for a moment, but his body is still tense beneath me.

Now's the time for me to look over my shoulder for my backup. Is he close or must I finish this myself?

Ooops—now he's loose again.

We're off and running.

He, like a deer, and me wondering if all my jogging will pay off.

Boy, I'm out of breath!

Hope my radio works.

Damn this heavy equipment!

I seem to be hobbling . . .

One block . . .

Now two . . .

Sure hope he poops out soon . . .

Turned this corner—now he's gone!

Must be hiding.

There he is! Back in the alley!

The troops converge.

He still wants to fight.

Don't hit him in the face, he's my prisoner!

He's finally cuffed and in the wagon.

Jeez, my damn ankle hurts.

Probably should have hit him harder in the first place.

Damn!

HEARTS IN BARBED WIRE

BY RICKY D. COOPER

Chicago PD, retired.

Police officers put up barbed wire around their hearts to protect them.

The popular public perception is that police officers are unfeeling and uncaring. Individuals who are unfeeling or uncaring do not risk their own well-being, often their lives, for others. Cops in movies or on TV are generally portrayed as emotionally detached. The valiant sacrifice police officers and firefighters made on 9/11 when they went into the Twin Towers refutes this.

Police officers put up barbed wire because they do care. While they might suffer a prick from those sharp barbs, the wire protects them from the impact of the worst blows.

Everybody has suffered a prick at one time or another. No big deal. Police officers bear witness to shocking acts of inhumanity, guard grisly crime scenes, and endure exposure to all that is evil, cruel, and perverse in human nature. They have to protect themselves somehow. Stoically, police officers endure a thousand tiny nicks and scratches and cuts on their hearts, sometimes dripping blood on some barroom floor when they've had too much to drink.

Cops seldom reflect on these minor injuries. They are generally grateful the primary organ is still functioning. Injuries and wounds are part of the Job. Cops have hearts tough as saddle leather. Leather gets worn. And barbed wire rusts.

Every cop that ever worked the Street has a hundred war stories. I was a Chicago police officer for twenty-nine years. I have my share of war stories, too. This is the one where I got wounded. This is the one where the eighteen-wheeler, doing seventy, hit the barbed wire.

I was working on the Tactical Team in the 21st District and at the time the Youth Division, as well as the Detective Division, was desperately undermanned. As a result, follow-up investigations were assigned like injured patients at a trauma center; detectives and Youth officers handled the smoking gun cases first—the cases that were newsworthy or political hot potatoes. The deadend cases got put off until somebody had some spare time, and nobody had any spare time.

To relieve the backlog of cases, Tactical officers working in the districts were assigned to follow-up investigations where there were named offenders. Each day the Tactical lieutenant would distribute case reports with named offenders for the crimes committed in each team's sector. On the day in question I received my follow-up case, and as soon as I scanned the report I tried to wiggle out of the assignment. It was the rape of an eighteen-month-old baby, not very pleasant reading to begin with. The father had allegedly sexually assaulted the child. The mother had confided this information to a neighbor after he had complained about the baby crying all the time. It was the neighbor who notified the police. The beat officers who took the case report had been unable to interview the mother or the father. The case report had been written purely on the basis of what the neighbor told them.

I knew the mother personally. She came from one of those families that every copper who worked the area came into contact with on a regular basis. Mommy Dearest was a crack whore and my introduction to her had been memorable. Thinking I had rolled up on an on-view rape, I had almost popped a cap at a bunch of guys running from a warehouse dock across the street from the projects, where a naked woman was hunkered down on all fours. As it turned out, it was the eighteen-month-old's mother, Sheila, pulling a train. Consensual group sex on a dilapidated warehouse dock—what a delight. And there I was, thinking I'd rescued some damsel in distress, and ending up getting chewed out by the "un–fair maiden" for interrupting the free flow of trade and hindering the economic growth of the community. I had grave doubts about the rape of the baby being bona fide. Why would Sheila confide in the neighbor? It certainly wasn't out of concern for the welfare of the child, otherwise she would have called the police herself and reported the incident, or at least would have taken the child to the hospital. Then the hospital would have notified the police. While perusing the case report, I noted the fact that the witness who reported the incident was a senior citizen. It seemed to me that a more likely scenario was that the old man's complaints about the baby's crying had agitated Sheila and she had retorted with the first or worst thing she could think up that would shock the old man and shut him up.

Even if the incident had actually occurred it was hearsay, unless Sheila verified the neighbor's story or the offender confessed. If some guy was living with Sheila and he was bringing in any kind of money, I couldn't imagine her sacrificing her crack ticket. This was all a paper shuffle, going nowhere. I tried to hand the case report back to the lieutenant.

"This is a waste of time," I said. "The neighbor didn't actually see anything. He just heard the baby crying and asked the mother about it."

"Interview the mother," the lieutenant said. "See what she has to say."

"I know this broad," I argued. "She's a crack whore. She's never gonna give her old man up."

"Then bring him in, and talk to him."

"We got no leverage with this guy," I insisted. "Even if he did this, which I doubt, the only way he's ever going to be charged with it is if he confesses. I don't see that happening."

The lieutenant gave me his special look, cocking one eyebrow like the Rock, a signal that the debate was over. "Then arrest the guy. Bring him in and process him. If nothing comes of it, I'll have the watch commander release him without charging."

Looking at the determined set of the lieutenant's features, I knew I was beating a dead horse. My partner and I sallied forth to the glorious high-rise project buildings on State Street where the crime occurred, enjoying, as always, the soft rustle of litter in the refuse-strewn hallways, like palm fronds whispering in a tropical breeze, and the subtle fragrance of urine wafting from the elevators.

We took the stairs up to the third floor. Once you've gotten stuck between floors on those elevators a time or two, with nothing to do but read poorly spelled graffiti and hope for a quick response from the fire department, you get a little leery of riding in them. By the time we reached the third floor, I had so much stuff stuck to the soles of my shoes I was about two inches taller.

We interviewed the neighbor first. The old man couldn't add anything to what was in the report. When I knocked on the door of Sheila's apartment I was hoping nobody would answer. That way, I reasoned, I could go back and tell the lieutenant we tried but our efforts to locate the offender were unsuccessful. Then I could forget about the whole thing.

Sheila opened the door while I was still rapping on it. Stunning as ever, she was resplendent in stained pink sweatpants and a halter-top that revealed a tiny Buddha belly like a kangaroo pouch. Her hair was straightened and slicked down, so she looked like James Brown after a sex change. There were so many scars, scratches, and scrapes on her face, neck, and arms, that she looked like she'd had a shoelace caught on the bumper of a car at the Indy 500 and had been dragged around the track for the duration of the race.

She was holding the baby, a cute little girl.

"We need to talk to your old man," I told her.

There were two young boys, about eight and ten, inside the apartment, sitting on the sofa watching cartoons. The alleged offender was sitting at a wobbly kitchen table. When he looked up at me, I knew.

When the street speaks, it doesn't use words. It conveys its message through body language, like a deaf-mute signing. The bowed head, the flickering, nervous eyes, the slumped shoulders, all screamed guilty. Up until that instant, I hadn't really considered the fact that the guy might actually have done it, that he had sexually assaulted the tiny bundle the mother was cradling, that he had raped an eighteen-month-old child. It seemed absurd, like somebody trying to have sex with one of their kid's rubber dolls. Maybe I hadn't wanted to consider it. The thought made me nauseous.

Child molesters usually evoke a frightening rage in me. I was never particularly courteous or unduly gentle with any of them. Yet in this case, because of the incomprehensible nature of the crime, despite the full confession his body language gave, I still had reservations about his guilt. It was his eyes that tempered my anger and outrage. There was something compelling in those eyes that I could not identify, some emotion that I had never encountered before as a police officer. I recognized the guilt right away, but I couldn't put a name to what else I was seeing.

"There's been an accusation made against you," I told him. "Why don't you come with us into the station where we can hear your side of the story?"

He nodded agreement.

"Get the kids ready," I told Sheila. "You're all going in to the station."

"What we all got to go fah?" she demanded.

"You want me to go digging around in here to see if I can find a rock you misplaced?" I asked.

She thought about it a while, chewing on her lip. Then she shook her head.

We loaded everybody into our car, one of the boys sitting up front with me and my partner, the rest of the family crammed into the back of our unmarked squad, and hauled them all into the station. During the ride, I kidded with the two boys so they wouldn't be scared. I noticed that both of their voices were strained and they sounded like their throats were full of phlegm.

When we got upstairs to the Tact office, I situated the family inside, then waved the lieutenant out into the hallway to huddle with my partner and me.

"This guy did it," I declared. "The only way we're going to nail him for it is if we can crack him. The two boys are sickly. I think we ought to call out Youth officers now and get all three of these kids examined at the hospital."

Everybody agreed. My partner made the notification to Youth Division while I took Sheila out of the Tact office. I led her down the hallway to an interview room where I could talk to her alone. I threatened, I pleaded, I cajoled, but I couldn't move her. She denied ever telling the neighbor about the rape. She insisted the old man made it up because he was mad about the baby crying all the time and he wanted to get them thrown out of the apartment. I left her in the interview room so that she was separated from the offender.

I read the arrestee his rights while he hung his head and tapped his toes up and down.

I tried the lie first.

"Your old lady gave you up," I said. "She told me what happened. She's going to be a witness against you. Now, you want to give me your version of what happened?"

He wouldn't speak. He just shook his head from side to side.

"It'll go a lot easier on you if you cooperate," I told him. "When you get to court the judge will consider that as a sign of remorse."

I gave him some time to think about it while I typed up my report, studying him out of the corner of my eye. He was never still for an instant; he bounced his hands on his knees, rocked back and forth on the bench. Every once in a while I would stop typing and talk to him in a soothing and persuasive voice, telling him how I understood compulsion, chronicling how many times I had tried to quit smoking.

All that afternoon, I picked at his head, probing for some weak spot, some button I could push to open him up so he would spill his guts.

The Youth Division officers arrived. They transported the baby and the two boys to the hospital to be examined.

"You know, you don't have to talk to me," I told the suspect. "But you better tell somebody about it. There are some things you can't keep inside. They'll eat your guts up."

I gave him the whole "confession is good for the soul," you-can-tell-Father-Cooper routine, but he wouldn't budge.

When one of the Youth Division officers called from the hospital and informed me the baby had been examined and the doctor confirmed that she had been sexually assaulted, I winced involuntarily, the same as I did when a mortar went off back in 'Nam. But it was what the officer told me next that made me feel like my brain had short-circuited. I was so upset, I slammed the phone down and bolted to the men's room to regain my composure. I walked around and around in circles in the second-floor men's room until I could regulate my breathing normally. I splashed cold water on my face. I smoked a cigarette.

The Youth Division officer had informed me that the examinations of the two young boys had revealed that both of them had syphilis in their throats. It was the venereal disease that was causing the wet, liquidy sound in their speech that I had noticed and attributed to phlegm. When I regained some measure of composure, I flipped the cigarette out the window and went back in the office.

"You know what this sick pervert did?" I asked my partner.

The suspect jerked upright at the insult. I spoke through my teeth, glaring at him the whole time.

"He abused all those kids," I yelled, raising my voice. I stormed over to the bench where he was sitting.

"Didn't you?" I demanded.

He didn't move. He didn't speak. My hands were clenched into fists at my side. I towered over him, presenting as menacing a presence as I could, hoping he would think I was on the knife-edge of losing all self-control, ready to beat him to death.

"They examined the baby," I hissed. "The baby's been

raped all right, and both of those boys have syphilis of the throat."

He stared at the floor. I grabbed his chin with my left hand and raised his head up. I held my right fist cocked like I was ready to punch him.

"Now," I said, "look me in the eye and tell me you didn't do it."

He looked me in the eye, without blinking. His eyes were wet.

"I ought to knock you right off that bench," I said. "I ought to beat you within an inch of your life just so you get a taste of the pain you put those poor kids through."

Maybe he knew I was bluffing. As outraged as I was, as sickening as the crime was that he had committed, there was no way I could have hit the guy, not after staring in those eyes. There was pain in his eyes, terrible pain, and remorse, but something larger and more torturous than remorse; there was self-loathing and helplessness, and hopelessness.

He had the eyes of the damned.

As bad as I wanted to punish him—and by now I had worked myself into an actual rage—as much as I thought he deserved it, I didn't have enough bully in me to hit him. It would have been like beating up a cripple.

My hands went limp. I shook my head. I felt drained.

"How could you do it?" I asked, my voice a whisper now. "How could you put those kids through that? They're your own blood. What kind of monster are you?"

Tears ran down his cheeks. I walked away from him, so I didn't have to look at him anymore. I sat down at one of the desks. I folded my hands on the desktop and stared off into space. My partner stopped typing. The lieutenant put down the newspaper he was reading. It was as quiet in the room as a church.

The next time I looked over at the offender, he was

trembling like somebody having a seizure, his whole body jerking spasmodically. He was crying so hard that tears were splashing on the floor at his feet like raindrops. He looked like he was ready to come apart at the seams. I knew he was ready to crack if I could just reach him. By then I was so filled with disgust I didn't want to talk to him anymore; I didn't want to even be exposed to him. But I knew if I didn't get the confession, he would walk out of the station. The nightmare those three children had endured would continue for who knew how long. I knew if I could just find the right words, I could flip him. Looking down at my own hands, folded on the desktop, I saw that they were trembling.

I felt weak. I tried to gather my resolve.

I was determined he wasn't going to walk even if I had to spend the rest of my life in that office with him.

Taking a deep breath, I stood up. I took out my cigarettes and walked over to the bench where he was sitting. I opened one of the windows behind him to blow the smoke out. I lit up.

"You want a smoke?" I asked, sitting down on the bench next to him. He shook his head. By then his head movements had become part of his spastic physical manifestations.

"I want to talk to you, okay?" My voice was calm and reasonable, although all I felt was emotional exhaustion. "I want you to look me in the eye while we talk."

He nodded. Our eyes locked. I put my hand on his knee.

I didn't know what an empathetic bond was back then. I only know how it felt to me, that when our eyes locked and I made physical contact, I felt the connection between us. I knew we were joined on some level. It was almost like he had transmitted an electric current from his body to mine, like when somebody gets an electric shock and you grab them. I genuinely felt his pain. It was like a blow.

"If we live long enough, we all do bad things in our lives," I said. "We can rationalize what we do, make excuses, but we still did them; we're still ultimately responsible for them. We find ways to compartmentalize these things, so we can live with the guilt.

"That doesn't work with some bad things we do. Some things are too horrible to justify to yourself. The guilt, the remorse, it'll eat you up like a cancer. What you did is sick. You're a sick man. I know you think you couldn't help yourself because of the sickness, but that's not true. You need help. You won't be able to live with this. It will drive you completely mad in time, or you'll kill yourself. You need a doctor. You need a doctor for your mind. You tell me what really happened, I'll get you some help."

His head bobbed up and down. When he spoke, his voice trembled.

"You'll get me a doctor? You'll get me help?"

I knew he would have a psychiatric examination before his trial. Once that awful connection between us occurred, I did feel actual sympathy for him. I pitied him, but my concern was for the children and their future, not for his well being or his mental health. I wanted that confession.

"You'll see a doctor," I said. "I promise."

He burst like a dam. The words poured out of him in a torrent. He admitted to assaulting all three children, while I cringed. It was more than his story that he shared with me. As he recounted the horrors, his emotions assaulted me so that I felt violated. I wanted to jerk away, but I was afraid if I broke the connection he would stop talking. We needed every detail of the crimes to get him charged; I had to walk him through them.

I was like a tourist visiting Hell.

I tried to memorize his words, retain all the details of the crimes, while at the same time warding off visions of the events. It was like watching a movie with my eyes closed. The whole time, his anguish, his torment, his guilt, his own personal suffering traveled through the connection from him to me. I didn't understand his compulsion, I didn't want to, but sitting beside him I knew how he felt. To get his full confession, I was forced, like the damned, not to break the bond between us, not to flinch.

When he was done, I felt dizzy and feverish, like I was coming down with something. I patted him on the thigh, while he wept.

"We'll get you some help," I assured him. "You did the right thing telling me."

I don't know what I was thinking at the time. I was confused, disoriented. I went out in the hallway and splashed water from the fountain on my flushed face. I digested the information he gave me. There was still something that nagged at me, something I didn't understand. I went back in the office and stood in front of him.

"There's one thing I don't get," I said.

He nodded, inviting me to continue.

"I don't see how the sight of a baby could excite you. I don't understand how you got aroused in the first place."

He looked at his feet, twisted his hands together.

"Sheila played with it," he said.

I know my voice went up three octaves. *"What?!"*

"Sheila put the baby between us," he said. "She played with me until I got hard enough to do it."

I was more outraged and horrified by Sheila's conduct than I was by the torture their father had inflicted upon the children. She had brought them into the world; she had nursed them through infancy, then betrayed them, allowing somebody else to abuse them while she stood by, mute and indifferent, to their suffering.

I didn't trust myself to go down the hallway to interview her. My nerves were frayed; I was emotionally wounded and I knew it. The leash I had on my self-restraint was ready to snap. If she gave me a song and dance there was a real good chance I was going to put a beating on a woman for the first time in my life.

Maybe Sheila saw all that in my eyes because as soon as I told her what her old man had said she gave it all up, including her part in it. When the assistant state's attorney came out to take written statements from both of them, Sheila was eager to cooperate, as excited as an actress in her first audition for a starring role.

The detectives were just as offended by Sheila's callous behavior as I was. We did everything we could to get her charged as an accessory to rape. When the assistant state's attorney refused to charge her, we called the first deputy superintendent and tried to get an override. But the ASA prevailed; he wanted her cooperation as a witness and his research of case law revealed that no mother in Illinois had ever been charged as an accessory to rape regardless of the circumstances involved in the incident.

All we could do was charge Sheila with a misdemeanor for neglecting her children. But at least that way she would spend a night in jail and we would have some kind of handle on her if her husband or she recanted their stories later.

Once the father was put in the lock-up and Shelia was sent to women's detention, I went into the men's room to wash up. No sooner had the door slammed than the Tact lieutenant walked in. I was scrubbing away at my hands. They were filthy.

"That was one of the best interrogations I've ever seen," he said. "You did a great job."

I nodded, smiled. I was distracted. The cheap soap coming out of the dispenser wasn't doing any good.

"Thanks," I said.

He just kept hanging around in there, leaning against the wall, frowning.

"I know it was rough," he told me.

I shrugged; big tough guy, that's me.

"We got him charged," I said. "We got him off the street. That's the main thing."

He nodded.

"How long you been washing your hands?" he asked.

I shrugged. It seemed like a weird question. Why would the Tact lieutenant be concerned about my personal hygiene? "I just started when you walked in."

"You know how long you been in here?"

I wondered if he thought I was trying to milk some overtime. We were almost off the clock.

When I didn't answer, he said, "Twenty minutes."

I still didn't get it.

"I'll be right out," I assured him. "I'm almost done."

About three weeks later, my skin started falling off. It would just flake away, a thumb-sized piece of it here and there, all over my body, like I was a leper on a slow schedule, losing a half inch of flesh at a time. I felt like a bird, molting. When I went to my family doctor he sent me to a dermatologist.

After I explained my problem to him, he asked, "How many times a day do you bathe?"

"I don't take baths," I said. "I can't stand lying around in dirty bath water."

"Okay. How many times a day do you shower?"

I had to think about it for a minute. I wasn't really keeping track. If I felt sweaty or dirty, I hopped in the shower, like everybody else.

"I don't know," I admitted. "Three times a day, maybe four sometimes."

"That's your problem," he informed me. "You're drying your skin out. You have to cut back on the showers."

I thought about what he said for a few minutes, struggling with the idea of showering with less frequency.

"You don't understand," I argued, shaking my head. "I can't get clean."

Police officers put up barbed wire around their hearts to protect them. But sometimes it's not enough.

TWENTY-SEVEN TIMES

by Justin Paquette

Patrolman, Atkinson PD, New Hampshire.

I work for a small rural agency in southeastern New Hampshire. My town is just minutes away from the Massachusetts border, and about an hour north of Boston, Massachusetts. Atkinson is a bedroom community that is quickly growing, with a population pushing over seven thousand people.

Within our police department, we have four full-time officers—I'm the fourth—and ten part-time officers, but we only run one patrol car per shift. Our newly created Patrolman's Union is fighting for more officers to provide increased service and for better officer survival/safety as the town grows, but right now we are just pleased that we have coverage twenty-four hours a day.

In a small agency such as ours, and in a town that is expanding rapidly, we deal with all kinds of complaints and problems. Many of them involve four-legged culprits, as opposed to our usual two-legged ones. It is not uncommon for us to respond to all sorts of calls for service regarding animals. Whether the call concerns a marauding moose or bear, a beaver hit by a car, or escaped livestock, we see it all in terms of the animal kingdom of the rural

Northeast. Sometimes we feel that we wear our police officer hat one minute and our animal control hat the next, but it comes with the territory.

I consider myself fairly well acquainted with the outdoors. I regularly hike, backpack, and rock climb. One thing I am not, however, is a hunter. But, on November 11, 2001, I wished I had been one.

I had just finished my Field Training Program and was on my own, riding solo. It was a busy night, and since I was the only car on patrol I had to take each and every call for service. As a matter of fact, just after the incident I'm about to relate, I responded to a call of a barricaded female subject who was trying to kill herself with a claw hammer. Even in a small town we have our problems, but that's a story for another day.

Anyway, the call came in at 2200 hours (ten P.M.). A deer had been hit by a motor vehicle and the animal was reported to be struggling at the side of the road. The person who hit the deer called it into our dispatch center but did not give any further information.

When I arrived, I found that the street was dark, with only one or two streetlamps a couple hundred feet from one another. After a few minutes of searching on foot with my flashlight, I found the deer. Just like the caller had described, it was hurt and struggling at the side of the road.

I radioed into dispatch and told them the deer's condition. I also advised them that I would be discharging my weapon to put the animal down. Our police department issues the Beretta Model 92FS 9mm handgun as the service weapon and our ammunition is Speer Gold Dot hollow point 147-grain, 9mm Luger.

I took my shooting stance and aimed my weapon just like my instructors had taught me in the Academy. Where was I taught to shoot? Center mass. How many rounds had I been taught to expend? As many as it takes until the threat is neutralized. Am I a hunter? No.

I shot the deer twenty-seven times.

Whenever I am cornered and asked the inevitable "why?" question, I have two answers. 1) I am not a hunter; 2) consistent with my training in police/combat shooting, I aimed at center mass. When I am forced to explain further, I say that I began to realize that something was wrong when my center mass shots were not having any effect. So with a magazine change, I aimed for the neck. When that was not working, I aimed for the head and finally killed the deer.

Of course, it doesn't end there. I had to call my sergeant and explain what I did and how many rounds it took for me to do it. Word of my "shoot-out" spread like wildfire, and soon all the officers from the surrounding towns with which we have a mutual aid agreement started calling me Dead-Eye. Even my town's selectmen got in on the joke when he turned to my chief during a meeting, winked, and asked, "So, Chief, how's your ammunition budget doing?"

My misadventure with the deer even became a training issue for future recruits going through Field Training when they added to the curriculum, "Where to Shoot a Deer."

But the icing on the cake had to be when a neighboring town discussed the incident at length in an interdepartmental newsletter:

"Recently an unidentified Atkinson officer, in an attempt to put a deer out of its misery, shot the animal twenty-seven times. Was this payback for the deer running out in front of his cruiser, or did he just not know where to shoot?"

What can I say? Now I know what to do, but this is something that will follow me around for my entire career. At least I can laugh about it and be a good sport. We all make mistakes. The important thing is that we learn from them. I have. Just don't call me Dead-Eye or let me hear, "So, why *did* you shoot that deer twenty-seven times anyway?"

I am not a hunter. I aimed for center mass. That's the whole story, plain and simple.

LINE OF DUTY

THE "ROUTINE STOP" THAT CHANGED MY LIFE

BY RICHARD AUGUSTA

California Highway Patrol, Antioch, California;
retired after twelve years.

I joined the California Highway Patrol in January 1967 and ten years later my career almost ended in tragedy. It was the night of May 29, 1977. My partner, Darrell Todd, and I were on routine patrol in Contra Costa County. It was about 1:30 A.M. when a car coming from the opposite direction on a two-lane road passed us by. It had been weaving across the centerline so I made a quick U-turn to stop the vehicle. The car immediately turned onto the first side road and came to an abrupt stop. The driver, a female, got out of the car and walked back toward us, meeting me halfway between her car and the patrol car. I told her why I had stopped her and asked to see her driver's license, which she told me was in the vehicle. I followed her back toward her car, and as she neared the driver's door she turned to say something to me; it was then that I noticed two men in the car. Suddenly, the man in the left rear seat jumped up and opened his door. As I pivoted to face him, I saw that he had a gun resting on the door frame, pointed at me. I had a moment's insight: as usual, the element of surprise goes with the bad guys—he had me cold, there was nothing I could have done.

We weren't wearing vests in those days so all I could do was spin sideways to reduce the size of his target. He uttered "Okay, mother——!" and fired two shots from a distance of two or three feet. One shot missed. The other hit me in the left side and the impact knocked me to the pavement. Now I know that the bullet punctured my left kidney and lodged near my spine. But then it just registered that my trousers had been torn in the right knee and the palm of my hand had been cut when I fell to the pavement. Even though everything happened in just seconds, the whole sequence felt like it occurred in slow motion.

I had fallen right behind the gunman and he immediately turned his attention to my partner and started firing. He got off a couple of quick shots, then jumped back into the rear seat of the car and slammed the door. The female bolted for the open driver's door. At this point, while lying bleeding in the roadway, in terrible pain and certain that I would die, I drew my service revolver (six shots in 1977), determined to take one of them with me. I fired three shots into the left rear door where the gunman was sitting and, as the female was not as quick to react, I fired one shot at her as she was closing the car door. As the car began to accelerate away, I fired one final shot at the other male occupant in the right front seat. That bullet shattered the left rear door window.

This exchange of gunshots took about fifteen seconds. I had fired five shots, had one left. Despite being seriously wounded, I got to my feet, holstered my weapon, and walked slowly back to the patrol car. As my partner frantically put out an 11-99 call, I lay down on the front seat and propped my feet up on the door, hoping that by elevating them I could keep from going into shock.

I was transported to Delta Memorial Hospital, where a Catholic priest was summoned to administer last rites before I went into emergency surgery.

Unbeknownst to us when we had made our "routine stop," the three people in the weaving car, which turned out to be stolen, had been on a Central Valley crime spree which included numerous robberies and even murders. I guess our paths were destined to cross that night, there's no other way to explain it.

A week later the trio was apprehended during a bank robbery in Bakersfield, California. Both my partner and I lived to testify at their trial in Fresno.

A PAIR OF JEANS

BY BRIAN PARR

Sergeant, NYPD, eleven years.

It was sometime in the summer months of 1994; I was partnered and on routine uniform patrol within the confines of the 114th Precinct, Astoria, Queens, NYC. The weather was clear and it was late in the evening. At the time the area was plagued by gun violence, and shootings in the housing developments nearby were not uncommon. So I was alert to my surroundings and wary of any suspicious persons, particularly those on foot late at night. As I turned the corner in my cruiser, I observed a black male, approximately twenty years of age, walking alone toward me down a dimly lit side street with his hands under his shirt. When he saw me, he quickly turned and started walking in the opposite direction, looking at me intermittently over his right shoulder. Interpreting his actions as suspicious, I was confident that I had caught him fixing a firearm at his waist area. I ordered him via loudspeaker to stop walking and to face me. He ignored me and continued to walk away. I could not see his hands at this point, only his elbows sticking out from the side of his body, and by his motions I could see that he was doing something under his shirt and pulling at his pants.

Fearing that he was going to pull a firearm on my partner and me, I pulled over and we both ran up on him. Without hesitation, I seized him with one hand while quickly reaching into his pants with the other in order to grab the gun before he could pull it out and turn on us. Well, I got a big disgusting surprise. My fingers encircled not a gun, but a pile of feces. The startled kid tried to talk to me but I couldn't understand a word he was saying so he began to cry. It was then that I realized that he suffered from mental problems and was terrified.

What had happened was this: he was taking a dump on the sidewalk when we turned the corner in our cruiser. When he saw us, he got scared and automatically pulled his pants up before he had finished his business. When we called out to him, he hurriedly walked away while trying to fix his pants because he didn't want to get in trouble. Then, after I stopped him and ended up getting his little secret all over my hand, he was embarrassed and began to cry. I was just so relieved that what he was hiding wasn't a gun and that everything was okay that I wasn't even mad about the whole thing. I just told the kid to stay where he was and that I would be back in ten minutes. I went back to the precinct, washed my hands—catching a lot of abuse from the rest of the guys, hahaha—then went to my locker and took out the clean jeans that I wore to work that day. I took them back to the kid and gave him the jeans along with a roll of paper towels and I explained to him why we had stopped him. He sniffled a bit but then smiled shyly and went on his way, still muttering in a language I didn't understand.

AUGUST IN DECEMBER

BY GEORGE BOOTH

Detective, Breckenridge Police, Colorado.

On December 10, 2000, at 8:24 A.M., I was driving south-west on Village Road in Breckenridge, Colorado. It was a mild winter morning, the sun was shining and there was a light breeze. I had no inkling that this would be the day that I'd watch a man die, that this day would haunt me for the rest of my life.

I was on duty and on patrol in my marked police vehicle. This day felt like any other—I was expecting to spend the better part of it sitting in front of a computer writing police reports. As I drove up a road that makes a twist upward to an area called Beaver Run Resort, a famous ski resort that has thousands of visitors every year, I thought about what a beautiful day it was. People from all over the world bring their families up here to enjoy the Rocky Mountains. On normal winter days during the ski season, the sidewalks in front of Beaver Run are filled with people, mostly small children. The joy on the faces of those children, looking forward to their ski lessons or just happy to be outside in the mountain air, is always evident. But for some reason this day seemed different. The children seemed more subdued, or maybe I just had a sense of foreboding, a premonition of what was to come.

As I was driving along, I suddenly observed the inexplicable: the Breckenridge Ski Area bus was coming toward me on the sidewalk. Dumbstruck, I thought, "What the f—— are you doing driving down the sidewalk?" There was a sense of unreality to the whole thing—as if time had slowed down. The bus, almost gracefully, silently, like an airplane sweeping through thick white clouds, entered the pedestrian area. The terrible reality of what was going to occur struck me with such force that I felt as if all my wind had been pushed violently from my lungs. But before I could react, I heard a loud thump as the bus struck a light pole. The bus's front passenger side jumped violently up into the air. At the same time I observed a blur in front of the bus that was a darker color than the white bus. As the bus came down and continued down the sidewalk I realized that something was underneath the bus. Finally, the bus came to a complete stop at the exit to Beaver Run guest registration. As I called on my radio to dispatch for help I observed that a body was lying on the sidewalk behind the bus.

Now, when I review the incident in my head, I think about how police officers are expected to act. We are taught and encouraged to hold back, to fight down our emotions. A police officer is not allowed to display feelings, not ever. Sure, I've had to deal with death before and sometimes the deceased has been a young child, sometimes an older person or even someone in the prime of life. But in all of the situations I'd faced before, there had been time, precious time, to prepare myself mentally for what I was about to face. Before that day I had never appreciated the "prep" time that was afforded me on past calls for service. Even during emergency calls, an officer has seconds, sometimes even minutes, to mentally prepare himself for what he's going to find. For example, if an officer is sent to a bar fight in progress he has time to go over his responses; he asks himself "Where do I park?", "Where are my backup officers?", and so on. But in this case I was simply not prepared for the sight of a bus careening down the sidewalk into a pedestrian zone.

As a cop, I have no choice; I can't choose not to take a call, I can't choose to simply turn away if it all seems like too much. Police officers take calls for service on a rotating basis; sometimes we get to help locate a lost child, sometimes we answer a "black bear at large" call. Now I wish that on this day, rather than patrolling up this mountain road, I'd been dispatched to a parking complaint. But that wasn't my choice to make.

My coworkers told me that I was too calm in the face of great danger or tragedy. I remember my radio transmissions to the dispatcher that day. They were slow, calm, and precise. I was told later that I was so composed on the radio that very few people realized the gravity of the call.

I left my patrol vehicle and started running toward the body on the ground; even from a distance I could see blood filling his hair. It must have been only ten to fifteen seconds from the time the man had been hit by the bus until I was beside his lifeless body, but it felt as if time were moving in slow motion. I remember being thankful that no children had been killed. I remember people screaming and running. I knelt beside the man I would later know was August Berndt and always think of as August. He wasn't moving and I told the radio dispatcher that I believed the victim had "cored," cop jargon for a fatality. The dispatcher asked me to clarify and I told her the accident was an obvious "Frank," more cop jargon for a fatality. I could hear the radio chatter as emergency personnel was dispatched, everyone was now scrambling to get to my location.

I looked up as a young man came toward me. I could

see panic in him, panic that was running through him, deep and thick. "Did I kill him?" he whispered, his voice cracking. He was shaking uncontrollably, his trembling hands near his face. I knew then that he was the bus driver. I yelled for him to get back onto the bus and to keep any passengers inside. But he just stood there, looking at me, then down at August, his face pale with shock. I knew he was experiencing the kind of fear that will turn the stomach of even the most hardened individual, the kind of fear that is completely debilitating, that takes over your senses and will not release you from its unrelenting grasp. I've seen that look before on the faces of people who have been arrested and know they are going to prison for a very long time, or on those who have just received word that a loved one has died. It's that look of incomprehensible horror that people get when they realize a situation has gone too far and nothing can change it or turn back the clock.

I watched as the driver stumbled back on the bus, swaying like an old hobo. I looked up and saw that there was a small gathering of people by the main entrance to Beaver Run and I recognized one of them as the resort bellman. I yelled to him to call security for additional help. I wasn't thinking clearly; I was thinking that the Beaver Run security guard would be able to assist me even though he wasn't a member of Emergency Services and wasn't trained for these emergencies. And when he came over to me, he had the same physical and emotional response that the bus driver did. I could see it in his face and hear it in his voice. He asked, his voice breaking like an adolescent's, "What can I do, George?" I knew he couldn't help so I told him to stay with the bus driver.

When I put on my latex gloves and checked for vital signs, I saw what appeared to be a large sponge soaked in blood lying next to August's right ear. There was also a large amount of blood at the back of his head. On the left ear, I saw blood and a grayish-white substance that could only be brain matter. A large flap of hair and skin had lifted from his head and I found myself wondering if that was where his brains were seeping from his skull. I thought about looking closer but I couldn't bring myself to do so. It seemed amazing that this grayish matter was what had fueled this man just minutes before. The same thing that made it possible for him to walk down the sidewalk was now letting him die. That separation of the brain from the body, which I was witnessing, served to define his death. The bus was the instrument, but his mortality was much more intimate, it was something inside of him, amid the blood, the viscera.

His wrist was warm to the touch but I couldn't find a pulse. He had a scarf of some type around his neck and I moved it in an attempt to locate a carotid pulse but I couldn't find one there, either. I found myself wondering if he had bought the scarf himself or if it was a gift that he wore to make someone happy. His eyes were open and his head was leaning slightly toward his right shoulder. His mouth was wide open and full of blood. I wondered if the gently rising steam from the warm blood inside his mouth was his departing spirit. Was that what it looked like? I remember feeling scared that there was no one there to help him, or me. Had I the choice, I would have been anywhere but there. But I no more had a choice than August Berndt had; fate put us both there—him to confront his mortality, me to simply do my duty.

The pool of blood did not bubble or rise and fall so I knew that he didn't have an airway and his breathing had stopped. His eyes were grayish and there appeared to be a fuzzy film over the pupil area of his eyes. Based upon my training, I knew that CPR or other rescue measures would be futile. I studied his face, trying to decipher his last thought but his facial expression told me nothing. I have often regretted that I did not honk my horn or activate my siren in an attempt to warn him of the impending danger. It wouldn't have saved him but maybe he would have had that moment to prepare himself mentally for what was about to happen. Though maybe not—his last thought might just have been, "What the hell is that cop honking at?" Was it better to let him die lost in his private thoughts as he strolled along on this beautiful winter's day? And was there something I could have done to at least try to prevent his death—could I have turned my patrol car in front of the bus in some desperate attempt to save his life? Or in the end would that have cost both our lives?

All these things ran through my mind like a torrent of images in the few moments that it took me to run from my patrol car and kneel beside him to check his vital signs. I know my facial expression revealed nothing. I was just a cop doing my job.

It was then that an unidentified male approached me. He started asking me questions completely unrelated to the incident. I clearly recall the man. He was tall and thin with his hair parted down the middle and feathered back like a hairstyle from the 1980s. He was wearing a red sweater with cleaned and pressed blue jeans and cowboy boots.

"Excuse me, do you know where I can get some lift tickets?" the man asked me. His back was to the sun and he was almost a complete silhouette—I could barely see his face. Later I wondered if he was an angel or maybe the devil; after all, he was wearing red. Or was he a typical tourist, self-absorbed to the point that he didn't look close enough at me to see that I was kneeling next to a dead man who had his brains seeping all over the sidewalk?

I had been warned about being harsh to citizens in these types of situations. My supervisors told me, "The average citizen doesn't understand police work and you should take the time to help them to understand." I didn't have the time to explain to this guy what was happening. I asked him, "Sir, are you a doctor?" secretly hoping that he was and would take over, relieving me of this awesome responsibility. But he just looked at me blankly, saying nothing, waiting, I suppose, for me to answer his initial question. For the first time that day I lost my composure and yelled, "Get the hell out of here!" He stepped back and just seemed to dissolve into the crowd.

Now I find it curious that I never saw that man before and I never saw him again. In fact, I asked other people if they had ever seen him and no one had.

Officer Joe Staufer arrived. I briefly told him what had happened and that I was going to cover the victim with a blanket because of the number of pedestrians in the area. I was thinking of the onlookers. There is always someone who wants to videotape a gory accident or to snap a quick vacation photo. I thought, you want to look, go ahead, get a good hard look—as a matter of fact why don't you get close enough to inhale the sick sweet smell of death? The smell that gets in your clothes and doesn't come out for several washes, that lingers in your hair long after you've left the scene. But I didn't say anything like that; the good police officer in me took over and more out of respect for the victim, for August, than anything else, I covered the body with a blanket I kept in my patrol vehicle. I had watched him die; I was in a strange way his next of kin here on the street among those who had never known him in life.

I moved my patrol vehicle forward so that the arriving emergency personnel could get close to the scene. The fire department arrived and I directed them to park in such a way as to shield August Berndt from the eager onlookers and to protect any roadway evidence left by the bus.

I watched as the fire department personnel pulled back the blanket. I assisted them with opening his jackets and cutting open his shirt. They connected him to some emergency equipment and stated the obvious: that he was deceased. I went to secure the area with crime scene tape.

I was doing okay, holding it all together, until Officer Staufer approached me. He grabbed my arm and looked into my eyes and asked if I was all right. I nodded—I certainly wasn't going to tell my supervisor what had been going through my head, what I was feeling. I was lucky that he didn't press it—he just stared at me for a long moment and then went off to tend to other matters.

I recall walking around the accident scene, wondering why I was chosen to witness the death of August Berndt. Or was there no reason—was it all random and just some crazy happenstance that I was there at the last seconds of his life? While I was standing next to the bus trying to make some sense of it all, a very large Colorado State Patrol trooper approached me. He asked if I was all right. I didn't reply. Then he looked deep into my eyes as if he could see all the way to my soul.

I felt my face flush and a trembling in my bones. I thought for a moment that I would lose it right there but that big trooper grabbed me and hugged me. I felt like a small child being hugged by his father. Then he let me go and said, "It's all right, brother, go take five in your car, I'm here now."

Cops always refer to other cops as "brother" when they don't know your name. He knew what I was going through without me saying anything like only another cop, or a brother, could. There's a pain and harshness in being a cop. He knew what it was like to experience too much. He later told me that he recently had to work a two-car head-on traffic accident where both parents of a little girl were killed. He told me that he was so upset about seeing the little girl alive, trapped in a car with her dead parents, that every night since then he awoke in a sweat, waking his wife by screaming out the radio traffic he gave out during the night of the dreadful accident. He said his wife would hold him and try to comfort him but I wonder how cops ever rest at all when they are condemned to relive the horrors they've seen whenever they close their eyes.

It was some months later that I saw a photograph of the trooper who had comforted me on the front page of a local newspaper. I thought, good for him, maybe he saved someone, and maybe he got a medal. But Trooper Jason Manspeaker was dead, killed in a traffic accident. He died that day for all of us. I felt as if I had failed, that I had never repaid his kindness, nor would I ever have the chance to now.

Life passes us all too quickly. I think the only way I can repay the debt I owe to that kindhearted trooper is by sharing kindness with other officers as they struggle through the events that will forever scar their lives and careers.

In an odd twist of fate, I later learned that August Berndt had a brother named Marc. He had been killed in a fatal traffic accident years earlier in Breckenridge. Marc had been driving down the highway when a logging truck turned in front of him, extending the logs so that they struck him in the head, killing him instantly. Ironically, my wife, who was also working for the police department, happened to be there and witnessed Marc's death much as I later witnessed his brother's.

A few months after August Berndt's death, I was issued a subpoena to appear at a jury trial concerning the death of Marc Berndt. I felt so bad for the family and all their losses that I approached a family member, a sister, introduced myself, and tried to tell her that August did not die alone. She looked at me and cried, thankful I guess, but I don't really know if I helped or not.

During my experience on a mountain road one December morning a few years ago, I did not face my own mortality but I did come close to another's, so close in fact that I was there for the transition, the crossing over from life to death. The death of August Berndt, and the subsequent death of Trooper Jason Manspeaker, changed my life, because now I find myself thinking that no matter how difficult things may be, or how hard life and the job can get, at the very least I am alive.

ANOTHER DAY, ANOTHER QUARTER

BY DAVID L. WOOD

Deputy, Edwards County Sheriff, Texas.

In August 1993 I had lost my rookie cherry and was just beginning to scratch the surface of what being a cop was all about. It was a typical miserably humid morning in East Texas and I yearned for the arid, breezy mornings I'd grown up with in the western region of the state. But this was where my law enforcement roots were and I was doing my best to "make a hand."

The dispatcher's voice seemed edgy as she detailed my call: "Hearne . . . one nineteen, respond to the three hundred block of Peale, reference dog bite victim."

"Nineteen clear, en route," I answered and a couple minutes later I pulled up behind an ambulance in a residential area. Paramedics were attending to an attractive, but bloody, young woman who was seated on the curb and cradling an infant.

"Hey, Drew, what have we got?" I asked, approaching one of the medics. He was fortyish and a reserve patrolman who I knew well. He stepped aside and filled me in.

"This young lady was walking from her apartment to her mom's house to use the telephone—she ain't got one at home. Anyhow, she says this big-ass female pit bull comes out of nowhere and takes a chunk out of her thigh, unprovoked. The poor gal's doing what she can to defend her baby and the dog gets a piece of her elbow."

I looked a little closer at the young woman's bandaged arm and leg, noticing that her lower lip was trembling and dried blood was sprayed all the way into her hairline. I shook my head.

"Damn!"

Drew nodded, shook his head along with me, and then continued his narrative.

"So she fights the mutt off and makes it over here to this house and screams for the residents to call for help."

"Pretty tough chick."

"No kiddin'."

"Any idea who owns the dog?"

Drew looked over at the young woman, then met my eye, leaned over and said confidentially, "I just happen to know exactly who owns the dog."

I raised an eyebrow. "You have my attention."

"One of our EMTs, son. He lives just around the corner."

"Damn." I opened my cruiser door. "Jump in. Take me over there."

On the way I advised dispatch of the situation and requested that an animal control officer meet us at the dog owner's residence. Drew pointed out the window and we pulled up in front of a ramshackle wood-frame house with a $30,000 two-ton Chevy pickup parked out front.

I shook my head. "It never ceases to amaze me."

"What's that, Dave?"

"These folk's priorities. Drive a high-dollar vehicle and live in a shack."

We contemplated this mystery for a moment and then Drew nodded. "I hear ya, son."

The yard was bare and unfenced and two pit bulls were chained securely to the side of the house.

"It looks like he's got 'em chained."

I looked too but wasn't completely convinced. "Is that all of them?" I asked, not wanting to leave the safety of the Caprice to become dessert for an ornery canine.

"He may have one inside but that's all that's normally out here."

Well, okay. I checked out with dispatch and Drew and I cautiously approached the front door. Since Drew was working in a medical capacity and was unarmed, if anything blew up our defense would likely fall to me. My intention was simply to advise the dog's owner of the incident and to investigate the situation further. But as we crossed the street, cussing in the sticky heat, I caught sight of a brown blur just out of the corner of my eye. Before I had time to react, there was a shrill and slobbery bark as a pit bull bitch lunged at me and hit me full force in the chest. I collapsed backward, lucky that my protective vest cushioned my fall, and lay sprawled on the dimpled pavement. I'll always wonder why I made the more attractive target, but right then I was wondering why I ever got out of the Caprice.

I became a witness to Drew's instinctive act of heroism; he slammed his fist into the dog's head using a closed lockblade buck knife as a fist load. The strike was effective but not before the dog claimed a fleshy piece of my left forearm just in front of my elbow. I had raised my arm defensively and I thank God for those instinctive reactions. The eighty-pound dog also managed to rip out a healthy chunk of my left leg just below my knee before Drew's blow distracted it. The dog jumped back, startled but not down, ran a few yards back, and then readied itself to lunge again. But by then I was on my feet and bringing up my Sig Sauer P 226 into a Weaver lock. I had a good background and a too-close-for-comfort shot but I am reasonably sure that any shot taken under stress is somewhat uncomfortable. I took the shot and the dog buckled and started to run for the house, but it slowed, staggered, and fell. Not taking any chances, we approached the downed beast with caution.

At about this time the dog's owner, a young man of about twenty-five, came rushing out of the house, the screen door banging shut behind him. He knelt by the dog but the 115-grain, 9mm silvertip had done its job. The bullet had entered the dog's brisket, wreaked havoc with its insides, but had not exited. The three of us stood there in the heat for a moment or two, thinking our private thoughts as flies buzzed around the newly deceased. My two wounds were leaking generously and Drew said we had better get me patched.

As we stepped back toward my idling patrol unit the animal control truck arrived. I noticed my empty shell casing in the street and, though its value as evidence would be inconsequential and the situation demanded that I seek medical help that was not available at the scene, I bent down in the street to retrieve it as a keepsake. I also decocked the pistol and secured it in my holster.

The dog's owner was sad but also apologetic. We later found out that the female pit bull had just had pups and was ferociously defensive. But the investigation also revealed that he was raising the dogs to fight and so, in lieu of criminal charges being filed, the dog owner agreed to board the animals outside the city limits.

I mended quickly and had a new war story to tell. Believe it or not, the dog's owner had a homeowner's liability policy and the insurance company insisted on paying both the young woman and me $1,500 apiece beyond our medical expenses for a signature on a release of responsibility. I used some of the funds to invest in extra practice ammunition so as to remain proficient in defensive firearm skills. I wanted to be able to defend myself against whatever threat I encountered, human or otherwise.

I recall reflecting on the entirety of the incident as Drew drove me to the hospital that muggy morning.

"You doin' okay there, son?" Drew asked me.

"Hell," I said. "Another day, another quarter."

Drew just chuckled.

THE CYCLE OF VIOLENCE

BY PHIL BULONE

NYPD, retired after fourteen years.

The dispatcher's voice broke the silence of the police radio. "In the 8-8 Precinct, we have a 10-10. Investigate aided at 4134 Tremaine Street, apartment 4C. Unit to respond . . . K."

Being the rookie, I immediately grabbed the transmitter from its cradle and announced, "8-8 Sector Henry will respond . . . K."

"10-4 Henry. We have no additional information—advise if you need a bus . . . K."

As I returned the transmitter to its resting-place my partner, Jimmy O'Rourke, took his eyes off the road and gave me a dirty look. I knew exactly what he was thinking.

"Dumb rookie—why would you pick up that radio? It's not even our sector."

Jimmy was a huge Irishman towering over six feet four inches and weighing more than three hundred pounds. He was in his twenty-fifth year on the force and retiring at the end of the year. He was my training officer, attempting to teach me to forget everything I had learned in the Police Academy and how to really survive on the streets.

Jimmy parked the RMP in front of the apartment

building on Tremaine Street. As we entered the building by walking up the steps leading to apartment 4C, we found that the apartment door was partially opened. Jimmy stopped me as he removed his .38 Smith & Wesson from its holster. I did the same as I followed him through the half-opened door. We came into a large living room. The decor was Early Depression—there was a broken couch, a small card table with three folding chairs, and an old black-and-white television set showing Big Bird doing some kind of dance.

I killed Big Bird as we headed down a long corridor leading to a bathroom and two bedrooms. At the first bedroom, Jimmy carefully entered and checked it out. Nothing looked suspicious. I took the next room, a bathroom. The sink was red with what appeared to be blood. As we entered the second bedroom, I placed my index finger on the trigger of my gun. Jimmy entered first and I heard him say, "Oh, shit."

When he moved his bulky body out of the doorway, I could see a young woman lying on the floor, her face bloody. On the bed next to her was a little boy lying on his stomach with his underwear down around his ankles and his legs spread-eagle—bleeding from his rectum.

"Call for a bus and the sergeant," the big Irishman yelled. I did as instructed as Jimmy picked up the little boy in his large hands and held him close to his massive chest.

As I bent down next to the woman, I heard this tough, hard-ass cop say to the boy in a gentle voice, "Don't worry, lad, everything will be okay."

The woman on the floor was Hispanic and looked to be no more than nineteen or twenty years old.

"What's your name?" I asked.

"Elena Javier."

"What happened here?"

She told me her boyfriend, Enrique Lugo, had been drinking and had wanted to have sex with her. When she told him she didn't want to "do it" with the child in the house, Enrique informed her that if she didn't, he'd beat her and "do it" to the kid. As she went to grab the child to leave, Enrique punched her in the face, splitting her lip. When she fell to the floor, he kicked her several times in the stomach. Then he grabbed the boy, threw him on the bed and raped him. Finally, he left.

I looked out the window and saw the ambulance and the sergeant's RMP pulling up outside.

When Sergeant Tony Mancini, known in the precinct as a "cop's cop," walked into the room, Jimmy filled him in as he shook his head in disgust. Then he said, "Let's get these two over to Cumberland Hospital. Put a description over the radio. If we're lucky, maybe one of the sector cars will pick up this piece of shit."

Just then we heard someone entering the apartment and a male Hispanic walked into the bedroom, took one look at us, and turned and started running for the stairs. Louie Robinson, one of the precinct's scooter cops, tackled the fleeing male and threw him down on the concrete landing. He picked him off the floor with one hand and asked, "You guys looking for this prick?"

"Cuff him," Sergeant Mancini ordered.

When Louie brought the cuffed prisoner into the bedroom the woman screamed, "What are you doing? You can't arrest him!"

I looked over at the young woman whose swollen face had just been bandaged by a paramedic and said, "What are you talking about? This guy just beat the shit out of you and raped your son and you don't want him arrested? He can't hurt you anymore."

She looked at me with her huge expressive eyes. "If he goes to jail, who's going to pay the bills? Where will I go? I have no money and my family is in Puerto Rico. I need Enrique—he takes care of my son and me. I love Enrique!"

And, as if on cue, Enrique yelled from across the room, "Tell them, baby—tell them you love Poppy."

Louie Robinson quickly quieted down the big mouth by tightening the cuffs. Sergeant Mancini instructed the paramedics to remove the woman and her son to the hospital. Jimmy and I were directed to take Enrique to Central Booking.

As the woman and her son were being taken out, she turned to Sergeant Mancini and pleaded, "Please, I don't want to press any charges."

Mancini looked at her. "Listen, you're going to the hospital. If you don't want this guy arrested then you go down to the DA's office in the morning and tell him you want the charges dropped. For now, Enrique will be spending the night in jail, compliments of New York's finest."

As we drove to Central Booking, Jimmy explained that what we just went through was pretty common in this neighborhood. Too many women living in abusive households, getting beaten by their boyfriends, their kids also abused sometimes to the extent of being sexually attacked.

Jimmy said, "You take the collar. See for yourself. This guy will be cut loose—he won't even be arraigned."

The next morning I stood in front of the judge's bench. Next to me was an assistant district attorney fresh from law school, holding a bunch of case files. To his left, an attractive female Legal Aid lawyer was talking with Enrique Lugo.

The bailiff called the case.

"What are we going to do here, counselor?" the judge asked the young ADA.

"Your Honor, the complainant in this case refuses to

press charges. She said she is willing to forgive the defendant."

The judge interjected, "I see there was also an assault on a six-year-old. Has Child Protective Services been notified?"

"Yes, Your Honor. I just got off the phone with them. They said they would not pursue the child's case unless they get full cooperation from the mother and she refuses to cooperate. They said they have too many cases and not enough case workers to investigate something that's going nowhere."

I could see the judge was pissed off with what he was hearing. He looked over the rims of his reading glasses at all of us standing in front of the bench. Fixing the ADA with a withering look he said, "Counselor, I have no choice but to dismiss these charges. The defendant is released from custody. Next case."

It was just like Jimmy said it would be. I finished up my paperwork and signed out from the courthouse. As I drove back to the 88th, I passed by Tremaine Street. There, walking hand in hand, were Enrique Lugo and Elena Javier. Her face was still bandaged. The little boy wasn't with them. He'd stay in the hospital a few more days.

There would be an apology from Enrique—a promise to change. He would swear that he would never hit her or the little boy again. He would tell her that "everything will be better." Then, not too far down the road, she would say something to set him off and the cycle of violence would begin all over again.

Jimmy was right by telling me to forget everything I learned in the Academy because this was the reality of the street. It was something I could never learn from reading a book.

THE BOOT

BY JACK SOMMERS

Sergeant, Los Angeles PD, thirty-three years, retired.

Several years ago when I was a training officer, I was training a new rookie. We called them "Boots." Part of my training M.O. was to emphasize that the Boots were to do exactly what I told them to do. This was to ensure officer safety and that proper procedure was followed. This particular Boot was very talented and he would do anything I told him to do.

On this particular night we were walking a foot beat in downtown LA. This area is full of winos, pimps, prostitutes, and gang members. We were walking past a liquor store when I saw a Ninth Street gang member who I knew always had warrants. I told my Boot to stop the suspect. He followed proper procedure by taking a position of advantage while stopping the individual. I acted as the cover officer while my Boot requested identification. I told my Boot to conduct a quick pat down for officer safety. He did this perfectly. I took the suspect's identification and told my Boot to watch the suspect while I ran him for warrants.

The warrant check came back and showed that the suspect had recently been arrested for drugs but the arrest had not gone to warrant yet. I told my Boot that the suspect was clean, and said to "kick him." As I happened to look away for a second, I heard this *thud* and then the sound of a body hitting the pavement. I turned back and saw the suspect lying on the sidewalk. The suspect was screaming, "He kicked me in my ass! I think I broke something!"

I helped the suspect up and said to my Boot, "What did you do? *I said to kick him!!*" With that, my Boot nailed him again, sending him to the sidewalk with a beautiful sidekick. The suspect was screaming like crazy, "What's wrong with this crazy motherf——er? Why you kickin' me in my ass? I'm gonna sue, you crazy motherf——er!!"

I helped the suspect up again. I told my Boot, "I meant you were to kick him loose, not *kick* him!"

I patiently explained to our "victim" that this young officer was a Boot and he had misunderstood what I had said. After several minutes of explanation and eating a little crow, my victim understood and went on his way. Needless to say, from that day on I was more explicit in my instructions to my Boots.

MY SURVIVAL

BY TOM SCHULTE

*Lieutenant, Overland PD, St. Louis County,
Missouri, more than thirty years.*

One of the toughest jobs that I have ever had in thirty
years of law enforcement has been that of the department's sex abuse investigator. I am not the sensitive type,
but looking into the eyes of an abused young girl, whose
age would usually be between eight and twelve, to see the
hurt and confusion there, would have a profound impact
on even the most hardened cop. Knowing that I could
never make the world a safe place for her again was a bitter pill to swallow.

My assignment as a sex abuse investigator spanned
nine years. During that time, I tried to keep in touch with
some of the children to see how they were progressing. It
was a result of these continued contacts with the young
victims that my feelings of pain and helplessness really
started.

From my experience, in the majority of these cases,
there are no happy endings. The bad guys are arrested
and put away but anyone who has conducted these types
of investigations knows what happens to the victims. For
the most part there is no follow-up therapy. After they testify at the trial, that's it, case closed. I always tried to

make the victim's parents promise me that they would take their child to a counselor to get some help in dealing with the abuse, but this was seldom done. Adding to my frustration, the victims lived in the areas that I patrolled and every time that I saw them, the pain and confusion that I had initially witnessed from the child-victim would be renewed in my mind.

The effect of the abuse usually manifested itself in the little girls in one of two ways. They either totally withdrew, never having anything to do with men again, or they tried to find someone who they thought would protect them. Often the protector was just as bad as the perpetrator. The only difference this time was that it was the victims who chose their protector/abuser rather than the other way around. A number of abused children become addicted to drugs or alcohol at an early age in order to cope. I knew of one young girl who became a shoplifter to support her habit. After numerous arrests, she went to prison under the persistent offender law. I began to wonder if my efforts ever really made a difference in their lives at all.

It was hard for me to accept that the victims of abuse never stop being victims. I have seen mothers ignore their children and choose to stay with the perpetrator. These cases affected me the most but I did not become hard and uncaring because that would have hurt the other children I was dealing with.

I never fell into the trap of denial—there are enough officers who choose not to believe the kids who report a rape or ongoing abuse. It is much easier for some cops, especially newer officers,to believe that these unthinkable crimes didn't happen than it is to believe that they did. However, I learned to listen to the children because the incidents that they are reporting are so embarrassing and painful that few would make up this type of story. Most sex abuse investigators have a sixth sense when it comes to differentiating truth from fiction and "cry for attention" investigations are usually stopped well before an arrest is made. I made a conscious decision that I did not want to distance myself from the emotional aspects of a sex abuse investigation, although this would have been the easier path to take.

Instead, I went the other way. I felt that I should try to save all of those kids. I knew that I could not help each one but at least I needed to try. In one case, a mother gave up her daughter and the twelve-year-old was placed into the foster care system. I attempted to be a part of her life. I even brought her to my home to help her feel like a part of a family but it just didn't work out. She had many problems, too many to be overcome in our twice-monthly visits, and living in a state-run institution just did not help. Yet to this day, she still calls me to say hello and to see how things are going with me. I look upon that as a win. It is a win by a narrow margin but it is a win nonetheless.

Each investigator has his/her own way of dealing with these cases, but I really didn't know how to cope. I did not know what to do; whom could I turn to in order to work out some of the stress and inner turmoil these cases were creating? I tried to deal with this on my own but I now know from experience that dealing with emotions on your own never works. The only thing I accomplished was keeping the feelings hidden from view until the stress got so great that they started to resurface.

Eventually, I received a promotion and moved out of the bureau. At last, I no longer had to investigate child abuse cases. I took all of the emotions from handling these cases and put them on a back shelf, never to be thought of again, but I soon discovered that not dwelling on problems was not the same as dealing with them. I only stuffed the feelings inside, just as if I had put all of the cases into a big box on a shelf and hidden it behind something bigger.

There came a time when I had to take one of the cases off the proverbial shelf and review the facts in order to help the victim. While going over the details of the child's abuse, however, I also found I had to relive the pain. Not just the pain from her case—the floodgates opened and I began to relive the horrors of all the sex abuse cases I had investigated during nearly a decade. The case in question was one of recurrent child rape, the ultimate parental betrayal. It ended in a homicide where the victim killed her father in order to escape the abuse. It was necessary for me to make a deposition regarding my initial investigation. I told the lawyers that reliving the case was going cost me a great deal in emotional upheaval but they didn't care, they were preoccupied with this one case. I knew as soon as I began the deposition that all the pent-up emotion would come flooding back. I was right. It was like pouring salt on an open wound. I tried to put up a brave front, but as always when a child is a victim, I could not appear dispassionate.

This time it was not possible to put the emotions on that back shelf. I realized that if I tried to do this again, it would be a temporary fix and the next time I had to review a child sex abuse case, the agony would again rise to the surface. It was finally time to deal with the things which were starting to affect my outlook on my job. I realized that I needed to talk to some friends about my feelings, friends who weren't necessarily in the police field, just people who could be trusted. I also began to write about some of the cases and I found this also helped. What is put down on paper can be left on the paper and does not have to be picked back up. This approach may not work for everyone but it helped me.

What I realize now is that cases often came up so fast and furiously that I was not allowed the time I needed to dwell on them. I just did my job and continued on. In a sex abuse investigation, the "rule of three" is true more often than not—when one abuse assignment is received, two more are sure to follow. This case overload only makes it more difficult for an officer to assimilate the feelings of a particular case. Soon the cases all become an indistinct jumble of young victims, pain, and the loss of innocence. We think that if we don't dwell on the feelings that they will just dissipate. Therefore, we ignore them. We just keep stacking the mental boxes higher and higher until the stack falls over. Then we have a mess. This is the time when officers experience what is recognized as "burnout."

Burnout is a coping mechanism. Some cops become burned out when they feel that the reward for doing the job is not worth the effort they put into it. I have let this feeling creep in on a few occasions but, to be honest, I believe that giving in to it is just short of a full-blown bout of feeling sorry for oneself. We all know someone afflicted with the "poor me syndrome." I can only tolerate these types of people for a short amount of time so it is very disconcerting for me when I'm the one with the case of the "poor me's."

I've known officers who look to others to measure their sense of self-worth. This, too, can be a trap. If, at any time, their cheering section is silent they will be alone and will still have to face themselves and who they really are. No matter how hard we may try we are not always the sharpest knife in the drawer. Everyone has days where nothing seems to go right. These are the days where everything we touch, we break. What should this type of officer do on those kinds of days? To survive, all of us need to be able to look inward and get our rewards from the simple fact that we have tried our best.

I realize that as an investigator, I may not ever be able to make the world a safe place for the victim again but I know I was instrumental in beginning the first step in the healing process. For that reason alone, it was vital that I learned how to take care of myself for that was the only way I could have survived my tenure as a sex abuse investigator—the hardest job in the entirety of my career.

In fact, sometimes just trying to make a difference is all it takes. Sometimes that is all that can be done.

HEADS & TAILS

BY CHUCK SPRINGER

*Police Officer, Warren PD, Warren, Michigan,
five years.*

*These stories are much more amusing over a beer, but I'll
give them a shot anyway . . .*

One time, early on in the first phase of my FTO (Field
Training Officer) program, my FTO was all over me for
being a magnet for disaster. Shortly after his tirade, we
received a deceased person call in one of the less than ad-
equate areas of our city. The dispatcher informed us that
the death was a hospice death, which made things easier
for us as it would have been expected and probably not
violent. Upon arrival, we made contact with the departing
hospice nurse on the front lawn. She informed us that
everything was in order and that the paperwork was inside with the mother of the deceased.

When we went in the front door my FTO and I both
noticed immediately that the deceased woman was quite
young, not more than late twenties. She had very long
blond hair and she was lying on the couch in the front
room. As my FTO and I were looking over the hospice
paperwork, our attention was drawn to the deceased's
mother who was brushing what I first figured to be a cat.

However, we slowly realized that the "cat" looked an awful lot like the deceased's long blond hair. Simultaneously, my FTO and I both swiveled our heads in unison to look over at the dead woman on the couch. Sure enough, the deceased was completely bald (she had died from cancer). We were not humored at this point, but rather shocked and offended. Had the mother been sitting next to her recently departed daughter while crying and brushing her hair, we wouldn't have found her behavior to be so hardhearted. However, she was standing on the other side of the room talking to us, casually and without emotion. Sure, everyone deals with grief differently so I forced my attention back on what the deceased's mother was saying. She told us that she was going to have to raise her young grandsons on her own now that her daughter had passed away. She kept on with her tale as the two boys, her grandsons, came into the room and began aggressively to play hockey right next to the couch where their dead mother lay. Sure, we realized that they were young and probably did not understand what had happened to their mother. But their grandmother never told them to settle down, to go outside, or anything. I know this is Hockeytown, but this seemed a little extreme. She kept talking to us while she let them duel it out between the blue lines. Sticks swinging, elbows flying, police in the living room, and Granny never breaking sentence while brushing her dead daughter's hair! It was at this instant that I realized why officers have such unusual senses of humor—reality gives them no choice.

As we walked out the door, my FTO and I did everything possible not to bust out laughing. Something so sad had just turned into the most bizarre run of my short career. After getting back into our car we regained our composure while waiting for the mortuary service to arrive at the Addams Family home. As we pulled away, I could hear my FTO mutter, "God, this is going to be a long month." And he was right.

Another time . . .

One night while I was off-duty, my partners were working together (three officers are assigned to the car; two work together while the third is off) when they observed a he/she hooker cross the street, heading toward one of our sleazy hotels. They stopped him/her and discovered he/she had several minor warrants. After playing the cop game, "What can you give me to keep yourself outta jail," he/she said that he/she was going to the hotel to have sex with a man who would then smoke crack with him/her in exchange for sex. My partners felt that this potential bust was worth a shot, so they let him/her knock on the hotel room door. The door was opened by a naked man who stared in shock at the officers standing there on either side of the door. Because standing naked in a doorway constitutes a lewd act, my partners began to place the subject under arrest. But the naked man had another idea: he made a run for the small bathroom at the far side of the room. My partners began to chase after him but they stopped in shock. The naked man had a tail. Because they had hesitated, the naked fugitive easily beat them to the bathroom, tearing off his tail and throwing it on the bed as he went. Okay, my partners didn't really want to investigate this but as they were duty-bound to do so, they poked at the tail on the bed . . . It was a set of anal beads.

And though the several bags of crack they had uncovered was a nice bonus, both of my partners were permanently scarred (okay, nauseated for a long time) by what they had seen. All in all, it was a good night to be off.

WHAT SEEDS WE PLANT

by Ray Majeski

Police Officer, twenty-four years: Baldwin Park and Chino, California; Grangeville, Idaho; Sitka, Alaska.

My career in law enforcement has covered almost twenty-four years and, in looking back, one moment stands out above all the rest for me.

Several years ago I was sent to an apartment in response to a domestic dispute. When I arrived, a woman who had been brutally victimized by her husband was sitting in a living room chair unable to even see me through her swollen eyelids. Her husband was gone; he had fled the scene when he heard that a neighbor had called the police.

The young woman, who was consoling her two small children, sat totally broken and humiliated by the circumstances. After the normal formalities involving such a call, she asked me what I thought she should do. Without hesitation, I told her to divorce the man who had treated her so. She didn't balk at my suggestion as one would expect, but seriously asked me how she could support her children without her husband's help. I told her that there were many people and organizations that would jump at the opportunity to assist her, but first she had to think about herself and the safety of her children and rid herself of such an abusive man.

Two days later I returned to the young woman's apartment to check on her welfare and to give her some additional words of support. She still looked lost and frightened but told me she had started divorce proceedings. We sat and talked for a while and I told her that I had contacted the local high school and had learned that she had been a straight-A student prior to marrying. She nodded and told me she had quit school to marry, against the pleas of her teachers and parents. She looked so sad that I tried my best to bolster her spirits, to give her some sense of courage so that she might be better able to face the road ahead of her. I tried to convince her that she and her children would be fine, that all she had to do was put her mind to it and she could accomplish anything. I believed she had it in her and I let her know this as best I could.

Over the next few months I ran into the young woman several times after those earlier events which had caused our paths to cross and each time she would tell me she was doing her best to get on with her life as a single mother. I would always tell her that she had what it takes, that all she had to do was take the first step and there would be people there to help her with the steps that followed.

Eventually she moved away and for several years I heard nothing from or about her. Seven years had passed and I, too, had moved away to the small community of Sitka, Alaska. One evening when I was working a graveyard shift, the dispatcher called my office to inform me that there was a personal call for me. When I picked up the phone, I was greeted by the voice of the young woman; she asked me if I remembered her. For a moment, as I was flooded with memories of her and her difficult struggles, I didn't speak, but then I found my voice and asked her how she was and how things were going in her life.

She told me that she was sitting on the edge of her bed and that she had been thinking about me. She sounded so serious. She said she had to call me because it was such a special day for her. She went on to tell me that after that terrible day when I had shown up at her apartment on the domestic dispute call, she had taken my advice and returned to school. She said that because of the faith I had shown in her and in her abilities, she had found the confidence to move ahead with her life. And now she just wanted to share one of the greatest moments in her life with me because that day she had graduated from the University of Washington. And she wanted to thank me.

One never knows what an impact we, as police officers, can have on someone's life unless we take the time to show we truly care.

GROUND ZERO

GROUND ZERO

WTC RESCUE 1982

BY ROBERT GATES

NYPD, Detective, retired after twenty years.

This story is about an incident that happened at the WTC long before the terrible events of 9/11, when there were still two towers and when terrorism was just an ugly word. What has remained the same is the bravery of the men and women in law enforcement who worked lower Manhattan.

On May 21, 1982, at approximately 1730 hours, a deranged man identified as Benjamin C., approximately thirty-four years of age, defeated the security system on the roof of the World Trade Center South Tower in an attempt to commit suicide. It was his intention to jump off and plunge to his death in much the same way as dozens of people did nearly twenty years later as their building was consumed by a fire ignited by jet fuel, their escape exits blocked. Only Benjamin C. had a choice of living or dying, whereas the others only had the choice of how to die.

Emergency Service Truck 1 was dispatched along with other Emergency Units including ESU Sergeant Alfred Baker. The members of the WTC police, the Port Authority Police Department (PAPD), were the first on the scene and they were able to establish and maintain valuable verbal contact with Benjamin C., and through a dialogue, managed to gain his confidence and establish a rapport until the arrival of the NYPD Emergency Services.

I was a member of NYPD's Emergency Services Unit (ESU) and we arrived soon thereafter and met with the PAPD officers on the scene. We learned that after Benjamin C. had defeated the rooftop security system, he had scaled a parapet of the main roof and slid down a metal facade about eight to ten feet, finally landing on a five-inch steel beam which was a part of the roof's construction. As the situation was desperate, a rabbi was summoned for Benjamin C. and the press was informed as to what was going on.

Sergeant Al Baker decided that Officer Paul Kawas and myself, being partners and with the first Emergency Services Unit on the scene, would volunteer our services in the event a rescue had to be made. Meanwhile, the conversation between the PAPD officers and Benjamin C. had reached somewhat of a stalemate so it was decided that the rescue operation should go ahead.

The rescue plan was as follows: I would rappel over the side of the building, following the path of the would-be jumper while using a three-quarter-inch life line and a Morrissey belt; Officer Kawas would be the second officer to assist, and if there were problems, Officer Michael McCrory would go over the side wearing the parachute harness. In addition, Officer Albert Staab would maneuver himself just inside of an access plate on the facade.

When we all managed to get into position, hanging precariously more than hundred stories off the ground, Sergeant Baker tried to engage Benjamin C. in a dialogue. It seemed that despite his mental disturbance, the jumper was highly intelligent and astutely knowledgeable in many intellectual subjects. For about forty-five minutes we listened as Sergeant Baker and Benjamin C. discussed philosophy and religion and various aspects of esoteric theology. Because Benjamin C. seemed distracted by this dialogue, it was thought that the rabbi would be instrumental as a diversionary tactic and so he was invited to join in the discussion.

Thus, while they were so engaged, I noiselessly maneuvered myself into position to conduct, or at least begin, a rescue attempt. But things did not go as planned—the conversation between Benjamin C. and the rabbi grew heated because of some quirk in their discussion of religion and the jumper became enraged. This seemed like a good time for me to rappel over the roof and down the facade so I did so and managed to land solidly on the five-inch steel beam several feet from Benjamin C., who at this time was demanding a cigarette and threatening to jump. In an effort to make my sudden presence on his beam seem unremarkable, I casually offered him a cigarette and tried to engage him in conversation. Unfortunately, the first cigarette slipped from his fingers and we both watched as it floated the 110 stories to the ground below. He accepted my offer of a second cigarette and stood there smoking it as I assessed the situation and tried to inch my way closer to him. Benjamin C.'s back was to the North Tower and I wasn't sure if he was carrying a concealed weapon, but it was at this point that Sergeant Baker gave me the signal to make the grab. I sprang at Benjamin C. and seized his left wrist but he jerked it free; in my second attempt I lunged at him and held him in a bear hug, literally holding on for dear life as he struggled to break loose. Luckily, and simultaneously with my grab, Officer Kawas rappelled over to assist, while Officer McCrory appeared like Spider-Man and pinned the three of us to the wall of the Tower. Officer Staab scrambled out of the access plate and the four of us lifted the jumper to safety.

Benjamin C. was removed to a nearby hospital for observation and I, along with the rest of the rescue crew, took in the view. We had rescued a seriously deranged person from the highest point in New York City, at a place where the Hudson River far below appears no more than a foot wide to the naked eye. It was a view I will always remember and appreciate for it's a view that is no more. I have wondered lately if Benjamin C. now appreciates the value of life and if he marvels at how he was someone who made it alive out of the South Tower, where over three hundred public service heroes gave up "all their yesterdays" so we all could enjoy our tomorrows, where thousands of civilians perished in a single day.

INSOMNIA REVISIT

by Harry Fagel

Las Vegas Metropolitan PD, nine years.

How much awake can ya be?
Sitting in the chair staring at the electric glass
Images bouncing off the eye orbs
Firing the synapses too
Sleep not really sleep
Just a smearing of conscience interrupted by dreams
The brain sizzling and popping
Hot steak in hot pan
And ya think and think and think
About airplanes and cutthroats and demons in disguise
Typing and tapping the keys extensions of the moment
Wishing for a way out of this alert fiery state and find-
ing only sighs
Sleep is a wishing stone
Just out of reach and holographic and unattainable
Hovering on desire and washed in want
Can't drug or drink or think your way out of it
Fury burns away every attempt
I hear the cries in my half dreams
Cabin filled with blood and people rushing the final door

  Long last conversations on air phones to already griev-
ing families
  Who bite nails and watch it all unfold on CNN
  Holes in the ground with vaporized souls
  Clinging to the tops and bottoms and sides like rem-
nants of sunlight
  Heroes cashing the last check and
  Dying with their boots on
  I know it resides down deep
  Coiled in my mind shifting and sliding
  Images of peace collapsing in dust and ruin
  I try to stand
  United we stand
  United we stand
  And wave my flag and swallow my fear
  Not give murderers any ground to steal the joy at just
being alive
  I just can't help looking over my shoulder
  Just a little more than before
  And wonder and
  Wonder and
  Pray for the innocent and
  Stay
  Awake
  Again

HEROES

BY PAUL RUBINO

Lieutenant, Jersey City PD, New Jersey, retired after twenty-eight years.

It would have been a picture perfect day if not for the smoldering ash wafting across the Hudson River. Gazing to the north and south of the river one could see the azure sky, feel the sixties temperature. But yesterday had also started as a beautiful morning. As the ferry left the dock from Jersey City, New Jersey, to its destination across the water, the occupants of the boat, almost all public safety personnel, were in a somber mood but resolute at the task facing them. It was Wednesday, September 12, 2001, and the past twenty-four hours had turned beautiful mornings into dreadful nightmares.

As a recently retired lieutenant from the Jersey City Police Department I sat with officers I had worked with for years, some who had become close friends, yet the unimaginable destruction we stared at across the river left little energy for conversation. This crime scene we were going to would be like no other any officer could envision. We all had responded to shootings, stabbings, domestic disputes, motor vehicle fatalities, drug arrests; the usual eight-hour tour of carnage. But this would be different; this was mass destruction of human life at which the most hardened law enforcement officer would cringe. As we took the three-minute trip to the World Trade Center site I thought about the many hours of riding patrol through the streets of Jersey City with the Statue of Liberty and the New York skyline a stone's throw from our side of the Hudson. To think that most of us took for granted what thousands travel to see every year. Now there was something missing from that magnificent vista, not just from the skyline, not just a piece of concrete, steel, and glass, but a piece of our lives.

We disembarked on the New York side and made the slow walk up the ramp, past Moran's Bar and Restaurant, looking like it had been abandoned for years. Less than forty-eight hours ago it had been bustling with patrons unwinding after the business day or having a "quick one" before their ferry arrived. Soot, debris, and ash were everywhere. This did not resemble the area I had so often walked through on my way to the city's points of interest. From the Plaza to Battery Park, devastation surrounded us. The buildings that remained, with windows blown out and steel girders jutting and hanging perilously, large sections of the upper floors of the World Trade Center embedded deep in the ground, "the Pit" as Ground Zero was called, all gave an eerie feel of both awe and trepidation. It seemed like a newsreel of a bombing in Beirut or another bad Hollywood action flick. But this was real and up close, it happened in our country, our neighborhood. Although there were hundreds of workers and volunteers at the site the only sounds that could be heard was the machinery removing the debris. Any conversations were held in a low tone. No one had to make an announcement to that effect, it was just understood. This area had become sacred ground. It was the burial place for thousands of lost souls and an observance of reverence was expected.

After doing what little service we could provide at

Ground Zero we made the trek back to Jersey City. If the ferry ride to the World Trade Center was quiet, the return trip was deafening silence. Most slumped on benches, exhausted, not just from the physical labor, but also from the emotional strain. There was no need or desire for talk, everything that needed to be said could be read in the eyes of these volunteers. As we walked up the dock, past another crew waiting to take the ferry over to do their "duty," the numerous people on the dock broke into applause in appreciation for those who just returned from Ground Zero. I looked around at the faces of the brave men and women who were coming off the ferry, those getting ready to leave, the volunteers who worked tirelessly unloading supplies from the many trucks that had arrived with every item imaginable, then loading them onto the ferries to be brought over to Manhattan. I thought about the people who would be at Ground Zero for weeks to come. I remembered the men beside me as we formed a human chain to pass the supplies off the boats that docked by the marina of the financial center. One was a fireman from Pennsylvania, the other a police officer from Baltimore. I had observed so many different badges and uniforms from across the country. Police, Fire, EMTs, rescue workers. Those in public safety who do not hesitate to serve when they are needed. They just ask, "When and where do you want me?" At this country's darkest hour they answered the call to duty just as they do every day in their own communities. At a time when we witnessed our worst disaster, we also witnessed what is an innate quality of the American people: to rise to the occasion and band together when we are threatened.

The thousands of lives lost in this tragedy will always be remembered as heroes. Those who were at their jobs, working to support their families when the attacks occurred, the public safety officers who rushed to the scene to save lives, the people who volunteered after the disaster to help in any way they could, the workers still at the site day and night trying to bring some closure for the suffering families. They are all heroes, each and every man and woman who felt that spirit and determination to show the world how much we cherish our freedom. The public safety personnel who made the ultimate sacrifice are members of our law enforcement family and should never be forgotten. Honoring them with plaques and memorial services is not enough. To truly honor them as heroes we must make sure their families and especially their children are supported emotionally, financially, and spiritually. They were our brothers and sisters on the job; they will be our heroes forever.

I'M WALKING AND TALKING
I'M NOT BITCHING ABOUT ANYTHING

BY PATRICK ZWIEBEL

Lieutenant, NYPD, twenty-one years.

On September 11, 2001, I was off duty when I heard on the radio that two jets had struck the World Trade Center. I knew that the NYPD would be calling a full citywide mobilization so I went home to get ready to go to work. While at home I left the TV tuned to a local station and frantically tried to call my wife, who is a nurse in Manhattan, the kids' school, and my mother to arrange baby-sitting for our three daughters. The TV reporter was talking about traffic and not looking at her monitor when the central station anchor suddenly interrupted her saying something like, "I think the World Trade Center is collapsing . . . Oh, my God! The building is coming down!" They saw what I saw but nobody could believe what was happening. And with the rest of the world I watched in horror as the first World Trade Center tower collapsed.

I grabbed my gear and jumped into my car, starting on a journey I will never forget. I took some side streets to the Long Island Expressway and headed for my command in the northern part of Brooklyn (about two miles from the World Trade Center). There was little traffic and I made good time but then the traffic got very heavy. I tried flashing my car lights and honking my horn and, surprisingly, most of the cars got immediately out of my way; it was as though they knew I was an emergency worker. A little while later I noticed another emergency worker had come up behind me. And then another and another. More and more vehicles joined our little convoy. Over curbs, up onto the grass, weaving in and out of traffic, we made our way into the city. Finally a marked car came by and we all fell in behind it. We managed to get closer to the Midtown Tunnel but when I took the exit for Brooklyn, traffic had stopped dead, nothing was moving.

Suddenly from behind me I heard an air horn blowing and then I saw a fire truck coming up; it was almost pushing the cars out of the way. I knew those on board were thinking of their brother and sister firefighters who were in the World Trade Center when it collapsed; a few stopped cars were not going to prevent them from getting there to help rescue them. At one point, four firefighters actually got out of the truck and threatened the obstinate driver of one car with their axes. Their desperate insistence worked: what was gridlock a minute before became a wide-open road. It seemed like it took forever to get to work but when I arrived and looked at my watch I found I'd gotten there faster than normal.

The procedure in the NYPD for an off-duty mobilization is for all members of the service (MOSs) to report to their commanding officer (CO) at their normal work site to then be redeployed in an orderly fashion to their appointed area. My problem was that I was the CO and getting to my command, the police academy (PA) in Manhattan, was out of the question. The phones were working only sporadically and all the landlines to Manhattan were out. I wasn't sure what to do. I asked the local precinct if they needed more help, but they needed more cops, not more bosses. I gave the desk officer my spare radios and the keys to my marked department van and then waited. It was the longest wait of my life. I went up to the roof where, less than two miles away, I could see the thick black smoke as it spread all over lower Manhattan. In the distance I could hear the never-ending sound of sirens from fire trucks, ambulances, and police vehicles of every type going into and out of the city. Finally, there was a broadcast over the police citywide radio frequency stating that all available MOSs were to report to a command post on West Broadway. I took that as an order and started toward the WTC.

I got a lift from a passing police car to the foot of the Brooklyn Bridge. What I saw before me was truly amazing: there was literally a sea of people coming over the bridge from downtown. All lanes of traffic were filled with people making their way toward Brooklyn and the fresh air. Most were covered with a fine dust; some had makeshift masks on. These people were very orderly, no panicking, no running, no yelling, and they were helping each other. Yes, they were helping each other. And as the days passed, I would continually witness this strength and magnanimity in ordinary citizens; the unhesitant giving of themselves to help total strangers was the norm rather than the exception.

I got another lift from someone who worked at 1 PP (One Police Plaza, the NYPD headquarters). When he dropped me off, I got my first scent of the WTC. The odor was like a combination of sheet rock, firewood, and chemicals all mixed together. I put on my paper medical mask and started walking toward the Hudson River. Within just a few blocks the dust layer grew to an inch or two deep. Most of the parked cars had their windows blown out on the side facing the blast. As I made my way across town I didn't see any civilians, just an occasional police officer. The closer I got, the stranger it became. It seemed as if I was in a snow blizzard; there was no sound, no movement, just fine, four-inch-thick gray dust covering everything. The red glow to the south, where the fires around the WTC were still burning, was the only indicator I had for direction.

When I arrived, I couldn't find either the Temporary Command Post or anyone of higher rank so I headed toward the WTC (we were not yet calling it Ground Zero). On the way I noticed a marked police department car dumping a case of water off at a corner and then going on to the next. Then I saw dust-covered figures coming out of the buildings, coming from all directions to pick up a bottle of water. They were all members of the NYPD, the FDNY, and the EMS who were searching the buildings for victims. They stopped only long enough to take a drink and then they disappeared back inside.

As I approached the WTC I could see that Emergency Service Unit and fire department personnel were all over the place. The EMS workers were covering or picking up things on the ground; as I got closer I realized they were pieces of human beings. Although it was hot and sunny out I remember feeling very cold.

When I was about one block from the WTC I had to climb over some rubble in the street. After tripping three times and getting my foot jammed I realized that no matter how much I wanted to help with the actual rescue effort I would just get in the way and would end up having to be rescued myself. So I located a captain and he told me he wanted only trained personnel at the site and sent me again to that nonexistent command post but instead I went to One Police Plaza.

When I entered 1 PP, an odd scene greeted me. The building was swarming with people, both uniform and civilian, but no one was in a state of panic, no one was running or shouting. No one seemed to be in charge either but everything was being taken care of: a triage area was being formed; a communications system was being established; people and equipment were being mobilized at a rate I would never have thought was possible. I reported in and was given command of a group of Police Academy recruits who, I learned later, had been getting their identification cards at 1 PP and were just about to go back uptown when they happened to witness the first plane crashing into the World Trade Center. So there I was with twenty-eight recruits with no guns, no shields, no vests, no radios, and very little training. Not only that but we were given multiple assignments in different locations. But we got to work. Three recruits joined with other EMT-qualified officers to form a triage center at One Police Plaza. Others off-loaded food, water, and masks and delivered them to Ground Zero. Still others helped with outside security, with directing traffic, and with assisting the stunned citizens.

Sometime later that afternoon I met a friend who was covered in gray dust and limping. I noticed he had a few small cuts on his hands, too. I asked him if he was okay and he said, "I'm walking and talking . . . I'm not bitching about anything." In retrospect, that seemed to sum up the attitude of people at Ground Zero who survived when the buildings collapsed. They might have some injuries but they had perspective. All day long ordinary citizens kept coming up and asking if they could help in any way. At first we turned them away—cops never need help from civilians, right? But many of them would simply not go away so after a while we let them help in off-loading supplies. They worked determinedly in the heat, building up a sweat. Then they would come up to us, dripping from all their hard work, to shake our hands and say, "thank you." They needed to help in some way and they felt better when they did—cops and citizens were united that day. I'm sure this violated every safety regulation imaginable but on September 11 the precautionary rules were simply not in effect.

Toward evening we began to get reports that workers at Ground Zero needed water and other supplies. We now had cases of bottled water stacked up but every time I would send some cases down there they would get diverted to some other place that needed it. By then it was getting dark so I persuaded a few recruits to accompany me (actually they all begged me to take them) and we headed for Ground Zero with a case of water and a dozen flashlights each.

The dust was still flying, but now it was a finer dust, almost like a fog. The closer we got to Ground Zero the quieter it became even though there were hundreds of people on the scene. Or perhaps it was that my senses were overstimulated and were blocking out the noise, like in the beaches of Normandy scene in the movie *Saving Private Ryan*. But it was not like what I would see later in news photos or on TV. I don't remember much of the details, but I do remember that it was like walking on the moon in slow motion. Most of the lights were out, yet you could see what remained of the WTC because of the hundreds of little flashlights bobbing over the rubble. They looked like lightning bugs swarming over a dark hill.

I stopped and stared at this ten-story-high hill of . . . what? What should I call it? It was a pile of construction material, twisted metal, concrete dust, dirt; it was all this, yet none of this. It was just there, a mound of junk. It was hard to imagine that both buildings of the Trade Center could fit into this hill. I kept thinking that most of the buildings should be lying on the bottom of the Hudson River or in the middle of some street.

I lost all sense of where I was. The biggest manmade landmarks in the city were gone. New Yorkers always knew where they were by their relationship to the WTC. If the WTC was over your right shoulder, you're walking downtown; if it was straight in front of you with the Hudson River on your left, you're going north; if it was to your back, you were headed for City Hall. This was something you could depend on.

I don't remember seeing all the damage to the surrounding buildings. We had goggles on by then and they kept getting covered by the dust. Every time I would take them off to clean them my eyes would get dust in them so I put them immediately back on. Most of the time I would keep my head tilted down so that I could see where I was going and also keep my goggles clean. All that day and night, it seemed, I never looked straight up.

There was some twisted metal lying in the street (at least I thought it was a street, it could have been anything) that we had to climb over. While looking down at it, trying to figure out what it had been, I noticed a white stripe on a red background and I suddenly realized that it used to be a fire truck. And I couldn't understand it . . . how could this happen to a ten-ton fire truck?

After we finally managed to drop off the water and flashlights, we headed back toward One Police Plaza. We took a different street back and we saw a patrol car on its side and bent around an Emergency Service Unit truck. The really strange part was that, though people were all around, no one was paying any attention to what would have been a major accident scene. Again, perspective had changed.

It was around eleven P.M. when I finally needed to eat something. Earlier, I had eaten a bag of Cheez-It crackers from my pocket. I remember that after finishing the bag I looked around for a garbage can to put it in and, finding none, I put it back in my pocket. A few days later I was cleaning my uniform pants and found the empty bag. It made me stop and think: there had been thousands of tons of debris on the street but I hadn't wanted to litter.

Cases of the civilian versions of the military Meal, Ready to Eat (MRE) had arrived so I tried one. You open the box and pour one chemical on top of another, then put the food carton and the heating pouch back into the box and it works like a chemical oven: after a few minutes it heats the food. I don't think I'll be serving this for dinner, but it wasn't that bad, or maybe it just didn't seem so bad since I hadn't eaten anything (except crackers) in fourteen hours.

At about one A.M. the families of missing members of the service started to arrive at 1 PP. It was distressing to see all those people coming into the building. Most already knew that their relative was missing in the collapse. But some, judging by their looks of disbelief, had no idea why they were being asked to come down there. And that was the start of this tragic sense of hope. Even after many days some of these relatives still held out hope that their loved one was still alive under all that debris.

Finally, at about four A.M., they started to release the day tour police officers so I called the Police Academy to tell them that we were being dismissed. After waiting to take a shower (there is only one working shower at my Brooklyn station house) I drove home. When I arrived home it was almost light. I sat on the steps of my house for few minutes trying, unsuccessfully, to de-stress. I looked up when I heard a low rumbling sound coming from the morning sky. After spotting what I originally thought were two slow-flying birds very high up, I finally figured out that they were F-16 fighter jets on high Combat Air Patrol. Nowhere in the U.S. had there been the need for Combat Air Patrol since World War II, more than fifty years ago. I was relieved, yet saddened to see this.

My home and my country had become a battle zone so quickly. The world had changed in a few hours.

I went in and kissed my wife, then went upstairs to lie down for a few minutes with each of my three daughters. That morning, as I held my wife and we cried softly in each other's arms, I thanked God for sparing my family and I prayed for all those who were not as lucky as I had been.

FIREFIGHTER, COP, MARINE, FRIEND, HERO

BY LOU SAVELLI

NYPD

Firefighter John "Chip" Chipura died on September 11, 2001, when the South Tower of the World Trade Center collapsed. He was an extraordinary man, a hero, who died while trying to save the lives of the thousands of ordinary people working at the World Trade Center on that day. His unselfishness and bravery was typical of Chip. Kind-hearted, polite, and brave is how I will always remember him. A Marine Corps veteran who had fought in Beirut, with a smile that could warm the toughest adversary and a baby face to match, he never had a bad word to say about anyone. Chip was the kind of guy who would ask, "How are you?" and mean it sincerely.

Before Chip became a firefighter, he was a cop in my Anti-Crime squad. He had been a very respected Community Policing beat cop in the precinct and was rewarded with an assignment to the Anti-Crime Unit in 1993 because of his outstanding performance. But when Chip and his partner, Police Officer Gerry Ahearn, were assigned to my team, I felt like I was the one being rewarded. These two young cops were so full of pride and integrity and so dedicated that my job as sergeant automatically became easier. They were the kind of cops that could handle any assignment with both zeal and a positive attitude.

One of my fondest memories of Chip was a night we spent working plainclothes patrol in the 72nd Precinct in New York City's Sunset Park, Brooklyn, neighborhood. It was around midnight and near the end of a four-to-twelve tour. We had been trying to catch a gang of robbers who were sticking up people at gunpoint near the subway stations around Prospect Park. According to the robbery pattern alert, the stick-up gang was becoming increasingly violent and had shot their last few victims without provocation. Chip and Gerry were so determined to catch the stick-up team that I didn't even try to tell them it was time to call it a night. They were bent on catching the violent gang before they killed someone.

The night was unusually quiet and unseasonably cold and a strange fog had reduced our ability to observe from a distance. The streets were eerily desolate with only a lone car passing every few minutes and only the occasional commuter, walking hurriedly from the subway exits after a late night at work, was visible. Chip, Gerry, and I were on surveillance, sitting in our parked unmarked car on the lookout for the stick-up team. I was sitting in the rear seat so that these young Anti-Crime officers, who were excellent street cops, could do their job with me along just to observe. I was thinking that the night was a bust when Chip excitedly said, "Check out that car," and motioned his head toward an older model black four-door Honda Accord passing us on Greenwood Avenue. From what I could make out, it seemed to be occupied by four tough-looking males, quite possibly gang members. Chip, who was driving, allowed the Honda to completely pass us by before pulling out from the side street where we were parked and onto Greenwood Avenue, being careful to avoid letting the Honda's occupants get a good look at our 1991 dark blue Chevy Caprice unmarked car, which might as well have had "NYPD" written on it. He read the license plate aloud several times so that I could write it down on my notepad. Chip initiated a surveillance of the black Honda while I called the plate into our central radio dispatcher.

"Seven-two Anti-Crime sergeant to Central K," I spoke into my handheld Motorola radio.

"Seven-two Anti-Crime sergeant—go ahead K," responded the Zone 11 NYPD dispatcher.

So as to ask dispatch to determine if the Honda was stolen and to let them know we were following a suspicious vehicle, I said, "Central, 10-14 rolling on a black Honda bearing New York registration Charlie-David-Adam-one-five-six!"

While we waited for the results of the plate check, Chip followed the black Honda by using the cover of the thick fog and shutting off our car's headlights. As the Honda neared the corner of East Seventh Street, we noticed an elderly couple walking toward the subway station after a late night at the bingo hall several blocks away. Chip and Gerry looked back at me with an expression I immediately understood. We were all thinking that the elderly couple could be the next victims of the subway station robbers. With their lives in the balance, we couldn't take a chance by waiting for a traffic infraction to happen, or for the dispatcher to respond to our registration check. We had to make a move right away.

"Let's take them now!" I replied to their unspoken request.

Then suddenly, the black Honda swerved toward the curb, cutting off the path of the couple. Chip accelerated and our three-thousand-pound unmarked police car sped toward the Honda. The suspected robbers were so intent on watching the elderly couple make their way to the corner that they never saw us coming. We were out of our car before the four males completely emerged, rushing them with our guns drawn and our flashlights blinding them. Shouting in loud voices that carried through the fog and darkness—*"Police! Don't move! Get on the ground! Now! Move and we'll shoot!"*—we sounded like an army of cops, not just the three of us, obviously outnumbered and unknowingly outgunned.

Chip shoulder-blocked the thug stepping out of the rear seat of the driver's side. He hit him so hard that he knocked him into the driver of the Honda, who was emerging with a gun in his hand. The driver bounced off his door and slammed into his compatriot and they both fell to the ground, losing their guns on impact with the cold wet sidewalk. At the same time, Gerry reached the perp stepping out of the front passenger side of the Honda. The perp was pulling a loaded 9mm pistol from his waistband as Gerry slammed him into the hood of the car and wrestled the gun from his hand. The rear seat passenger emerged and was making a move toward Gerry when he realized his gun was still on the floor of his car. He dove back inside and grabbed for it but before he could use it, he felt my Glock 9mm pressing into the back of his neck. He dropped the gun and I could also smell that he had dropped a load in his pants.

Gerry, a player from the NYPD football team, had slammed his perp so hard against the hood of the car that he was readily disarmed and handcuffed. My perp was so uncomfortable and cooperative that I cuffed him easily. I left him facedown on the sidewalk next to Gerry's perp while Gerry stood over them with his gun drawn shouting a few expletives to make them aware of the dangers of making any furtive movements. I ran over to Chip and helped him handcuff the other two dazed gunmen. Chip had already picked up one of the guns from the ground while I picked up the other and shoved it into my waistband. I knew I had to get us assistance to thoroughly secure our prisoners and to help search the car. I also was concerned that the perps may have had a back-up car that was in the area.

"Eighty-five forthwith! Greenwood and East Seventh, holding four with guns!" I shouted into my radio.

Meanwhile, the elderly couple, confused and frightened, stood huddled together against the nearby subway entrance watching us as we dragged the four perps along the pavement to the sidewalk. We arranged them into a neat line to make it easier to cover them. Within seconds, we heard sirens and the sound grew louder and louder until red and white lights could be seen emerging through the fog. One by one, marked blue-and-whites manned by two uniformed police officers arrived on the scene.

Each perp was thoroughly searched and shoved separately into the rear seat of an Radio Motor Patrol (RMP). I gave instructions to the uniformed officers to keep them separated at the station house so that when we questioned them we could play one against the other, and the four RMPs, now transporting a perp each, drove off and disappeared into the foggy darkness. Meanwhile, Chip and Gerry were busy searching the black Honda. The first thing they noticed was that the car was running without keys in the ignition and that the ignition was hollowed out. They also discovered ski masks, duct tape, bandannas, and handcuffs. While proudly showing me their spoils of war, a familiar voice came over our portable radios.

"Central to Seven-Two Anti-Crime, K!" said the anxious female voice on the radio.

"Go ahead, Central!" I replied into my radio.

"That registration Charlie-David-Adam-one-five-six is coming back 10-16 to a black Honda wanted in connection with robbery pattern 88-1993. Suspects are armed and dangerous!"

"10-4 Central—We have the vehicle and its occupants in custody and will be en route shortly to the seven-two station house."

"10-4 Seven-Two Crime. The time is now 0030 hours!"

We exchanged a look after hearing the time check. We knew 0030 hours, pronounced: zero-zero-thirty hours (12:30 A.M.) made the arrest time just before our end of tour so we couldn't be accused of making the collar after hours just to make overtime.

When we arrived at the 72nd station house, all the prisoners were secured in separate cells or rooms as I had ordered so that they couldn't talk to each other. Detectives from the precinct detective squad were already busy helping out with the paperwork since they heard the arrest transpire over the radio. They were also looking for fillers (look-a-likes) for the multiple impending lineups we had planned for the four gangsters to see if we could tie them to the other robberies from the pattern. Gerry went right to work filling out the mounds of arrest processing and related paperwork, which tended to discourage one from making arrests.

Chip, in his unique and compassionate style, bought each perp a soda and a bag of potato chips and then spent the rest of the night talking to each of them about straightening out his life. Chip was the greatest conversationalist I have ever known and one of the most likable people in the world. He really had a way with people. He was kind, pleasant, and he listened attentively. I believe he actually reached one of those gangsters that night, maybe even changed his life around.

That night was just one of many interesting nights with Chip . . . God bless him and those who gave so much of themselves on 9/11/01.

LOSS OF A CHILD

BY JAMES SCARIOT

*Sergeant, Internal Affairs, Monterey County Sheriff's
Department, California, nineteen years.*

*I submitted these two life experiences for two purposes:
the first is to remind us how precious and precarious life
really is. We all must cherish life and the lives of those
around us. Secondly, is to remind others that when they
see a firefighter or law enforcement officer, remember that
we are flesh and blood just as they are. Some of us carry
very heavy backpacks but we never stop serving.*

My September 11 story started unfolding on January 14,
1996. At that time, my family consisted of a son and
daughter from my first marriage and a son from my
wife's first marriage. That night I received a call from
James Jr., our youngest child. James started by telling me
how sorry he was for letting me down. Since I had no idea
what he was talking about, I asked for more details—always the cop. James was completing his senior year at
Willamette University in Salem, Oregon. All during
Christmas break he had worked on his senior dissertation
for one particular class, which he needed to pass in order
to earn his bachelor's degree. When James returned to
class after the break, he listened while his fellow class-

mates made their respective presentations. He also listened while the professor ridiculed what the students were saying. James had gotten angry with this and had confronted the professor. He expressed his opinion that the professor's responsibility was to teach, not to ridicule. Because of this confrontation, James told me he thought the professor was going to fail him in the course and he would not graduate, thus letting his mom and me down.

I told him he had not done anything wrong. I told him he done just what I would have expected him to do. The professor was wrong, not him. I told James if he received a failing grade for doing the right thing, for standing up on behalf of his fellow students, he needed to file a grievance with the university's administration. James told me he would know by Tuesday as the grades were being mailed out on Monday. I again told James he had done the right thing and our conversation ended.

On Tuesday, James phoned again. He always called me "D" or "Pops." He said, "Hey D, you're talking to a college graduate." He received a 4.0 GPA, the highest possible. We talked about how he had beaten himself up and worried for nothing. James then talked of his future. He wanted to enter graduate school in the fall. He was going to pursue a master's degree in education so that he could teach. Once he obtained his degree, he was going to go to the Oakland Raiders' summer camp and try out as a wide receiver. If he didn't make the cut, then he was going to try to play Canadian football. If he didn't make the cut in that league, he would be happy to be a teacher and coach. Our conversation ended with James saying, "I really love you, Dad." I said, "I love you too, baby. Please be careful." "Yeah," he said, "I know."

On January 28, 1996, at approximately 0500 hours (five A.M.), I was working patrol and was returning from a call for service in the Big Sur area. I received an urgent request to call our dispatch center. I called from the car and was told I needed to call the Lynn County Sheriff's Department in Albany, Oregon regarding my son, James Jr., as soon as possible. My first thought was that James was having some type of trouble in regards to his dispute with his professor. I called and was told that James Jr. had been night skiing with his roommates and had disappeared at approximately 8:30 P.M. the previous evening. They had searched the mountain once but suspended the search when a late blizzard came in. They planned on starting the search again at daybreak.

I drove back to the office, went off duty, and drove home. I woke up my wife and told her what they had said. I told her that I believed our son was dead. She said that I shouldn't talk like that. She said I should believe in God and that James would be found on the mountain injured somehow so that he couldn't come down by himself, but that he would be found alive.

We made plans to fly to Oregon to help search for our son. I made the flight and hotel arrangements. As we were about to leave for the airport in San Jose, I called the Lynn County Sheriff's Department for an update on the search. We were told that our son's body had been recovered from a tree well off the ski run at approximately 0625 hours (6:25 A.M.). We were told he died instantly from head injuries. We made our flight not to go and help search for our son but to bring his body home for burial.

I returned to work the last week of February 1996 and six days later, my crew received a call for a suicidal, barricaded person in Pebble Beach. The man was bipolar and had stopped taking his medication. As I was the on-duty supervisor, I drove over to the house. Two of my deputies had convinced the suicidal man to open his bedroom door. When I walked up to them, I saw the man standing in the bedroom holding the blade tip of a folding pocketknife in the recess of his neck below his Adam's apple. He had several nicks on both sides of his neck over his jugular vein.

I began a dialogue with the man. He told me that no matter what I said or what I did, he was going to die that night. I patiently explained to him that I couldn't let that happen and we began a lengthy conversation about incessant mental pain and anguish, something I was very recently familiar with. The man told me he hated his medication because it made it so he couldn't feel anything. As the conversation continued, he began to chide me about not understanding him and not understanding what kind of pain he was in. I told him I had a very real understanding of what he was going through. He just stared at me and challenged me: If I was such an expert on pain, then let me tell him what it was like. So I just stood there and related the story of James Jr.'s death. After I had finished the man just looked at me for a long moment, then he dropped the knife away from his neck, walked over, and handed it to me. I promised him that I would personally take him to the hospital and would stay with him until he felt he was safe. I also promised him that I would stop by his house and share my favorite drink with him. He put his arm around my shoulder and walked with me out to my car and he apologized several times for being responsible for all that transpired that night.

The man had one other relapse but did not become suicidal. His parents said it was because he remembered my promises, and that I had kept them. What I had done was stop by his house and leave a bag containing two cans of my favorite drink. I asked him to share those drinks with his family—two cans of Barq's root beer.

It was more than five years later, on September 11, 2001, at approximately 0645 hours (6:45 A.M.), that I was at our kitchen table reading the local newspaper and drinking coffee. My wife came down from our bedroom. She walked in saying, "The whole world has gone crazy!" My immediate thought was two-fold: What the hell did I forget to do this time; my wife needed to be included in an inventory of the crazy world. But I dutifully asked her what was wrong. She picked up the remote and turned on the TV. I sat and watched the replay of the aircraft smashing into the South Tower of the WTC and my thoughts immediately went to my daughter Kristina (Tina).

Tina had been married the previous December and had moved to New York. She had a job in Lower Manhattan but we had no idea of her proximity to the WTC. I made the frantic call only to hear those dreaded words, "We're sorry but all circuits are busy. Please try your call again later." For almost two hours we had no idea if we were going to have to bury a second child.

But this time we were granted a reprieve. Tina was all right. When we finally spoke to her, she told us that she had arrived at work just as the first plane hit the North Tower. She said she heard the loud noise but had dismissed it, as Manhattan is always noisy. She had just sat down at her desk when the second plane struck. Debris from that aircraft and the tower landed on her building and she and her coworkers had to evacuate via the stairs.

I thought about how close we came to losing another child and I remember thinking that I felt God had promised after James's death not to give us a cross too heavy to bear. 9/11 was a life-altering experience for many American citizens but our life-altering experience came in 1996 and actually helped us to survive 9/11.

UNTITLED

BY PETER DEMONTE

Sergeant, NYPD, seventeen years.

On September 11, 2001, I was assigned as the bicycle patrol supervisor of the Manhattan Traffic Task Force. Two of my officers and I were on patrol near the Waldorf-Astoria Hotel at Fiftieth Street and Park Avenue in NYC when, at 0846 hours, the call came over the radio that a plane had struck the World Trade Center. I immediately commandeered a passing van, threw our bicycles in the back of it, and told the driver to take us downtown. At that time we were several miles north of the site. The van driver was very nervous and was driving so slowly that I had him pull over. I unloaded our stuff, stopped a passing police car, and had the patrol officers take me the rest of the way. On the way, I could feel the tension in the city. I called my wife, Alissa, from my cell phone to tell her that a plane had hit the World Trade Center and that I was on my way down there to help. This type of phone call was not unusual as I always tell her about the events that are happening prior to her hearing about them on the news, but this was different. This was unlike any other call that I'd ever made.

When we arrived downtown the patrol officers let me

out a few blocks north of the WTC, as they needed to return to their precinct, so I rode my bike the rest of the way. I passed the mayor and the police commissioner and noticed that they did not look confident. I then rode into a surreal world where building pieces, airplane fragments, and body parts were scattered all over the street. As I looked up to see smoke and flames issuing from the tower, I saw people jumping from the their office windows; I knew this would not be good.

I left my bike propped against the door of One World Trade Center and went in the building to begin the evacuation, and inside I came upon a scene I will never forget. Water was cascading from the ceiling sprinklers, causing the floor to be flooded with several inches of water. People were exiting in a single file line, some bleeding, some burned, and all had a dazed look on their faces. One man came up to me to tell me that there was a defibrillator in his office if I needed it. I thanked him, but looking around at the scene, I knew it wouldn't be necessary. A hysterical woman told me, "There are bodies everywhere up there!" and that was all that she could say, over and over. I took her arm and led her to the exit, reassuring her that everything would be okay. Though people were moving in an orderly fashion they were moving very slowly, so I found a maintenance man and had him fold back the revolving doors so that people could exit more freely. I got the people out as fast and as far away as I possibly could while all the time encouraging them to keep moving and to not look back.

I went down to the mall level of One World Trade in order to make sure the evacuation there was proceeding unimpeded. I saw Sergeant Timothy ("Timmy") Roy, a friend and a member of my command, helping a burn victim. Little did I know at the time that I would be one of the last people to see him alive, and not only him, but also many others. It was the last few moments of their lives but I didn't know it then; many were fine people, some of whose names I will never know. But I continued leading people out and making sure they stayed calm.

During this period, I tried several times to call Alissa from my cell phone but I couldn't get through. Finally, after one last try, it rang and she answered. I told her where I was and that I was helping people get out. I felt conspicuous being on the cell phone so I told her I loved her and, in saying good-bye, she told me that another plane had crashed into the Pentagon. (She later told me she had mentioned this almost as an afterthought.) It was then that I realized that this plane crash at the WTC hadn't been an accident but was an act of terrorism. I was prompted to action and I immediately headed out of the mall level to seek out the deputy commissioner, who I knew was in the area. I wanted get immediate authorization to tow all the vehicles from the area around the Center, since I knew that terrorists commonly plant explosives in trucks to kill and injure the rescue personnel.

As I exited the Center and retrieved my bike I heard a loud, reverberating rumble. Somehow I knew what it was but I turned anyway, and saw the top of Two World Trade Center beginning to bend and collapse. I jumped on my bicycle and rode as fast as I could while yelling to people to run and to get out of the way. I managed to stay just in front of the huge rolling cloud of smoke and dust that threatened to engulf all in its path. Remarkably, I managed to make it into the clear. I stopped and looked back, fearing that we had lost at least 250 officers, 25 just from my command. Later I was relieved to find out that most of them had made it out alive.

Then I realized that when my wife had heard on the radio that the tower had collapsed she would think I had died. My cell phone wouldn't work because of the devastation and it wasn't until three hours later that I found a working telephone and could call her to let her know I was okay. Meanwhile, when I was on my way back to help search for my comrades, the second tower collapsed. It struck me that I had used up all my luck not only for that day but maybe for the rest of my life.

I was present when they pulled the last survivor, a Port Authority police sergeant, out of the rubble. I spent the next several months at the site, looking for my friend, Sergeant Timothy Roy, and making sure that vehicles did not clog the streets so that all rescue personnel and heavy equipment could reach the site. I wanted them to have unhindered access so that they might have every chance to dig and rescue anyone who might still be alive. But there was no one else.

We finally found Timmy's body on the day of the St. Patrick's Day Parade (March 16, 2002) some six months and five days after I last saw him. I was fortunate to be working overtime when he was found, just getting ready to go home, so I was there as they dug him out, and was able to help escort him over to the morgue.

UNTITLED

BY ROBERT BRAGER

Police Officer, NYPD, twelve years.

On September 11, 2001, I was assigned to the Street Nar-
cotics Enforcement Unit at the 77th Precinct in Brooklyn,
New York. I usually work some form of night shift but
that day I was scheduled for a day tour because I had to
attend court. Though it was almost the middle of September I remember it being a bright, sunny day which started
out routinely. But as I was about to leave the precinct to
go to court one of my partners told me that there'd been
an accident, that a plane had struck one of the World
Trade Center towers. I went into his office to see it on TV.
When I saw the camera shot from the circling news helicopter showing the tremendous hole in the side of the
building and the billowing smoke from the fire, I thought,
"This does not look good," but no one yet thought it was
anything other than a terrible accident. In New York
large-scale incidents happen all the time, so it was still
business as usual as I prepared to leave for court. As I
walked out the back door, someone told me that if I went
up to the roof of our four-story building I would have a
very clear line of sight to the Manhattan skyline. He said
he could see the fire clear from where we were in Brook-

lyn. I went up to take a look. I couldn't believe how big a fire it was; as far as we were from the World Trade Center, the amount of smoke and fire was still enormous. While I was standing there, someone pointed out what we thought was a helicopter approaching the second tower. About a dozen of us watched in horror as we saw this aircraft go straight into the building. I can still see the huge fireball and remember the delay until the sound of the tremendous explosion hit us in Brooklyn. The reactions from those on the roof ranged from tears to disbelief to sheer anger; we knew then that this was no accident. Almost instantaneously the alert went out around the city putting the NYPD on its highest emergency response, a Level Four Mobilization (which hadn't happened since the Crown Heights riots nearly a dozen years ago).

I ran down to my locker and threw on my uniform faster than I ever have in my life and grabbed my second gun thinking this was an attack and we were at war. Don't ask me what my backup weapon, a small .38, would do against a terrorist with an AK-47, but I felt better carrying it. As I ran upstairs I called my wife and left her a message on the machine to go to our five-year-old daughter's school and to take her home NOW! I was thinking that schools would be another target and I wanted my daughter out fast. I reminded my wife of where the shotgun was in the attic and I ended by saying, "We are under attack. Don't answer the door or open it for anyone, I'm going into the city and I will call you later. I love you."

As part of a Level Four Mobilization every one of the 72 precincts in the city plus all the Housing Units and the Transit Districts must send one sergeant and eight police officers as part of the response to a predetermined mobilization point near the incident. I quickly volunteered to be one of the eight officers sent from my command along with three others from my unit and a mix of other guys from patrol units. We jumped into a van and followed a caravan of other emergency units, which grew larger and larger as other vehicles joined us as we headed toward Manhattan along the route toward the Brooklyn Bridge. The sight going over the bridge is something I'll never forget. The towers seemed to stand so tall against the backdrop of the rest of the city, while the immense amount of smoke pouring out made it surreal. Usually a ride from that part of Brooklyn into downtown Manhattan during the morning rush can take nearly an hour and a half to go only a few short miles, but we made it in twelve minutes flat. When we arrived at Pike Street, just a few blocks east of the burning towers, we found that a staging area was being set up to deploy the arriving units. We were only there for a few minutes when we received our assignment to accompany a lieutenant, two sergeants, and sixteen other cops to evacuate the New York Stock Exchange buildings. As we climbed back in the van someone began screaming over the radio that the tower was collapsing. We tried to back up to get a clear view of the WTC from between the other buildings but all we could see was smoke. We found ourselves stuck amid a crush of vehicles that had been abandoned in the middle of the street by fleeing civilians; we were ordered to leave the van and to go in on foot.

In a column of two-by-two, we began to trot the five blocks west toward the World Trade Center complex. Visibility was non-existent; this cloud of gray dust consumed us. It was like what I always thought a nuclear winter would be like, as everything became a single shade of gray. There were no colors at all and the sun was almost completely blocked out. As we continued onward toward the WTC we passed hundreds of civilians in various states of shock and disbelief. Many had minor injuries and were running away from the towers, but we kept going in. I now realize that because of the enveloping dust the lieutenant we were following was lost. We were only three blocks from the tallest buildings in the city and we couldn't find our way toward them because we couldn't see a foot ahead of us. But we kept going.

As we headed into what seemed like a glimmer of light we found ourselves just north of the remaining tower near Chambers Street, behind Seven World Trade Center. I knew that the World Trade Center was a complex of eight buildings with the two towers being numbered one and two. Number Seven was forty-seven stories high and it stood about fifty yards north of the base of the second tower. As I got my bearings I looked up in horror to see the remaining tower engulfed in flames about two thirds of the way up.

Our assignment was to block Chambers Street to anyone or anything going south toward the complex and to aid in evacuating the civilians fleeing north. But every couple of seconds I kept turning to look straight up at that enormous fireball raging out of control. That's when I first noticed a strange phenomenon. Above the floors consumed by fire, starting at around the ninetieth floor, people were starting to jump out of the windows. I couldn't grasp how desperate someone had to be to leap to a certain death from a hundred stories up, but then they were facing something too terrible to comprehend: they saw the collapse of the first tower from the vantage point of their office windows, a view that the rest of the world could only imagine. I saw groups of two and three people holding hands and leaping together to their deaths. I followed their bodies down until I lost sight of them behind Seven WTC. I heard the sound of their bodies slamming onto the mezzanine; it sounded like a series of small bombs going off. This went on for ten to fifteen minutes when suddenly there was a burst of fire from the floors consumed by smoke. I looked up and saw the top of the building beginning to lean. I began to run, yelling for everyone to drop everything and to run north as fast as possible. We ran, pushing and propelling everyone in front of us toward safety, or at least toward escape. I kept expecting to be crushed, imagining this 107-story building falling straight over and taking out ten city blocks as it went. As I ran north I pulled a newswoman who was struggling to run along with me, but the tremendous dust and debris cloud overtook us. I was struck by something in the back of my legs and had to stop running. We ducked into an office building where someone had broken out the windows to seek refuge. It became eerily silent as the cloud slowly lifted. I tried to look in the direction where the tower once stood but only saw an empty space in the sky with a huge cloud of smoke rising up. From where we were I could see the side of Number Seven where we had been just a few minutes ago. The entire building was engulfed in flames. I was told later that even though the rear of the structure was intact, the front looked like the federal building in Oklahoma City after the bombing there, with most of the facade torn away. It, too, would collapse several hours later.

It was an orderly chaos after the collapse of Number Seven, with everyone scurrying to try and locate the cops they were with just a few minutes before. I was left with only one of my partners from our original eight, Officer Feranola, but we didn't know what had happened to the rest of our group.

Rumors began to circulate about how many hundreds of cops and firemen were missing or killed instantly in the collapse, and word spread of other attacks around the country. At different times throughout the day I was told that the Empire State Building, the United Nations complex, the White House, the Pentagon, and many other places might have been hit. You can't imagine the flow of distorted information during a time like that. Here we were in the greatest city in the world in the middle of the news capital of the country and we couldn't find out anything because all cell phone sites were down.

During the next few hours I would make many attempts to call my wife to let her know I was okay, as I didn't know what she saw or heard on the TV. But it wouldn't be until one o'clock in the afternoon when I got word to her that I was all right. She would later tell me it was the longest four hours of her life. She had been waiting for me to call and the phone kept ringing but it was only our relatives and friends calling to see if I was okay. She hadn't known what to tell them.

After the initial shock of it all wore off, the bucket brigades, crews of hundreds, began to work "the pile." Everyone believed that there had to be at least some people trapped alive since we knew there had to be thousands beneath us in the rubble. We worked by hand for the first few hours, removing crumpled metal and debris, filling the buckets and passing them down long lines from the top of the pile to the end. Every once in a while someone would yell for everyone to be quiet, thinking they heard something underneath the millions of tons of twisted metal. And for a moment everything would stop. As the night wore on it became increasingly discouraging to hear that out of all that debris not a single survivor was found. Seeing the hundreds of doctors and nurses at makeshift triage areas set up around the collapse site just waiting and watching for the influx of the wounded that would never come became mind-numbing.

Around nightfall Officer Feranola and I found the other cops we had been with at Number Seven and we shared our stories about where we were and what we were doing and how we managed to survive the building's collapse. We also shared what we had heard throughout the day about the number of people who were missing. Finally, around one A.M., we were relieved and told to go back to the Command to try to clean up for what was going to be a long few days.

The ride home was deadly silent as we reflected on what had happened over the last seventeen hours. When we arrived back at the Command at around two A.M. we were welcomed by our commanding officer and others who had feared we were all missing in the collapse. After a few minutes of relieved greetings, we were told to clean up and be back in two hours, at four A.M., to start all over again.

The next few days were a blur. Though a minor injury to my leg had limited what I was able to do, I, like every officer there, worked sixteen to seventeen hours with limited time off either at a traffic detail, as security, or on the bucket brigade at what was now being called "Ground Zero." I chose not to return to Ground Zero after 9/11 and to this day I have still not been back there. Since I live on Staten Island I volunteered to be sent to the Fresh Kills Landfill where all the debris was being sent. For the next few weeks I would do a couple of tours a week there sifting through debris piles with a hand rake, looking for anything identifiable. I never could comprehend that I was digging through the remains of what had been two of the tallest buildings in the world with a hand rake. I took solace in knowing that anything I found could bring closure to a loved one who didn't know what had happened to their wife, their husband, their mother or father or child. Yet, in all the time I spent up there I only found a few things: some jewelry, an ID and credit card, a number of shoes, and some very small fragments of bone. The largest piece of human remains that we found was the mid-section of a victim that was twisted into the middle of a piece of steel beam. It was very disheartening work but we knew we had to do the best we could.

Now, months later, every night before I fall asleep I still think about what I saw. The counselors we were sent to all said it's a normal part of what we went through. But nothing is the same now; everyone has changed a little bit because of 9/11. How can you be the same when your workdays are spent at the Ground Zero landfill and your days off are spent going to the hundreds of funerals for the 23 NYPD officers, 343 NYFD, 37 Port Authority officers, and thousands of civilians lost? You can't. We've all changed. Maybe forever.

UNTITLED

BY JAMES BOGLIOLE

Police Officer, NYPD, Transit Bureau Special Operations Unit, eighteen years.

September 11, 2001. Only a few hours after the first tower fell, I, along with members of my unit, responded to the scene. My account of what I witnessed is as follows. At approximately 11:30 hours we left our command in Coney Island not knowing what we were about to encounter. From the highway we saw an enormous cloud covering Manhattan. What I remember most vividly was the silence. Complete silence, as if you were deaf. When we entered the Battery Tunnel the falling ash looked like snow; you couldn't see five feet in front of you. We crept along hoping not to hit any other vehicles and as we exited the tunnel the "snow" grew thicker as if we were in the middle of a blizzard. As we drove on we observed many dust-covered and panic-stricken people fleeing the area on foot. Finally, the van came to a stop and we jumped out. It seems odd saying this now but it was like entering an amusement park where strange things were going on all around us. There was the acrid smell of jet fuel in the air and when I looked down I saw body parts lying on what was the West Side Highway. When I looked to my right I saw an aircraft landing gear tire; when I looked to my left I saw countless overturned vehicles; and in front of me I saw the most horrific scene of destruction I probably will ever see in my lifetime. We walked in a daze, overcome with disbelief that something so terrible could happen here in America. But we kept going and we climbed over tons and tons of rocks, wires, cars, metal beams, trees, tires, glass, and paper looking for any sign of life. It was if we had landed on a foreign planet.

As I stood looking at where the World Trade Center once stood, I thought back to only a few weeks earlier when I was staying there at the Marriott Hotel with my wife and four young daughters (ages three, six, eight, and eighteen). We had stayed there for a week because my six-year-old, Amber, was competing in a state pageant. Our hotel was attached to the World Trade Center. I thanked God that the pageant hadn't been this week.

As we continued eastward, we came upon a police officer lying motionless on the ground and covered with dust. Like many other areas, that spot was roped off. The officer was lying next to a small, bent-over tree. For some reason I can't get that tree out of my mind. It wasn't cracked or damaged, it was just bending over him. I kept thinking that somehow this bent tree was the cause of the officer's death but I don't know how that could be. I just keep seeing it in my mind's eye: the fallen officer and the yielding tree, and I wonder what had happened. I will probably never know. Maybe no one will.

We moved on, continuing our searching while listening to alarms going off everywhere. Finally, I was standing about fifty yards directly in front of Seven WTC and watching while massive flames were shooting from an entire floor. I heard someone say that the building was going to collapse and to get out of there. I started to turn back when my cell phone rang. It was my wife calling to see if I was okay. She told me that on the news they were saying that another building was in danger of collapse. I said, "Yeah I know, I'm standing in front of it, so let me go so I can get the hell out of here." I hung up and started jogging away from the building and within minutes I heard a loud rumble behind me. I turned around in time to see the building collapse. The swirling dust engulfed everything around us and added to the debris. Because of the devastation, it seemed that another building falling was inevitable. We walked cautiously onward, breathing in every type of airborne particle imaginable. My lungs felt as if they were filled with dirt; it hurt whenever I took a breath. We found an area and started to dig, trying to find someone alive. Digging through the rubble I found numerous identifications with the names of people and their photographs attached. I would read each one and look at the picture; it made things a lot more personal, a lot more real. Sometime during all of this my cell phone stopped functioning. I didn't know that my wife was watching the news as the building collapsed while knowing that I was near it. She frantically tried to reach me but couldn't. Hours later, when I finally was able to call her, she was so hysterical that I couldn't understand a single word she said. I reassured her that I was fine and not to worry.

This was the beginning of a two-month period in which my unit would go every day to our command post at Battery Park and from there on to Ground Zero, where we would begin again to search in the rubble and debris, hoping to find someone alive. Those long days blend together but certain ones stand out clearly in my memory.

For example, on our third day at Ground Zero we went underneath the World Trade Center where the subway and the mall were partially collapsed. Walking beneath all that rubble while listening to loud and unidentifiable noises coming from every direction was eerie and strange. As we walked through the subway it reminded me of the earthquake ride at Disney World. There was fire, smoke, water, and debris everywhere. Inside the mall it was pitch black so we shined our flashlights into the stores as we walked along, revealing the thick covering of dust and ash that blanketed everything. Unless you had a mask on it was nearly impossible to breathe. There was water dripping through the collapsed ceilings and wires hanging everywhere. You felt that at any given moment the entire place would cave in and you would simply cease to exist. Yet we had a job to do and so we went down there numerous times, taking measurements to see if there were any structural shifts or changes.

I remember working the high point of Ground Zero where you could look down at hundreds upon hundreds of people digging and working the never-ending bucket brigade. One day, there was this volunteer working next to me who was swinging a pick ax like a wild man. My partner Bob, a fireman, and I climbed a little higher on the pile, but I kept my eye on the volunteer because I thought he was a little too out of control. We found a hole or void that went straight down for two or three stories. We lay on our stomachs and peered inside looking for movement. Then something happened that I would never forget. The ax-swinging volunteer scrambled up the hill toward us. He pushed between us and fell facedown on the ground and looked down into the hole. He lay motionless for a few moments when all of a sudden he screamed, "I see the face of a little boy!" before his eyes rolled back in his head and he pitched backward as if he had fainted. We again looked into the hole, and strained to see into the void, but we saw nothing. Everyone stopped what they were doing; you could hear a pin drop it was so quiet. Then the volunteer awoke and crawled back to the edge of the hole, peering down almost hysterically. We finally realized that this guy was a little crazy and didn't belong. I yelled, "Get him out of here!" and my partner, who is 6' 2" and 250 pounds, escorted him to the beginning of the bucket brigade line. We watched as he zigged and zagged through the line straight into the arms of the FBI. It was a sight to see. A madman in a world gone mad. It turned out that he had been recognized as a "problem person" days earlier and was not authorized to be at Ground Zero.

We worked relentlessly and continued to assist in the recovery efforts every day for two months.

SOUL FOOD

BY BOB DVORAK

Police Officer, Des Plaines PD, Illinois.

The first time we dance with the darkest aspects of society, our internal meter starts ticking. Backward. Each tick of the meter stripping away another micro-layer of the varnish insulating our soul; if laid bare, without nourishment, it withers and dies as sure as a fish cast upon the shore. One's jurisdiction plays a part, as does life experience, but neither can be a factor in any mathematical sense. It's too subjective. For some, their meter bottoms out on day one. For others, it never does. The lucky ones find ways to feed the meter and maintain some sense of balance. Those who can't are lost, and may not even know it. Suicide rates among our ranks are disproportionately high. A young expectant mother is shot in the stomach, killing her and her unborn child. *Tick.* A widower, despondent over the loss of his wife, places the muzzle of his Army .45 under his chin and redecorates the kitchen. *Tick.* An intoxicated motorist hits a snow-encrusted retaining wall, launching his vehicle into a family of innocents. *Tick.* A mentally unbalanced mother of two leaps in front of a late night express train and explodes. *Tick. Tick-tick-tick-tick-tick-tick-tick-tick.* With only a handful of years under my belt, I can pinpoint, almost to the minute, when my meter first ran out, or rather, when I came to realize it. I'm sure it will happen again, but mere recognition of the beast should make it a little easier to digest the second time around.

September 9, a Sunday. As I was dressing for day watch, early guys from the midnight shift were filing past my locker, grinning: "You got a swinger." Goddammit. That's no way to start a day. Without stopping in at roll call, I drove down to Chippewa Street, where a number of units were already on scene, waiting for me to work my magic. Corner house with a long backyard. A private little paradise ringed by chain link and old growth trees. The yard was shady and cool, and a clean, earthy smell permeated the air. Quintessential Sunday morning.

Sixteen-year-old Pam Michaels was lying under a thick-trunked elm covered with a ratty old moving blanket. A well-worn child's swing, fashioned from a board and two pieces of rope, hung suspended from one of the tree's limbs. Pam'd hanged herself from another with a length of nylon dog leash. Innocence lost.

Her father had let the family dog out into the yard around 6:15, and had thought it odd that Pam would be outside at that hour, staring upward into the tree. I can only imagine what took place within that poor man's mind as he came to realize what had happened. I was alone with Pam when I uncovered her. She was in full rigor, her pale skin cool damp to the touch. Dark rings circled her eyes, which were open, staring up into infinity. Her tongue protruded from her mouth, and a deep ligature mark ringed her neck. Time had stopped. Nothing moved but the long strands of honey-colored hair dancing lightly across her face. She'd been pretty in life. Death made her a monster. I spent some time taking photos and measurements before allowing her parents a final moment with their daughter. Individually, they hunkered over her body, cradling her. Kissing her. *Tick*.

This case really bothered me, but not for the reason one might think—the sheer horror of a father finding his little girl hanging from a tree in the backyard. What bothered me was the fact that I didn't give a rat's ass. Didn't feel a thing. Oh sure, I was professional, and put on my best "I'm sorry for your loss" face, but inside I was empty, and it scared the bejesus outta me. I'd reached my limit. My meter had run out. Then came the eleventh.

I was car to car with my buddy Jim when dispatch typed us a message regarding the first plane to hit the towers, and like many hearing the initial reports I envisioned some type of accident involving a small private plane. When the second tower was struck, and we learned that both planes had been commercial airliners . . . My God. Guess it's how people must have felt in '41. Then the Pentagon, and western Pennsylvania. Incomprehensible. Patriotic blinders had made us all feel safe.

The days immediately following were eerily quiet. Wary eyes routinely scanned the horizons in spite of the airline shutdowns. Departments across the country came to share a common workload on top of their regional specialties: anthrax, real and imagined. Daily rations of suspicious persons, suspicious vehicles, suspicious mail. Hastily prepared department protocols wrapped in yards of evidence tape. I felt a tremendous loss for the country, particularly for the city of New York—for the families of the cops and firefighters who'd lost their lives. Shamefully, I felt little for the thousands of civilians who were lost. I realize how that sounds and I wrestled with it for a long time, but after the ninth, I was tapped out. It was those feelings, or lack thereof, that ultimately prompted my nine-hundred-mile pilgrimage to NYC.

By November, U.S. military efforts overseas were going well; Northern Alliance forces had taken Kabul, and fighting had shifted to southern Afghanistan. On the homefront, everyone had become a dyed-in-the-wool, flag-waving patriot. Operations at Ground Zero and Fresh Kills Landfill continued around the clock. November found me baby-sitting mosques, and trying to convince the Paplauskis that the ominous looking spots on their grapes were nothing more than common mold. I had to get to New York. I called my buddy Larry, who, since the attacks, had been steadily alternating between morgue details and shifts at Fresh Kills. I told him my friend Mike and I were planning a road trip and asked if he might be able to make some arrangements on his end. A few days later Lar called back and gave us a green light.

We rolled out on the morning of the twelfth, listening intently to the news about Flight 587 going down in the Rockaways. I wondered how much more the city could take. We pushed hard, making Pennsylvania well before nightfall, largely in part to our chief's providing us with a marked unit—our apologies to troopers in Ohio and the Keystone State. The fellas in Indiana are used to it. After rocketing through a couple hundred miles of rolling Pennsylvania countryside, we hit the Jersey border and began our descent into a funky netherworld of smokestacks and overpasses. Somewhere in the mix, I sacrificed our desired exit in order to keep our unit from being carried back on a flatbed, and as a reward ended up hopelessly lost in a nightmarish neighborhood of burned-out buildings and street zombies. Being in a marked unit did nothing for my confidence and neither did the guns. I'm no shrinking violet, but I was relieved when we snaked back out onto the highway. The guys who patrol that beat aren't making enough money.

A short time later we rendezvoused with Larry, who

took point, leading us to an old-styled motor lodge on Staten Island—a two-story horseshoe-type affair with a lone, burned-out Caddy in its lot. Hmmm . . . Admittedly, I had told Lar we were trying to get by on the cheap, but this wasn't exactly what I'd had in mind. The rat-faced kid in the office asked if we wanted a room for an hour; not having the energy to slap him, we rolled our eyes and signed on for the night. Our room, indicated by a number scrawled on the door in black marker, was a beaut—looked like something had been butchered in there. Welcome to New York.

We awoke to a cold gray dawn, fully dressed and feeling pretty rough, partly from the drive out, and partly from the sleep aids we'd consumed. Thankful our squad still had four wheels, we lit out, mainlined some caffeine, and headed toward the landfill. Fresh Kills Landfill, a.k.a. "the Dump"—a formidable sight silhouetted against the morning sky. Sacred ground now. Following a service road around its base, Mike and I were detained momentarily at a security checkpoint before being directed up a well-worn switchback. Upon reaching the summit we entered a post-apocalyptic frontier town, courtesy of the NYPD—a cluster of temporary structures surrounded by a hellish brown wasteland. The hilltop was bristling with activity. Cranes and front-end loaders incessantly worked ton after ton of powdery gray debris from Ground Zero; never-ending convoys of trucks and barges brought more. Ground crews armed with shovels and rakes monitored the process while combing through residual debris—continually searching for anything that looked out of place among the tangled gray masses of concrete and metal.

Larry met us up top, and after making a few brief introductions, ushered us into a prefabricated supply hut—a kind of Home Depot for survivalists—where personnel were outfitted with goggles, gloves, respirators, hard-hats, Tyvek suits, etc. We geared up and were assigned to a sergeant who was assembling a team to work one of the sifters. Conversations were friendly and genuine, but short. Maybe it was the hour. Maybe they'd slipped into their "zone." Together we strode out to the wastelands looking like an Apollo crew, passing by those we were re-lieving. They looked beat. Hell, everybody did. Their faces reminded me of the GIs on *Life* magazine covers from the forties. The sifters were mounted on platforms a good fifteen feet in the air, providing a bird's-eye view of the entire operation: the towering piles of debris. Cranes in constant motion like prehistoric metal monsters. An army of white biohazard suits contrasting sharply with the barren brown landscape. Spooky.

Debris fed into the receiving end of the sifters was subjected to a series of vibrating metal teeth before being moved along a wide conveyor belt, manned on each side by a half dozen officers. One had to yell in order to be heard over the clatter of the machinery and the slight in-crease in elevation made us take notice of the bitter winds, which relentlessly sought out exposed flesh. Fol-lowing the lead of my seasoned coworkers, I appropriated a suitable piece of rebar to utilize as a grappling hook. We examined all that passed, motioning for the sarge upon finding remains or anything that might be useful to detec-tives for identification purposes. What rolled down the conveyor on a given day was largely dictated by where within Ground Zero a particular load of debris had been recovered. A macabre soup du jour: severed limbs, joints and digits so severely burned they resembled fossilized wood, clothing, jewelry, photographs, bone fragments, shoes, teeth. By contrast, what wasn't found sometimes evoked deeper emotions. A charred firefighter's hood.

The sleeve of a navy blue uniform shirt. Anything of interest was set aside in five-gallon plastic buckets earmarked for the morgue; regular runs were made between the on-site facility and the city morgue.

Mike and I worked with enthusiasm. We were rookies. The guys and gals we worked with were thorough but they'd been at it for quite a while. They'd seen enough; they'd witnessed the horror of the eleventh long before our arrival, and were slated to live with it long after our departure. Mike and I were interlopers, rolling into town well after the initial outpouring of volunteer help. We were in NYC for less than an eyeblink in the relative scheme of things, yet we were treated as brothers. Working shoulder to shoulder with these people was one of the proudest moments in my life: I have never been more proud to be an American—to be a cop.

Wherever we went in the city, citizens and officers undeservedly and embarrassingly treated us like royalty. We talked to a lot of cops with a lot of different units while we were in the city, all of whom were candid and heartfelt, sharing their stories about the eleventh—tales of undaunted bravery, the likes of which I'd never heard before outside of history books. Heroes all. I cannot imagine what that fateful day must've been like. And that's after seeing Ground Zero, and working at Fresh Kills, and talking to survivors. The scale and breadth of 9/11 is simply unattainable having not lived it. Those who might contest this are misguided.

Before we knew it, our week was up. We packed our squad, pointed her west, and headed for home—a week older, years wiser. It was quiet in the car as we pulled out of the city, each of us lost in his own thoughts. Then a wistful grin spread across my face as I came to the realization that in the course of a week I'd undergone a trans-

formation of sorts, a subtle change only I could have per-
ceived. My meter had been mysteriously fed. The victims
of September 11 were real. They mattered. Every single
one of them. And the single victim of September 9? . . .
Suddenly she mattered most of all.

THERE'S SO MUCH HOPE

BY JOE McADAMS

Sergeant, NYPD, six years; LEO with other agencies,
three years.

September 11, 2001, started out just like any other day in
the three years that I had been assigned to One Police
Plaza, NYPD Headquarters. I was in my office at around
8:30 A.M. when there was a very loud *Boom!*, a noise
everybody at first attributed to the construction going on
around the building. But we soon learned that a plane had
crashed into one of the Twin Towers at the World Trade
Center. My thoughts immediately turned to my wife's
forty-five-year-old brother, Jimmy Munhall, who I knew
worked in one of the towers. Looking out the window, I
could see the North Tower burning about ten blocks away.

Then my wife, Patty, called on my cell phone to tell
me that Jimmy had called their mother to say that he was
okay. He was in the South Tower, the one that wasn't hit.
I would later learn that he also called his wife, Sue, and
left a similar message on their answering machine.

As flames and smoke poured from the North Tower, I
watched as the second plane flew into the South Tower.
We've all seen it replayed on the news but to have seen it
actually happen is beyond description. Flames and smoke
instantly erupted from the side of the tower facing me and

then seemed to wrap around the tower. I just stood there, confused, before I realized what I had just witnessed. All I could think was, Where was Jimmy? Jimmy—who was Sue's husband, six-year-old Lauren's daddy, the man who had walked Patty down the aisle at our wedding.

I talked to Patty on the cell phone again and she told me that after she watched the second plane strike the tower on television, she tried to telephone Jimmy but got no answer. She was so upset that I assured her that he worked on one of the lower floors, though I had no idea if this was true or not. Then an announcement came over our building's public address system ordering an immediate evacuation. It had been determined that our building might also be a target. I told Patty that I loved her and that I would call her as soon as possible.

I don't remember the exact sequence of events in those early hours or even in the days and weeks that followed. But I do remember trying to call Patty again on the cell phone as I joined the police personnel assigned to headquarters as they "mustered up" for head counts and assignments, but there was no service. There were already long lines of people at the pay phones; everyone wanted to call home to assure their families that they were okay.

We lined up for assignments about two blocks from the Brooklyn Bridge and headquarters. The buildings obstructed my view of the towers across the street. At 9:50 A.M. there was a deafening roar, very similar to the sound made when the second plane approached the South Tower. The officers and detectives standing about twenty feet to my left obviously saw something terrifying and they ran like I've never seen anyone run before. And I was right behind them. I thought it was another plane aimed at the Brooklyn Bridge, Police Headquarters, or at the somewhat taller "telephone building" between the two but when I turned to look, I saw only a single "Twin

Tower" and an incredible cloud of smoke where the South Tower had stood only moments before. The South Tower, the one Jimmy was in, had fallen.

Within a few short minutes, the sidewalks and streets were swarming with people walking in a northerly direction away from the general area of the World Trade Center. It was like those old Japanese monster movies where the citizens of Tokyo, fleeing Godzilla, fill the streets— only multiply that image a thousand times over.

The air was heavy with a gray dust and the people in the crowd who had been in the immediate vicinity of the fallen towers were covered in it from head to toe, just like the images we've all seen on television. Many of us started to "do" crowd control, keeping people on the sidewalks and moving toward the bridges off Manhattan to Brooklyn. Emergency vehicles were racing south toward the towers; civilian vehicles were heading north. I saw more than a few people almost struck by news vans racing to the scene. I did my job as best I could. I scanned the crowds for Jimmy even though I had already convinced myself that he would not pass by here on his way home to Jersey.

I noticed an elderly woman with a cane who was moving very slowly, clearly distraught, as younger people quickly passed her. I asked her if she was okay. She said she was alone. I asked some young ladies in the crowd to help her and, despite their own fears, and surely knowing that she would only slow them down, they readily agreed.

I noticed two van-type school buses, double-parked, impeding traffic on the four-lane street. Some adults were trying to get disabled teenagers in wheelchairs across the sidewalk to the buses despite the enormous crush of pedestrians flowing past. I went over and offered to help. The man and woman helping these poor kids seemed relieved by the sight of my badge and the tone of my take-charge voice. It was not easy getting the wheelchairs through the crowd, between the cars parked at the curb, and onto the bus lift. The kids were distraught. While I tried to maintain an outwardly professional demeanor so I could be effective, on the inside I was not doing any better then these kids. Police officers learn to mask their real feelings in the normal course of doing "the job" and on this day I was trying to keep my mask firmly in place.

As I was getting one of the wheelchairs onto the lift, a superior officer directed the buses to go immediately because they were blocking a lane of traffic. I told him we just had a few more kids to load up and he, seeing my badge, realized the buses would be moving soon enough so he directed traffic around them while we continued getting the kids on board.

As I was helping one of the wheelchair-bound kids onto the bus she suddenly cried, "I want to go home!" A light coating of that gray dust was all over her. I held her hand and told her she'd be out of here soon. She squeezed my hand tightly as if she would never let go. I didn't try to say anything because I knew I was on the verge of tears and cops aren't supposed to cry. We're supposed to appear strong and fearless in a crisis and I tried my best to maintain that image. After a few seconds I managed to tell her, "I have to help your friends." She released my hand. We finished loading the kids in short order and they headed home. I had to believe Jimmy was also on his way home.

I remember hearing and seeing the second tower fall around 10:30 A.M. as I stood by a bus stop with Detective Ada Palacios. I don't remember if we said anything. Knowing that the noise was not another plane pointed at us, and seeing that we were not in any immediate danger, we didn't run. We just stood there as the North Tower fell. What else could we do? This couldn't be real.

By noon or so, the number of pedestrians had slowed to a trickle. I was assigned with another officer, Bob Mladinich, to a rooftop observation post on a public housing development about two blocks from headquarters. We had already heard rumors about numerous firefighters and officers lost in the towers and we knew there were catastrophic civilian losses as well. I knew Patty would be worried sick about Jimmy and me. I still could not reach her on my cell phone and the pay phones on the street were out of service. I told Bob I had to see if one of the building residents would let me use their phone. I walked along the top floor hallway until I heard a television. I knocked on the door and asked if I could use the phone to call my family on Long Island and the gentleman inside agreed.

I called my home first. Busy. I called my mother-in-law, Marie Munhall, because Patty would surely be there by now. Busy. I called my sister-in-law Kathleen Walsh who lives downstairs from her mother. Busy. I called my parents, Ann and Gene McAdams, and got their answering machine. I left a message that I was calling after the towers had fallen, that I was okay and to please get hold of Patty and tell her I did not know when I would be home. I was sure it would be at least several days before I saw Patty and baby James again but at least she would know I was alive after the towers had fallen. I later learned that the news was already reporting that unknown numbers of police, fire, and rescue personnel, as well as office workers, were missing in the collapsed towers.

I tried my home phone one more time and my mom answered. I had forgotten that she was baby-sitting James that day. She was relieved to hear my voice but she told me they had not heard from Jimmy yet. My voice quavered as I spoke though I tried not to let her know how worried I was about Jimmy. She told me Patty had gone to be with her mom and Kathleen to await Jimmy's call. I asked Mom to call Patty and tell her I was okay, that I probably would not be home for several days at least, and that I would talk to her when I could.

I finally spoke to Patty later in the afternoon. I could tell that she was scared for Jimmy and me. He still had not called. I told Patty that most of the phones were out, and that many people were trying to get out of Manhattan and to call home at the same time. I told her not to give up hope until we had to, though I already knew it didn't look good. I was talking to her again that evening when I saw Seven World Trade Center, a forty-seven-story building, collapse at 5:25 P.M. Oddly enough, I merely told Patty another building had just gone down and continued our conversation. What else could I do? Jimmy still had not called.

I got off duty at 11:15 that night and had to be back at work at six the next morning. The commute home would be at least two hours if the trains were running, so I found a lumpy couch to sleep on at Headquarters. I listened to an all-news radio station throughout the night and got maybe thirty minutes of sleep. How could I sleep when I didn't know where Jimmy was?

The next morning I was assigned to a security traffic checkpoint under the Brooklyn Bridge with several other officers. The area around headquarters was a "frozen" security zone at this point. Only authorized personnel and vehicles were allowed to pass. Heavy construction trucks of all kinds were coming through all day. I saw a military tank drive south toward Ground Zero with two or three mounted and manned machine guns on top. Numerous refrigerated trucks, of the kind typically used to deliver frozen/refrigerated food to restaurants and stores, headed south toward the site. Some came back with police escorts, heading north. They weren't carrying food.

I got off duty around seven that evening. Fortunately, another officer was driving out to the Ronkonkama train station where my car was parked. My two-hour commute was thus reduced to forty-five minutes. I was finally going to see Patty and baby James. I don't remember the name of the officer who drove me that night. He was talking to his other passenger, another police officer, while I tried to doze off in the backseat. The driver said his buddy Pettit was among the missing.

"Glen Pettit?" I asked.

"Yeah," he said, "do you know him, too?"

I had taken the train home to Ronkonkama with Glen just the week before. I remembered Glen telling me that he had recently been at the scene of a parachutist who got hung up on the Statue of Liberty. Glen, with only four years on the job, was assigned to the department's Video Unit and had raced to the scene to film the parachutist's rescue by the department's elite Emergency Services Unit. I had first met Glen some four years earlier, also on the train, while he was in the Police Academy. I didn't run into Glen all that often, but when I did, that hour-plus train ride seemed like only five minutes. The man loved to talk and I didn't mind.

There is news footage of Glen running into one of the towers that day, past a line of firefighters, with a professional video camera on his shoulder, the kind you see news people running around with. He never came out. Ironically, the last time I had seen Glen on-duty was in the lobby of Police Headquarters with one of those video cameras. He was filming the Wall of Heroes, a memorial to all those officers killed in the line of duty over the years. Now his name will be added to the Wall along with twenty-two other NYPD officers.

When I finally arrived at my mother-in-law's I met Patty and her sister Kathleen out in the front of the house.

All three of us hugged each other in the driveway, crying. We still hadn't heard from Jimmy; we had not yet grasped that Jimmy wasn't coming home.

I walked into the house and hugged Patty's mom. We both cried. Our cousins Denise Matzelle and Geralyn Dicey were there, along with several other people. I went and picked up baby James, my little six-month-old. He gave me a big baby smile, the kind that communicates pure joy, as if to say, "Hi Dad, I'm glad you're here!" When my dog, Roxy, came in from the backyard, she stood up on her rear legs and put her front paws on my shoulders, a "Roxy-hug." I scratched her belly and gave her a kiss. Something I had taken for granted, merely returning home from work, had been stolen from so many families.

I got about five hours of sleep and was back on duty in Manhattan at six A.M. the next morning. We still had not heard from Jimmy. Although I knew better, I told Patty we should not give up hope yet. One of Jimmy's favorite expressions during a family crisis was "there's so much hope."

It was that first Friday after the attack, when we were assembling to get our assignments for the day, that I heard that John Perry was also among the missing officers. John was one of the first people I had met when I transferred to Headquarters in June 1998. Like me, he was also an attorney and one of the first things John told me was that he was waiting for the state legislature to pass a law whereby police officers could take a vested-interest retirement after only five years of service. The law was eventually enacted. On the morning of September 11, John was at headquarters to file his retirement papers to become an attorney in private practice. He had planned it to be his last day as a police officer. When John learned of the attack, he could have left the area and reported to the

Bronx precinct where he worked. He could have mustered up with those of us assigned to headquarters. Hell, he could have just gone home and started his new job the next day, but John ran to the towers to help. He was last seen alive assisting in the evacuation.

I was fortunate that I was allowed to be with my family that first Saturday after the attack. Patty, baby James, and I went to Jersey to be with Jimmy's wife, Sue, and his six-year-old daughter, Lauren. Sue has been amazingly strong throughout this ordeal. Jimmy loved her and she is a strong person, far stronger than anyone else I know. Perhaps it is because Jimmy had beaten cancer twice in the prior ten years. Maybe they had braced themselves for the worst during both episodes and that is somehow helping her, in some small way, through these difficult times. But how do you ever prepare yourself to lose your best friend, the love of your life, the father of your daughter? At least when someone is terminally ill you have a chance for final farewells.

Sue says she has to be strong for little Lauren and I guess we all have to be. Lauren is a sweetheart and the most well-mannered kid I know, a real credit to Jimmy and Sue. Jimmy was her idol, her buddy. They were inseparable on weekends. I guess because of his past battles with cancer and recognizing that the disease could come back, Jimmy made sure to make time for Lauren in his life. In fact, what the rest of us know as Saturday they called "Dadurday." There is not the slightest chance that Lauren will ever forget her Daddy, he was not just a blur passing through her life as he chased the almighty dollar.

Jimmy knew what mattered in life. He was an usher at the church and had volunteered on at least one Habitat for Humanity project. He and Lauren were big Yankee fans. Jimmy was truly a good guy who loved Sue, Lauren and his whole family. I know that often when somebody passes away, he can suddenly become a saint with no faults even if he was the black sheep of the family. There is no need to sanitize our memories of Jimmy. He really was a great and loving husband, father, brother, son, and friend.

The second Saturday after the attack Sue had the memorial service for Jimmy in Jersey. It was standing room only with an incredible overflow into the parking lot. I cried like a baby. The next Saturday we attended the memorial for Mark Rosen, Jimmy's best friend since college and a coworker in the same firm. Jimmy's family knew Mark very well and I had met Mark and his wife, also named Patty, several times over the years. It was like we had lost another brother. Again, I cried like a baby. The next day we went back to Jersey for little Lauren's seventh birthday party. We all did the best we could for her to make it a nice party. I disappeared into the backyard for a while and cried yet again.

On November 24 I was promoted to sergeant along with twenty-two others. Patty, baby James, and my parents all came to the ceremony at Headquarters. When I last saw Jimmy two weeks before the attack, he had promised to walk over from his office for the ceremony, just as he had attended my Police Academy graduation five years earlier. There is a *Heroes* video that they play for promotees and their families at the beginning of the ceremony. That video now includes the twenty-three NYPD officers lost in the attack as well as the Ground Zero rescue and recovery effort. Seeing those images made me think of Jimmy all the more. The whole day I couldn't stop thinking about how much we all missed him. While I am proud of the promotion and recognize that it means I will be able to provide more for my family, none of it seems terribly relevant anymore. Time spent with family and friends is what matters, not promotion and the money that comes with it.

They finally found Jimmy on March 19. Incredibly, his remains were intact and clothed. We buried him the Monday before Easter. We're supposed to consider ourselves lucky because we were able to give Jimmy a proper burial. What kind of world is it when we are considered fortunate to have a loved one's body? So many families will never have anything to bury, while others will have less then a full set of remains. I don't want the body. I want Jimmy alive and well but that's just not possible. I have no sense of "closure," whatever that means. We all loved him and miss him terribly. I told somebody at his memorial that we had had an extra ten years with Jimmy that we might not have had if he hadn't beaten the cancer. Just one of those mind games we play with ourselves to get through tough times. It's just not the same without him and never will be. To be quite honest, the passage of time hasn't eased the pain. Nevertheless, I'm thankful I knew him for the short time I did. To paraphrase a great poet, "'Tis better to have loved Jimmy and lost him, than to have never known him at all."

EPILOGUE

While the world as we know it may have changed as a result of 9/11, one thing remains as a constant: our nation's law enforcement officers will continue to serve their communities and to fight the never-ending battle against crime. Yet each day we will see the death or critical injury of another law enforcement officer in the United States. Each day another officer's family will be devastated by their loss and each day his or her fellow officers will swallow their fear and once again hit the streets.

The Police Memorial in Washington, D.C., has the names of over seven thousand fallen law enforcement officers carved into its marble walls: the names of men and women who gave their lives in the line of duty, for their communities, for their country. To these names will be added the names of those seventy-two officers who died in the infamy of 9/11. All of these fallen officers knew the risks involved when they took their oaths and pinned their badges on their chests, but that doesn't diminish their loss for the rest of us. With each of their deaths a little part of us has died too, and we owe them a debt that we can never repay. But we can honor them and to do so we must unite, not only with our fellow law enforcement officers, but with our citizens as fellow Americans, and this can only be done through revealing ourselves—our hearts beneath the badge. This is what I believe the authors in *True Blue* have accomplished; I hope that you, the reader, have come away with an understanding of how we see the world since it is, after all, the world we share. Cops really care about the people they serve and protect, cops are naturally patriotic and altruistic, cops believe in everything America stands for. Cops are just like everybody else. And no matter what the color of the uniform or the shape of the badge, it's the heart beneath that really counts. I hope you've had a glimpse of those hearts in these pages. That beat is always strong; it is always true. Always blue.

SGT. RANDY SUTTON

IN MEMORIAM

SEPTEMBER 11, 2001
OUR FALLEN OFFICERS:

NAME	RANK	DEPARTMENT
Leonard W. Hatton	Special Agent	FBI
Ronald P. Bucca	Fire Marshall	NYC, NY
John G. Coughlin	Sergeant	NYC, NY
Michael Curtin	Sergeant	NYC, NY
John D'Allara	PO	NYC, NY
Vincent G. Danz	PO	NYC, NY
Jerome M. Dominguez	PO	NYC, NY
Stephen P. Driscoll	PO	NYC, NY
Mark Ellis	PO	NYC, NY
Robert Fazio	PO	NYC, NY
Rodney C. Gillis	Sergeant	NYC, NY
Ronald Kloepfer	PO	NYC, NY
Thomas Langone	PO	NYC, NY
James Leahy	PO	NYC, NY

NAME	RANK	DEPARTMENT
Brian G. McDonnell	PO	NYC, NY
John William Perry	PO	NYC, NY
Glen Pettit	PO	NYC, NY
Claude Richards	Detective	NYC, NY
Timothy Roy	Sergeant	NYC, NY
Moira Smith	PO	NYC, NY
Ramon Suarez	PO	NYC, NY
Paul Talty	PO	NYC, NY
Santos Valentin, Jr.	PO	NYC, NY
Joseph Vincent Vigiano	Detective	NYC, NY
Walter Weaver	PO	NYC, NY
Thomas E. Jurgens	Sr. Court Officer	NY State Office of Court Admin.
William Harry Thompson	Captain	NY State Office of Court Admin.
Mitchel Scott Wallace	Sr. Court Officer	NY State Office of Court Admin.
Clyde Frazier, Jr.	Crime Specialist I	NY State Dept. of Taxation & Finance
Charles M. Mills	Director	NY State Dept. of Taxation & Finance
Richard R. Moore	Revenue Crimes	NY State Dept. of Taxation & Finance
Salvatore Papasso	Revenue Crimes	NY State Dept. of Taxation & Finance
William H. Pohlmann	Asst. Deputy	NY State Dept. of Taxation & Finance
Christopher C. Amoroso	PO	Port Authority of NY/NJ

NAME	RANK	DEPARTMENT
Maurice Vincent Barry	PO	Port Authority of NY/NJ
Liam Callahan	PO	Port Authority of NY/NJ
Robert D. Cirri, Sr.	Lieutenant	Port Authority of NY/NJ
Clinton Davis, Sr.	PO	Port Authority of NY/NJ
Donald A. Foreman	PO	Port Authority of NY/NJ
Gregg John Froehner	PO	Port Authority of NY/NJ
Thomas Edward Gorman	PO	Port Authority of NY/NJ
Uhuru Gonja Houston	PO	Port Authority of NY/NJ
George G. Howard	PO	Port Authority of NY/NJ
Stephen Huczko, Jr.	PO	Port Authority of NY/NJ
Anthony P. Infante, Jr.	Inspector	Port Authority of NY/NJ
Paul W. Jurgens	PO	Port Authority of NY/NJ
Robert M. Kaulfers	Sergeant	Port Authority of NY/NJ
Paul Laszcynski	PO	Port Authority of NY/NJ
David P. Lemagne	PO	Port Authority of NY/NJ
John J. Lennon	PO	Port Authority of NY/NJ

NAME	RANK	DEPARTMENT
J. D. Levi	PO	Port Authority of NY/NJ
James F. Lynch	PO	Port Authority of NY/NJ
Kathy N. Mazza	Captain	Port Authority of NY/NJ
Donald J. McIntyre	PO	Port Authority of NY/NJ
Walter Arthur McNeil	PO	Port Authority of NY/NJ
Fred V. Morrone	Superintendent	Port Authority of NY/NJ
Joseph M. Navas	PO	Port Authority of NY/NJ
James A. Nelson	PO	Port Authority of NY/NJ
Alfonse J. Niedermeyer III	PO	Port Authority of NY/NJ
James W. Parham	PO	Port Authority of NY/NJ
Dominick Pezzulo	PO	Port Authority of NY/NJ
Bruce A. Reynolds	PO	Port Authority of NY/NJ
Antonio Jose Rodrigues	PO	Port Authority of NY/NJ
Richard Rodriguez	PO	Port Authority of NY/NJ
James A. Romito	Chief	Port Authority of NY/NJ
John P. Skala	PO	Port Authority of NY/NJ
Walwyn W. Stuart, Jr.	PO	Port Authority of NY/NJ

NAME	RANK	DEPARTMENT
Kenneth F. Tietjen	PO	Port Authority of NY/NJ
Nathaniel Webb	PO	Port Authority of NY/NJ
Michael T. Wholey	PO	Port Authority of NY/NJ
Richard Jerry Guadagno	Refuge Manager	U.S. Fish & Wildlife Service
Craig James Miller	Master Special	U.S. Secret Service

TURN THE PAGE FOR A STORY
FROM RANDY SUTTON'S NEXT BOOK

A COP'S LIFE

Coming soon in hardcover
from St. Martin's Press

THE ULTIMATE
NINJA WARRIOR

Many years have passed since the night I killed someone. I have spent those years as any man might, seducing life with wild abandon while my companions cheered me on. I seized each moment for what it was—an unrepeatable experience, whether it be physical or sensual or, to a lesser extent as time went by, emotional. I always thought that I was propelled into living intensely by my pleasure-seeking nature, but now, as I more and more shun the company of others and live as a recluse, as loneliness has taken the place of my companions, as I undertake a sedentary life that I don't recall having volunteered for and which I still don't accept as belonging to me, I have begun to reflect, and to reflect with brutal honesty. All the roads in my long life seem to lead back to that one night when I took a human life.

Perhaps I have gotten ahead of myself, for in describing the results of an act I have omitted the event itself. If my plea for empathy is to have any merit at all, then the facts must be included for you to draw your own conclusions. Facts, unadulterated, speak insistently for themselves, and as a veteran cop I have spent a lifetime working with nothing but facts. How you will regard these facts is up to you; I can only describe that night as I remember it.

Las Vegas is known to the world as the mecca of hedonism. It is "Sin City," the capital of abandoned inhibitions, the neon bacchanalia where appetite dominates reason. For nearly half a century her pulsating lights have hypnotized her acolytes, luring them into her world of gambling, gluttony, and sexual pleasures. It is a world that most have only fantasized about. She is all she promises to be; what is rumored to be not only exists but flourishes beyond the wildest imagination. What isn't known, what isn't celebrated, is the parallel universe that exists beyond those neon sentinels, the same world of placid neighborhoods and shopping centers that dominates our nation's suburban sprawl. The same domestic melodramas erupting on a Saturday night after too many beers, the same youthful exuberance gone awry by way of a speeding minivan full of teenagers—these exist in the figurative back lot of Las Vegas just as they do in all our major towns and cities. It was within this unassuming reality, contained within a larger-than-life reality, that one man sought me out to end his life.

He was delusional. He heard voices. He believed that he had been appointed as an avenger, a liberator through death. He had lived with demons for a long time and had given up trying to keep them at bay with medication and moderation. No matter how tightly he closed the shades in his mind, they kept slipping through, howling and keening, to prey like demonic leopards upon what was left of his reason. Finally he embraced his calling, and they, the ubiquitous carnivorous "they," christened him "the Ultimate Ninja Warrior." He prepared himself to accept his appointed role. He donned black karate gear, strapped a shoulder holster holding a stolen semiautomatic pistol to his body, draped himself with ammunition belts and a samurai sword, and headed to the high school dance.

The Ultimate Ninja Warrior was a young man, not much older than the teenagers attending the event. When he appeared like a specter out of the trees lining the athletic field that cool autumn night, most of the boys and girls laughed, thinking it was one of their classmates pulling a prank. As the black-clad figure approached the gymnasium, he opened fire. For a moment the young people stood frozen in disbelief, but as the windows began exploding all around them, they panicked, and terror fueled their chaotic rush to escape. The Ninja embraced this confusion and charged into the building, his semiautomatic pistol held like a triumphant banner in his hand. He kept firing.

The teenagers scattered in every direction, some falling and others, propelled by primal fear and survival instinct, clambering over them without trying to help. Overwhelmed and terrified, each lost a part of himself or herself as the hail of bullets blasted the brick walls and shattered the windows, leaving fragments of glass and brick to rain down upon them like wrath on Judgment Day.

Within moments of the first shots, a 911 operator received the first phone call. At first she thought that the breathless young woman on the other end of the line was making a prank call, but then she, too, heard the *pfffttt* sound of bullets exploding in the background. The other operators began receiving similar calls. Soon the urgent tone of an emergency broadcast was flying out over the radios of patrol cars across the city.

"All units in sector Union 3, a report of a shooting in

progress at Torrey Pines High School. Caller reports that a male dressed in all black is armed with a pistol and is walking eastbound on Thrush Street shooting at students."

The dispatcher's voice was calm, but there was an edge to it that I could detect even before I turned up the volume on my portable radio. I had just left the diner and was walking with my former partner Dave and his young rookie. The three of us had eaten an enjoyable dinner, and we'd joked about what a quiet night it had been so far. We stood in the parking lot, listening to the dispatcher's summary of something that seemed more like the basis of a national news broadcast than an event transpiring in this quiet corner of the city.

"That's three blocks from here," I said, listening for the sound of gunfire.

"Sounds like bullshit to me," Dave said calmly, unwrapping a toothpick. "Some kind of prank call."

The rookie laughed nervously, nodding in hopeful agreement.

I laughed, too, but it was my sector, so I yanked the portable radio from the holster on my belt and told the dispatcher I was on my way. As I started to climb into my patrol car, Dave looked at me across the roof of his unit and said, "What the hell, we'll back you."

Since I was only about a minute away I didn't throw on my overheads, so I was flying dark as I punched the accelerator and screeched around the corner to where the shooter had last been seen. I could make out the lighted windows of the high school gymnasium up ahead, but so far nothing seemed out of the ordinary. Then I caught sight of another patrol car up ahead. Its brake lights came on as the dispatcher radioed that a man with a cellular phone who had been following the suspect had just been shot.

I pulled to a stop behind the patrol car as the two cops jumped out and used their open doors for cover. They both were pointing their pistols into the darkness, the tension evident in the arch of their backs. Then my headlights caught what they were aiming at: a figure striding toward them down the middle of the street. He was like a creature out of a low-budget horror movie—dressed from head to toe in a black ninja outfit, bandoliers of ammunition strapped across his chest and a pistol in his hand.

Shoot him! I thought, *shoot him before he gets too close to you—shoot him!* But the ninja didn't cross that invisible line that divides close from too close, and I watched him put his pistol back in his shoulder holster. Suddenly he turned and walked into the driveway of an apartment complex. The two cops stayed in position behind their patrol car doors, frozen, it seemed, with indecision. I didn't blame them; for a moment I wondered if I had seen what I thought I had. Then the police helicopter appeared overhead; my rocketing adrenaline made the blood pound so loudly in my ears that I didn't even hear it coming. Now there it was, so close that it was battering the palm trees all around us with its prop wash. It lit up the ninja with its powerful searchlight, and I made a dash for the trees lining the driveway of the apartment building, my 9 mm extended in my hand. As I ran, the staccato rhythm of the chopper blades in concert with the pulsing beam of the searchlight and the red and blue of the overhead lights of the first patrol car gave the confidently striding black-clad figure a demonic look.

I ran along the tree-lined path parallel with the driveway, almost alongside the ninja, shouting, "Police! Stop! Police!" I might as well have been talking to myself. He didn't look over at me; he didn't break his stride. I was starting to feel a sense of desperation. Since his gun was holstered, I didn't want to shoot him in the back, but people were beginning to emerge from their apartments, curious about the noise and lights from the helicopter overhead, and they were right in the path of the oncoming ninja.

I didn't have any choice, so I made the decision that will haunt me forever. I broke out of the bushes and ran up behind him, screaming at the top of my lungs to divert his attention from the people filling the apartment courtyard up ahead. He turned to look at me. In that same instant he drew his semiautomatic pistol from his shoulder holster and pointed it at my chest. My forward momentum wouldn't let me stop, and I plowed toward him while raising my own pistol and bringing my knee up to connect solidly with his torso. We both fired simultaneously, and as I was just three feet from him, I expected to feel his bullet searing through my body. But before anything could register, pain or fear, we both fired again.

Time stopped. The helicopter's searchlight was pulsing over us, the wind tore at my uniform, and the muzzle flashes looked like distant fireworks on the Fourth of July. Then my gun jammed—my worst nightmare; it had plagued my dreams for years. This madman, this ninja warrior, was standing only a yard away from me, still firing, and my gun wouldn't work. I had no cover, so I dropped to the ground and rolled, wondering if I was dead and just hadn't realized it. As I worked the slide of my gun, clearing the mechanism, he continued to fire. I rolled from side to side trying to avoid his aim. I fired again, but there was no reaction to my shots. I wasn't wearing any body armor; I wondered if he was.

Overhead the helicopter cops had seen the muzzle flashes and watched me fall to the ground. They thought I'd been shot. "Shots fired! Officer down!" a tinny voice screamed over the portable radio. The cops at the entrance to the apartment complex opened fire, thinking I'd been hit. I heard the bullets whizzing overhead as I struggled to my feet, trying to show the others I was all right.

I heard the roar of a powerful car engine, and out of the corner of my eye I saw a patrol car hurtling toward us, my old partner Dave at the wheel, his face grim and determined. *He's going to run the sonovabitch over!* I thought, both amazed and absurdly grateful. The patrol car slammed into the cement divider that kept cars from driving into the apartment courtyard, the engine revving, the tires burning rubber, but he couldn't get through those impervious concrete blocks even by ramming them while accelerating. My dismay turned to fury when I saw that the Ninja was distracted. As he looked over at Dave behind the wheel of the smoking patrol car, I emptied my magazine into him.

It was insane: My hollowpoint rounds had no effect on him whatsoever. As I reloaded, his attention once again turned to me, and he fired, missing me thanks to what seemed like supernatural intervention. Then I heard Dave's boots pounding on the pavement as he ran toward us. Inexplicably, the Ultimate Ninja Warrior turned and ran.

I slammed another magazine into my gun, and Dave and I ran after him around the corner of the building while exchanging shots. "Die, motherfucker, die!" I heard a shrill voice from behind a bush screaming as we turned the corner, one peeling left, one right. "Die, motherfucker, die!" Then I saw the muzzle flash from behind the bush, and we both fired into it until a black-clad body rolled out. As Dave ran up to handcuff the figure, I covered him, ready at the slightest provocation to fire again. Dave turned him over.

The searchlight of the air unit illuminated the scene just as the disco ball had illuminated the high school dance floor before this black-clad assassin had destroyed what had been innocent and pristine. I bent down to look at him. His face mask had fallen to one side, and I saw to my surprise that he wasn't much older than those whose lives he sought to end. He was hardly more than a boy. His blue eyes were sightless, bulging, staring into mine. Half of his face had been shot away, and what was left was mocking and macabre. He seemed to be grinning, his face shining wetly with bloody froth.

I don't know how long I bent over him trying to reconcile what I saw on the ground with what had stood before me in a hail of muzzle flash, seemingly immortal. Finally I stood up and met Dave's eyes. He was staring at me with the strangest look on his face. Before I could say a word, the brass, internal affairs, crime lab techs, and dozens of curious cops surrounded us. As is required, they separated us—the two cops involved in the shooting—and a grizzled homicide detective led me to an unmarked car.

"You did good, son," he said. "You survived."

I did, didn't I? I thought. For the life of me, I didn't know how.

The next few hours were a blur. I gave a taped statement about the shooting to homicide, and I was relieved of my gun so that it could be checked by ballistics for malfunctions. When my inquisition was all over, I changed out of my uniform and went to a bar where I knew I'd find other cops. I didn't want to be alone, but when I found myself the center of attention, answering questions about the shooting from all the curious cops I worked with, I realized I didn't want to be there, either. I suddenly didn't feel like I belonged. Anywhere.

This officer-involved shooting happened a long time ago, but in many ways it seems as if it happened only yesterday. While the intervening years have brought me close to death on many subsequent occasions, that particular night left me with far more questions than answers. Most of my questions begin with "why." Why was I spared that night when by all rights I shouldn't have survived? Why was I the one chosen to end that disturbed boy's life? Why did our paths cross that night? Why do I have to bear this for the rest of my life?

A couple of months ago, I met my old partner Dave for drinks. Both of us are nearing retirement age and have seen our share of combat. We seldom talk about our encounter with the Ultimate Ninja Warrior, but for some reason our conversation turned back to that surreal autumn night. We relived it, play by play, consuming more alcohol than we should have. We started our path of remembrance from our dinner break with his young rookie in tow and ended with our turning the ninja's body over and regarding his devastated face. Then I caught that look again—the same one he had given me when I leaned down to get a good look at the dead man.

"What? Why are you looking at me like that?" I asked.

"It's nothing," he said, letting his eyes return to contemplating the reflective light on his glass of scotch.

"Bullshit, Dave."

He ran his fingers down the side of the glass, gathering moisture on his fingertips, then he looked over at me.

"When we chased Ninja-man around the corner of that building and found him hiding behind that bush . . ."

"Yeah?" I prompted.

"What do you remember?"

I felt the alcohol driving through me as the memory vividly played out in my mind. I could see it as if it had happened yesterday, every damn detail. I looked over at Dave.

"We came running around the corner, and as he screamed, 'Die, motherfucker, die!' we opened up on him."

I shrugged. "Ninja-man was fucking crazy. End of story."

I took another swig of my scotch and emptied the glass. Dave was staring straight ahead, and I could see that he was looking at my reflection in the mirror above the bar.

"Will you fucking tell me what's on your mind, Dave?"

He turned toward me, swiveling on his stool.

"It was you."

I didn't get it. "What do you mean it was me?"

"You really don't know, do you?"

"Dave, will you please—"

"It was you. Ninja-man never said a word. It was you who yelled 'Die, motherfucker, die!'"

RANDY SUTTON